Layman's
BIBLE
Commentary

Acts thru 2 Corinthians

Volume
10

D1564964

Contributing

DR. PETER BARNES
ROBERT DEFFINBAUGH

Consulting Editor:

DR. MARK STRAUSS

BARBOUR
PUBLISHING

ISBN 978-1-62029-774-2

Produced with the assistance of Christopher D. Hudson & Associates. Contributing writers include Carol Smith and Stan Campbell.

Published by Barbour Publishing, Inc., P.O. Box 719, Uhrichsville, Ohio 44683, www.barbourbooks.com

Our mission is to publish and distribute inspirational products offering exceptional value and biblical encouragement to the masses.

Member of the
Evangelical Christian
Publishers Association

Printed in the United States of America.

TABLE OF CONTENTS

ACTS

INTRODUCTION TO
ACTS

One of the earliest titles for this book of the Bible was simply "Acts," with other early titles being, "Acts of Apostles," "Acts of the Holy Apostles," and the popular, "The Acts of the Apostles," which wasn't really accurate. The acts of Peter and Paul are highlighted in this book, yet many of the other apostles are hardly mentioned. A more accurate title might be, "The Acts of the Holy Spirit," but many modern Bibles have reverted to simply using "Acts" as the title.

AUTHOR

As was the case with his Gospel, Luke doesn't identify himself as the writer of Acts, though his authorship is seldom questioned. The information he provided in the book of Luke was a result of his research to verify the testimony of eyewitnesses (Luke 1:1–4). His involvement in Acts is even more personal. Much of this book, like Luke's Gospel, is written in the third person. But certain sections (16:10–17; 20:5–15; 21:1–18; 27:1–28:16) switch to first person. It is evident that Luke accompanied Paul on various legs of his missionary journeys.

Luke was a doctor (Colossians 4:14) who had an eye for detail. He seems particularly interested in seafaring, and he provides vivid descriptions as he narrates. Many of his first-person accounts are when Paul is traveling by ship.

PURPOSE

Like his Gospel, Luke's book of Acts is addressed to Theophilus (1:1). The purpose of the Gospel account was "so that you may know the exact truth about the things you have been taught" (Luke 1:4 NASB). With his follow-up book of Acts, Luke is sending his primary recipient (and perhaps his financial sponsor) a well-researched account of the spread of Christianity throughout both Jewish and Gentile communities. Since Luke was personally involved in the growth of the church, he was able to provide both an insightful historical overview and a corresponding apologetic emphasis.

OCCASION

Each of the four Gospel accounts provides a distinctive look at the life, death, and resurrection of Jesus. But none deal with what happened to Jesus' followers after He ascended into heaven and returned to His Father. In Luke's Gospel, we are told only that the disciples stayed at the temple, praising God (Luke 24:53).

The book of Acts picks up at that point to describe the coming of the Holy Spirit on the Day of Pentecost and records the growth, challenges, and miraculous happenings in the early church. Jesus had commanded His followers to make disciples of all nations (Matthew 28:19). Acts details the work of the Holy Spirit and the spread of the gospel "to the ends of the earth" (Acts 1:8). The offer of God's forgiveness and salvation is extended to the Gentiles, and new opportunities open up for mission.

God's Word went out in ever-widening circles from Jerusalem. Even as the book of Acts concludes, Paul had just arrived in Rome to speak before the emperor there. Though beset by relentless opposition and persecution, the followers of Jesus persevered and continued to carry the gospel wherever they went.

THEMES

From start to finish, the book of Acts emphasizes the work of the Holy Spirit. The Spirit was first evident in the lives of Jewish believers in Jerusalem on the Day of Pentecost, but later was evidence that Gentiles, too, were experiencing the forgiveness and salvation of God.

The establishment and expansion of the church is Luke's ongoing concern in Acts. The followers of Jesus first congregate in a single group and create a unique and exemplary model of community. As they increase in number and persecution pushes them out of Jerusalem, they gather in various other locations, led by pastors and elders. And rather than each body seeing itself as independent, the churches look after one another's needs, financially and spiritually.

The persecution of believers is repeated throughout Acts as well. It was persecution that drove the church out of Jerusalem into surrounding areas. Paul was regularly persecuted during his travels. And at times when Paul could not be located, his associates were persecuted instead. More intense and organized persecution would come later, but Luke describes many of the initial attacks against the early church.

Luke also records a number of impassioned speeches throughout the book of Acts. Many are presentations of the gospel by church leaders such as Peter, Stephen, and Paul. Every episode contributes in some way to the central theme of the book: the expansion of the church from Jerusalem to the ends of the earth, and from a Jewish beginning to a Gentile expansion.

HISTORICAL CONTEXT

Since Luke's coverage of world events makes no mention of Nero's persecution of Christians (AD 64 and following), the destruction of Jerusalem in AD 70, or Paul's death in AD 68, many scholars believe he wrote the book of Acts around AD 60–62. He had traveled with Paul to Rome at this time, and may have been writing Acts while Paul was writing his Prison Epistles.

CONTRIBUTION TO THE BIBLE

The book of Acts holds a distinctive place in scripture. It is the only follow-up provided for the Gospels and provides a revealing look at the interaction, blessings, and problems of the believers in the early church. The Gospels highlight the ministry of Jesus; Acts highlights the ministry of the Holy Spirit. Only when viewed together do readers get the complete picture of God's plan, and how He chose to include humankind in the work of His kingdom.

More importantly, Acts shows how the expansion of the church from Jerusalem to Rome and from Jews to Gentiles was the work of God and part of His plan of salvation. The accounts of this time period provided by secular historians are helpful, to be sure, but they were written by people outside the church, looking in. Luke's account as a participant and believer gives us a trustworthy report that emphasizes things important to those who share his faith. His book of Acts provides much information that amplifies our understanding of other portions of scripture.

In addition, Luke's mostly chronological account of Paul's travels is invaluable in establishing dates for and better comprehension of his Epistles. By combining Paul's references in his letters with Luke's in Acts, the details of Paul's ministry become much clearer.

OUTLINE

ACTS 1:1–26
MAKING A BIG TRANSITION

Setting Up the Section

The book of Acts picks up where the Gospel of Luke ends. Jesus has been making occasional post-resurrection appearances, but He is about to depart for good. He leaves His followers final instructions, and while they await the promised Holy Spirit, they try to attend to some business.

📖 1:1–3

FORTY DAYS OF ASSURANCE

Luke again addresses his writing to Theophilus as he did in his Gospel (1:1). The use of the title "most excellent" (Luke 1:3) suggests that Theophilus had a position of high social status. Perhaps he was a Roman court official with whom Paul was scheduled to meet, and Luke hoped to provide him with a less prejudicial and more reliable opinion of Christianity. If so, Luke was not only a skilled historian, but he was also an astute diplomat and knowledgeable apologist who argued convincingly for the cause of Christianity.

Luke also emphasizes in his opening statement that the entire earthly ministry of Jesus was only a beginning. What Jesus had begun would continue to expand in geographic and spiritual significance (1:1).

Jesus' public ministry had lasted about three years. Then, after His resurrection, He appeared numerous times in various settings over a forty-day period to prove that He was alive (1:3).

Critical Observation

The Bible records a number of appearances of Jesus between His resurrection and ascension. He appeared to Mary Magdalene (John 20:14–18), a group of women (Matthew 28:8–10), two men on the road to Emmaus (Luke 24:13–35), and numerous times to His disciples (Matthew 28:16–20; Luke 24:36–49; John 20:24–29; 21:1–24). He also appeared to Peter (Luke 24:34; 1 Corinthians 15:5), his brother James (1 Corinthians 15:7), as well as a group of more than five hundred people (1 Corinthians 15:6).

JESUS' ASCENSION

Luke describes four stages of development Christ instituted for disciples in the early church:

1) He chose them (1:2). None of the apostles were self-appointed.

2) He commissioned them (Matthew 28:16–20; Acts 1:2). He gave them specific instructions.

3) He showed Himself to them (1:3). It was no ghost or apparition that appeared to them during that forty-day period. In this passage He ate with them (1:4). These disciples were irrefutable eyewitnesses to the reality of Jesus' resurrection.

4) He promised them the Holy Spirit (1:5), who would provide the power and authority they needed to carry out His instructions.

The instructions of the resurrected Jesus to His followers were very specific (1:4–6). He gave them a command (not to leave Jerusalem) and a promise (they will be baptized with the Holy Spirit).

On what appears to be a later occasion when they were again together, the disciples had a question of their own (1:6). In his Gospel, Luke noted numerous times when the apostles either misunderstood Jesus or seemingly ignored what He was saying as they held their own discussions about position and power. It's not surprising that Jesus once again had to steer their attention to the need for simple obedience and witness rather than establishing rank in God's kingdom (1:7–8).

The clarification from Jesus in verse 8 provides an outline for the book of Acts. Reading through Luke's account, we first see the witness of the disciples in Jerusalem, then the surrounding areas of Judea and Samaria, and if not literally to "the ends of the earth," at least to Rome, Turkey, Greece, Africa, and perhaps even Spain. And perhaps Jesus had His followers begin in Jerusalem because that had been their source of greatest failure. Just a few weeks before, they had all abandoned Him in His moment of greatest need. But after they received the Holy Spirit, they would never again be the same. They would be witnesses first among the people who knew them best—those who were especially aware of their weaknesses.

The disciples' own lives would be the first to change, and then they would touch many others. Jesus' inclusion of Samaria in their mission (1:8) is significant because of the spiritual, cultural, and racial barriers between the Jews and Samaritans. Right off the bat, Jesus is drawing His followers out of their comfort zones.

Some people argue that the statement about Jesus being taken up (1:9) reflects a naïve and prescientific view of cosmology, with heaven being somewhere above us and hell somewhere below. Yet such an argument seems to press the point too far. Christ's ascension is not about the order of the universe or the physical location of heaven. Rather, it shows a distinct break as Jesus leaves His human companions and returns to His Father. He had been appearing and disappearing for forty days. What better way to show He would not be coming back than to let everyone observe His final departure into the clouds? Angels confirmed with certainty that He wouldn't be returning for quite some time (1:10–11).

No one had witnessed Jesus' resurrection, yet they saw its effects in the continued presence of the risen and living Lord. And they did witness His ascension, but not the effects—at least not for a while. Their understanding would begin ten days later when the Holy Spirit arrived.

📄 **1:12–26**

REPLACING JUDAS

The number of believers that gathered after Jesus' ascension was a meager 120 (1:15). With the exception of Judas Iscariot, all the apostles were present (1:12–13). And by this time, Jesus' brothers, who previously hadn't believed in Him (John 7:5), were also among the believers (1:14). Though somewhat small, the group was constantly in prayer (1:14).

Peter's awareness of scripture led him to propose finding a replacement for Judas. The Bible never provides the reason that Judas betrayed Jesus. Luke refers to his wickedness (1:18); other translations of the original language describing Judas refer to his "infamy," "villainy," and "crime." Opinions are divided as to whether Judas was trying to save his own skin, acted out of greed, had come to feel out of place among the close-knit group of apostles, or was simply trying to coerce Jesus into declaring His role as Messiah and taking a stand against Rome. Whatever his motive, Judas's real tragedy is that, after realizing his mistake and experiencing remorse, he didn't attempt to seek forgiveness and restoration. His gruesome death (1:18–19) stands in stark contrast to the new life and fresh start the other apostles would receive.

Demystifying Acts

Matthew wrote that Judas went out and hanged himself (Matthew 27:5). The additional details in Acts 1:18–19 may suggest that considerable time passed before he was cut down. Another possibility is that an alternate biblical definition of *hanging* involved a large sharpened pole instead of rope. The person would be impaled on the pole and left there to hang.

Peter quoted portions of two psalms (69:25; 109:8) that had typologically predicted the betrayal of Jesus and what should be done in response (1:20). These two passages seemed to provide adequate guidance for what action they should take. With Jesus no longer available to consult, and prior to the arrival of the Holy Spirit, the apostles were using scripture to guide their decision-making and the discerning of God's will for their lives.

In determining who should replace Judas, they looked for someone who had belonged to their group from the beginning of Jesus' public ministry and had witnessed His resurrection (1:21–22). Two possible candidates were named (1:23). To ensure that the decision was God's and not theirs, they prayed and cast lots to determine which person should be selected (1:24–26).

Casting lots may seem like tossing a coin to us, but it had long been a highly respected method of determining God's will (Leviticus 16:7–10; 1 Samuel 14:40–42; Nehemiah 10:34; Proverbs 16:33; etc.). Yet it is interesting to note that scripture says nothing more of Matthias, the one chosen. In addition, this is the final mention of casting lots in the Bible. After the arrival of the Holy Spirit, it was no longer necessary.

Some people believe the apostles acted hastily and that Paul was intended to be the twelfth apostle. However, Paul would not have met either of the criteria they were using, and he was aware that his calling was quite unlike that of the others in Jesus' inner circle (1 Corinthians 15:7–8).

It's not fair to evaluate the importance of characters based on the amount of attention they receive in scripture. Many of the original Twelve remain essentially invisible throughout Acts. The very fact that Joseph and Matthias were chosen for consideration at all is testimony to their dedication and high moral character.

Take It Home

When we think of the apostolic nature of the church and realize that God chooses to work through His people, it is easy to rush forward and start trying to do things our own way. We design a plan to accomplish the mission of God and go full steam ahead only to discover many times that we've made a mess of things. Along with Jesus' promise that His followers would receive power and authority was His command to wait (1:4). Can you think of a time when you should have waited for God and suffered because you didn't? How about a time when you did wait and it paid off? What can you do to ensure that in the future you will wait on God to provide a clear calling and vision for your task?

ACTS 2:1–47

THE ARRIVAL OF THE HOLY SPIRIT

Setting Up the Section

Prior to His crucifixion, Jesus had tried to tell His followers that the Holy Spirit would come to replace Him after His departure (John 14:15–27; 16:5–16). After His resurrection, just prior to His ascension into the heavens, He instructed them to go to Jerusalem and await the Holy Spirit. He hadn't set a time frame, but their wait was only about ten days. The coming of the Holy Spirit was an unmistakable event that transformed the believers and initiated the establishment of the church.

📖 2:1–13

A SIGHT, A SOUND, AND STRANGE SPEECH

The annual celebration of Pentecost (2:1) was significant in both an agricultural and historical sense. It was originally known as either the Feast of the Harvest or the Feast of Weeks, and was the middle of three annual Jewish harvest festivals. *Pentecost* means "fiftieth," and relates to the fact that the event was held fifty days after the Sabbath of Passover week (Leviticus 23:15–16). During the years prior to the birth of Christ, Pentecost also came to be celebrated as the anniversary of the giving of the Law at Mount Sinai, because the event was thought to have taken place fifty days after the Exodus from Egypt.

It is no coincidence, then, that Yahweh's two covenant promises were fulfilled on the day of Pentecost. He had promised through His prophets to send His Spirit (Ezekiel 36:27) to the people of Israel, and to put His law in their minds and write it on their hearts (Jeremiah 31:33). While the people were ready to celebrate the harvest, the specific occasion would also become a memorable event regarding the "harvest" that Jesus had been concerned with (Luke 10:2). And the sound, fire, and speech that had been present atop Mount Sinai occurred once again on the Day of Pentecost (2:2–4).

The sound was that of a violent wind. The fire took the shape of tongues that came to rest on everyone present. And the speech was perhaps the most impressive sign of all. The group of uncultured and unschooled Galileans was suddenly able to present the gospel in the various native languages of all the visitors gathered in Jerusalem for the Feast. It was not a gift of hearing; it was a gift of speech.

Luke's list of peoples represented in Jerusalem included fifteen groups named (approximately) geographically from east to west (2:5–11). The fact that they all heard the gospel clearly explained in their own language represented the voice of God and the universality of the message.

Reactions to this amazing occurrence were mixed. Many people were amazed and perplexed (2:12). After all, these were the same people who had been too timid to even admit knowing Jesus during His trial and crucifixion. Yet here they were boldly proclaiming the wonderful things God had done (2:11). After experiencing such fresh new power, the followers of Jesus would never be the same. Yet other people weren't so impressed with the believers and looked for other explanations (2:13).

📄 2:14–41

PETER'S EXPLANATION

Peter made it clear that the phenomenon the crowds had witnessed was not the result of too much wine—especially not at 9:00 a.m.! He then used three passages from the scriptures to explain what was happening.

The first (2:16–21) was from Joel 2:28–32. Joel was a rather gloomy book, written during a period when an invasion of locusts had destroyed every green plant and created a national disaster in their rural, agricultural economy. And rather than attempting to soothe the people with promises of comfort and hope, Joel told them that their situation would get worse. The locusts were only a symbol of the more intense divine judgment to come. Yet in this context was the passage cited by Peter of God's promise to pour out His Spirit and provide salvation for everyone who calls on His name.

Peter's boldness on this occasion is striking. He had already stood and raised his voice to address the large crowd (2:14). And while it was one thing to quote scripture, Peter's additional remarks summarized the essence of the gospel and held his listeners accountable for their actions (2:22–36). He told them that Jesus, sent from God, was handed over to them. And, yet, they were the ones responsible for His death (2:23).

Critical Observation

The tendency for overzealous Christians to blame Jews for the death of Christ stands as one of the black eyes in the church's past. It is a fact of history that Jewish leaders did conspire to have Jesus executed, and the Gospels record that the crowd on Good Friday called for His blood (Matthew 27:25; Luke 23:23). Yet the Romans were the ones to crucify Him, and all the water in the world cannot wash Pilate of the blood that is on his hands for the death of Jesus. But at a more basic level, it is the sin of each and every individual that is responsible for putting Jesus on the cross.

Peter was addressing fellow Jews and all of those who lived in Jerusalem (2:14). He held his own people accountable for their actions (2:23). But the word *wicked* can also mean "lawless," and those without the law were the Gentiles. However, the act of putting Jesus to death is soon overshadowed by God's action of raising Him from the dead (2:24).

Peter's second passage is from Psalm 16:8–11, a psalm of David. Although this poem was written a thousand years before Christ and contains statements that apply literally to the Old Testament king of Israel, one portion could not possibly have referred to David. In Peter's speech, he pointed out that David's tomb was there in their midst (2:29), so David's body had certainly seen decay. Jesus was therefore the Holy One referred to in Psalm 16:10, who had overcome death and the grave as prophesied by David long ago (2:30–33).

Peter's third passage was from another psalm of David (Psalm 110:1). This verse is quoted or referred to in the New Testament at least twenty-five times. In the original Hebrew, the first reference to "Lord" is *Yahweh* or *Jehovah*, referring to the great God of Israel. The second word interpreted "Lord" is *adonai*, meaning an individual greater than the speaker. So David is saying that God invites another person, someone greater than David, to sit at His right hand. Peter again clarifies that this significant individual is none other than the Messiah.

Demystifying Acts

One might wonder how Peter is suddenly such a profound source of spiritual insight and theological acuity, enabled to realize that Jesus was the fulfillment of so many Old Testament prophecies. Perhaps a clue is found in the story of the two disciples on the road to Emmaus (Luke 24:13–35). As Jesus walked with them, "beginning with Moses and all the Prophets, he explained to them what was said in all the Scriptures concerning himself" (Luke 24:27 NIV). Similarly, Jesus spent numerous sessions with His disciples during His post-resurrection appearances discussing the kingdom of God (Acts 1:3). In light of the resurrection, surely the apostles began to grasp a better understanding of what had happened. And with the presence of the Holy Spirit, Peter was able to concisely summarize the facts and persuade his listeners.

It was painful for many in the crowd to hear that the person whose crucifixion they had endorsed had been made both Lord and Christ by God (2:36). Yet, rather than assigning blame or amplifying feelings of guilt, Peter promises forgiveness and salvation for those who would repent and be baptized. He warned them and pleaded with them, and in response, about three thousand people became believers that day (2:40–41).

📖 2:42–47

THE CHURCH GETS UNDERWAY

In one day church membership increased twenty-five times its original number, and new people were added every day (2:47). In a modern setting, such growth might create numerous problems. Yet in its earliest stages, it seemed that the new and growing church was doing everything right. It was, and continues to be, a model for worship (both collectively in the temple and in smaller groups in homes), in discipleship, in showing care for others, in evangelizing, and in serving. The godly awe that filled the people (2:43) was reflected in their attitudes, relationships, giving, and every other aspect of their lives.

Take It Home

In our post-modern world, the twenty-first century church has many of the same challenges that the first-century church faced. Christianity is again becoming a minority voice among the other beliefs in our nation and our world. In some countries, Christians are persecuted with the same cruel intolerance as the members of the early church were soon to face. What can we learn from their positive examples to make our body of believers stronger today? What can be done collectively? What might you do personally to make a difference?

ACTS 3:1–4:31

PERSECUTION BEGINS

Setting Up the Section

As the early church is formed, Peter quickly emerges as the prominent leader. After making an impassioned and persuasive speech to a large crowd (2:14–36), he soon begins to demonstrate spiritual power and authority similar to what Jesus had modeled. In this section he heals a beggar who had been crippled from birth. And as had been the case with Jesus, the healing didn't go unnoticed by the Jewish religious leaders, who respond with a show of their own power.

POWER IN THE NAME OF JESUS

Peter and John were on their way to the afternoon prayer when they encountered a crippled man who, we find out later, was over forty years old (4:22). Lame from birth and unable to get around on his own, he was completely at the mercy of others (3:2). No doubt his location outside the temple was a planned strategy to appeal to people on their way to prayer. He was hoping to benefit from their desire to gain merit as a result of almsgiving.

The temple gate that was called Beautiful (3:2) is usually considered to be the Nicanor Gate—the main eastern gate to the temple precincts from the court of the Gentiles. The story was told that the gate had been transported from Alexandria to Jerusalem by ship when a terrible storm began. The gate was about to be jettisoned, and a man named Nicanor requested to be thrown overboard along with it. When both survived the storm, it was considered a miracle, and the name and gate were forever associated. Josephus the historian described the gate as being seventy-five feet tall with double doors made of Corinthian brass. The beggar must have appeared a pathetic creature indeed at the foot of this gleaming, magnificent gate.

He asked Peter and John for a contribution, as he did everyone else who came along. But their response was different (3:4–5). The beggar had hoped for money, but what he received was much more valuable (3:6–8). Perhaps Peter had been observant when Jesus raised Jairus's daughter from the dead (Luke 8:54) because he didn't merely tell the man to get up; he gave the command, and then extended his hand to help (3:7).

The healed beggar's reaction is noteworthy (3:8). He praised God verbally while simultaneously walking and jumping. His physical enthusiasm was certainly praise as well. And as onlookers saw the commotion and recognized the man who was leaping around, they were amazed (3:10).

PETER'S SECOND SERMON

Even in his unbridled enthusiasm, the healed beggar held on to Peter and John (3:11). Consequently, it didn't take long for a crowd to form.

Solomon's Colonnade (3:11), next to the outer court of the temple, was a roofed porch supported by rows of tall stone columns. It was here that Peter, for a second time, found himself surrounded by curious onlookers wanting an explanation for the awe-inspiring events they had witnessed (2:14–36). He began by telling them, essentially, "Don't look at me. John and I didn't perform this miracle!" (3:12). The power, he said, should be attributed to God who has glorified Jesus (3:13).

Peter used imagery of the suffering Savior (Isaiah 52:13–53:12), an unfamiliar concept for many in the crowd who still anticipated a heroic military Messiah. He went on to provide three specific ways that Jesus had suffered at the hands of the people:

1) They—including those in the crowd—had demanded that Jesus be killed even after Pilate tried to exonerate Him (3:13).

2) They had demanded release of a murderer rather than God's own Son (3:14).

3) They had killed the very One who made life possible for them, but God had raised Him from the dead (3:15).

It was only through Jesus' power that they were able to heal the crippled man (3:16). And it must have been difficult to hear that, even though God had foretold that His Christ would suffer (3:18), the suffering had been at *their* hands.

Still, Peter wasn't attempting to instill guilt. He acknowledged that the people had acted ignorantly (3:17). Yet as a result of their actions, they needed to repent. They had missed the significance of Jesus and allowed Him to die; they must not overlook His eternal significance as their only source of restoration and salvation (3:19–21).

Peter made another point that would have been important to the people in the crowd. They hadn't just missed out on the message of the prophets concerning Jesus; even Moses (whom they revered) had told them to look for a prophet like him (Deuteronomy 18:15–19; Acts 3:22–23). The other prophets from Samuel onward had then reaffirmed Moses' message of a coming servant of God (3:24–26). Moses and the prophets had done as God had instructed, and now it was up to the people to do the same by turning from their wicked ways (3:26).

📄 4:1–22

TROUBLE WITH THE AUTHORITIES

As with Peter's first sermon, the second one had mixed reactions. Many people believed what Peter was saying and responded in faith (4:4). In fact, the church swelled from around three thousand people (1:15; 2:41) to five thousand men (4:4). (Many times, biblical head counts included only the males, referring to family units.)

Yet Peter's teachings about Jesus' resurrection had also gotten the attention of the Sadducees, who didn't believe that people were resurrected after they died (Luke 20:27). They came, along with security officers from the temple, and seized Peter and John. This was no small scrap with the law; the captain of the temple guard (4:1) held a priestly rank second only to the high priest, and he was responsible for the maintenance of law and order. Since it was already late in the day, the apostles were jailed for the night (4:3).

Demystifying Acts

The Sadducees were a ruling class of wealthy aristocrats. Politically they ingratiated themselves to the Romans and followed a policy of collaboration. Theologically they believed that the messianic age had begun during the Maccabean period (around 160 BC), so they were not looking for a Messiah. They also denied the doctrine of the resurrection of the dead, so naturally they viewed Peter and John as both heretics and agitators.

The purpose of their overnight incarceration was to convene the Sanhedrin (frequently referred to simply as "the council" in scripture). This was a seventy-member body plus its president, the high priest, comprised of members of the high priest's family, experts in the law (including scribes and Pharisees), and other respected members of the community (elders). They sat in a semicircle as they served as both the Supreme Court and Senate of the nation of Israel.

During their night in jail it surely occurred to Peter and John that they were about to stand before the very group that had condemned Jesus to death less than two months before. Was history about to repeat itself? They surely couldn't count on justice from this court that had listened to false testimony and unjustly condemned Jesus. Fear would have been justifiable, since many of the same authorities that had sentenced Jesus to death were presiding (4:5–6).

But the next day, rather than being afraid, Peter was filled with the Holy Spirit (4:8). His response is an emphatic demonstration of the truth of what Jesus had previously promised His followers (Luke 21:12–15). Peter certainly received the words and wisdom that Jesus spoke of. As soon as Peter and John were challenged to explain themselves (4:7), Peter took the offensive. There were three parts to Peter's defense:

1) He focused on the healing of the crippled man as being an act of kindness, brought about by the name of Jesus Christ of Nazareth (4:8–10). Peter was neither ashamed nor afraid to testify about Jesus.
2) He drew attention to the fact that the same Sanhedrin trying his case had been responsible for the death of Jesus, but God had vindicated the Lord by raising Him from the dead (4:10–11). He considered their actions a fulfillment of prophecy (Psalm 118:22). Jesus was the overlooked and rejected stone that had become the capstone, the crowning piece of God's creative work in the world.
3) He changed the topic from healing to salvation (4:12). He started by replying to a query about physical and temporal restoration, and moved from there to the subject of spiritual and eternal restoration. The healing of the crippled man was a picture of the salvation available to all people through Jesus.

Peter's use of "no other name" (4:12) proclaimed the positive uniqueness of Jesus. His death, His resurrection, His exaltation, and His authority constitute Jesus as the one and only Savior for humankind.

The Sanhedrin was astonished at the courage of Peter and John. Jesus had been an insightful and formidable opponent to the religious authorities who had repeatedly debated and criticized Him. These two were clearly ordinary men (4:13). But that had been an early assumption about Jesus as well (John 7:15).

The council members had to make a judgment, and the healed man stood before them, physically regenerated (4:14). So they could not deny the miracle, but neither would they acknowledge it. Even the miraculous power of God could not penetrate the Sadducees' preoccupation with protecting their vested interests. They shut themselves off from seeing and responding to the miracle that occurred. But they also realized that the crowds of people were certainly taking notice of what had happened (4:17).

The best they could do was to solemnly forbid Peter and John to speak at all in the name of Jesus. The ban on the apostles was intended both to serve as a warning and to provide a legal basis in the event further action should be needed. But the powerful Sanhedrin was certainly not expecting the apostles' response to its admonition (4:19–20). As with the prophets of old, God's Word was in the apostles' hearts like a burning fire, and they could not remain silent.

With all the people praising God for the miraculous healing of the crippled man, the council could see no way to punish Peter and John. So it threatened them more and then let them go (4:21).

Critical Observation

Consider Peter's newfound boldness in this passage. He had always been the impulsive one in the group of apostles. He got out of the boat and walked on water, only to falter and begin to sink (Matthew 14:27–31). He was quick to speak up but frequently said the wrong things (Matthew 16:22–23; Luke 9:32–36). Within hours of promising to go to prison and to death with Jesus, he had denied Him three times (Luke 22:33–34, 54–62). Yet immediately after the coming of the Holy Spirit, we see him stand boldly and proclaim the gospel to a large crowd, use the power of God to heal someone of a forty-year ailment, and defend his faith before an authoritative and rather resistant group of religious leaders.

🔖 4:23–31

THE RESPONSE TO PERSECUTION

At this stage in the early church, the believers were all together "and had all things in common" (2:44 NKJV). So when Peter and John had been arrested, imprisoned for the night, and tried before the Sanhedrin, all the other church members had a stake in what would happen to them. The fact that Peter and John were released with nothing more than a slap on the wrist was a cause for great rejoicing.

And their joy was not misplaced. While some may have felt a great sense of relief, the believers immediately lifted their voices in prayer and praise (4:24). They acknowledged God as sovereign Lord and Creator. And the words of Psalm 2:1–2 came to mind and took on new significance. The psalmist had written of nations, peoples, kings, and rulers gathering together to oppose God (4:25–26). Those same groups were still standing in opposition: Jews, Gentiles, Herod, and Pontius Pilate (4:27).

But at this point, after the resurrection of Jesus had put things into better perspective, they could see Jesus' (and their own) persecution as events that God had ordained (4:20). The believers did not pray for God to eliminate, or even reduce, their sufferings. Rather, they asked for boldness in the face of threats and opposition (4:29). And they asked for God's power, not to use against their persecutors, but so they could continue to heal and minister in the name of Jesus (4:30).

God acknowledged the believers' prayers, responding by shaking their meeting place and filling them all with the Holy Spirit. As a result, their boldness was intensified.

The believers withstood this initial problem of persecution from those outside their ranks and grew stronger as a result. The next threat, however, would come from within.

Take It Home

Notice in this passage that what the beggar was asking for was not what he really needed. He was looking for handouts from others, which had gotten him by for over forty years. But after Peter and John saw his real need and used the power of God to heal him, the man was absolutely jubilant. What can believers learn about their prayer habits from this story? Do you ever pray for something that is more of an immediate want than a real need? Could it be that the reason God sometimes doesn't answer prayers is because He is more concerned with meeting our needs than in fulfilling our current desires?

ACTS 4:32–5:42

NEW PROBLEMS FOR THE NEW CHURCH

Setting Up the Section

Led by the Holy Spirit, and inspired by recent positive results after an encounter with the Jewish authorities, the newly forming church is a model of unity and mutual sacrifice. So when the first threat to that unity is exposed, the consequences are severe indeed. Yet the believers get past that problem and continue to teach, heal, and share with one another. Meanwhile, opponents continue to intensify their persecution of the believers, which only strengthens the faith of Jesus' followers.

📖 4:32–37

ONE IN HEART AND MIND

From the arrival of the Holy Spirit on the Day of Pentecost, every mention of the gathering of believers has emphasized their unity. Here they are of "one heart and soul" (4:32 NASB). Beyond being just a mental attitude, the proof of their love for one another was seen in their selfless giving. Even though believers were by this time numbering in the thousands (4:4), none among them were in need of anything because they didn't even claim possessions as their own. The willingness of those with wealth to share with others more than covered the needs of the group. This was but one of the results of the grace that was on them all (4:33).

Generosity even reached the point where some people would sell their houses and property to donate to the needs of the church (4:34–35). One such person was named Joseph, yet he would become known throughout the rest of the New Testament as

Barnabas, a nickname meaning "Son of encouragement" (4:36).

The response of the church to such large (and public) gifts is not noted. With everything else said about the church to date, however, one would think that much praise would be given to God, with heartfelt appreciation expressed to the donor(s). Yet with the steadily growing numbers, it was only a short time until problems arose to jeopardize the unity the believers felt and the sharing they practiced.

📄 5:1–11

TWO EXCEPTIONS. . .AND THE CONSEQUENCES

The account of Ananias and Sapphira is one of the more difficult biblical passages to deal with. The offense of the couple seems insignificant in contrast to other sins that were quickly forgiven. From all appearances, Barnabas and Ananias did the same thing. Both sold a piece of property. Both brought the proceeds of the sale to the apostles. The only difference might appear to be that Barnabas brought all he received, while Ananias held out a little for himself.

Yet Ananias was guilty of the double sins of dishonesty and deceit. He and his wife agreed to misrepresent the selling price when reporting to the church. It is understandable that they might have wanted a positive reputation and the respect of their peers. But instead of acclaim, they both were put to death by God immediately after Peter's explanation that they had lied (5:3). They weren't killed because they held out some of the money for themselves; that was their right. Instead, what they thought was a subtle attempt to make themselves appear better was actually a lie to God (5:4, 9).

The church members became fearful after hearing what happened (5:5, 11). The situation was a classic example of what Paul would later teach: "Do not be deceived: God cannot be mocked" (Galatians 6:7 NIV). And the story is a graphic reminder that there are no "little" sins.

Critical Observation

Perhaps the severity of the punishment of Ananias and Sapphira was the result of their being the first to break the unity within the early church. Throughout scripture, as God leads His people to new opportunities and a closer relationship with Him, those who are first to disobey are treated more harshly. A few examples include:

- Nadab and Abihu, two sons of Aaron who tried to make an offering of incense in a different manner than God had prescribed (Leviticus 10:1–2)

- Achan, who stole and hid plunder after the fall of Jericho (Joshua 7)

- Uzzah, who touched the Ark of the Covenant against God's instructions, even though he had the best of intentions (2 Samuel 6:6–7)

PHENOMENAL HEALING AND CONTINUED GROWTH

As the story of Ananias and Sapphira spread throughout the community, the result was beneficial. Although verse 13 says that no one else dared join the apostles and believers, the reference appears to be to those who might be joining merely out of curiosity or with less-than-total commitment. The very next statement clarifies that additional men and women continued to be added to their number (5:14).

Those who chose to be involved with the new movement were witness to incredible things. Few of the numerous signs and wonders (5:12) are detailed other than healing of the sick and those tormented by evil spirits (5:16). Yet the method of healing listed is but a single clue as to the great spectacle of how God was at work among His young church (5:14). People began to flock in crowds to Jerusalem as news spread of the many wonderful things taking place (5:16).

ANOTHER BRUSH WITH THE AUTHORITIES

The Sadducees weren't happy that the apostles had ignored their warnings to quit talking about Jesus (4:18, 21), so this time they had a larger group arrested and jailed (5:17–18). Their real motive is recorded as well: jealousy (5:17). Clearly, God was at work among the believers in Jesus, and all the Sadducees could do was observe (and complain) as outsiders.

The apostles were supposed to be in prison overnight, but their sentence was commuted by an angel who released them (5:19). Rather than take the opportunity to hide or escape, the apostles followed the angel's orders to go tell people about the gospel.

The truly miraculous aspect of the apostles' prison break was that no one knew they were gone. The cells were still locked and the guards still at their posts. It wasn't until the Sanhedrin had assembled and sent for the apostles that they were discovered missing. Someone finally had to tell the council that the apostles were teaching in the temple courts—one of the most public places in Jerusalem (5:25).

To avoid a potential stoning by the people, the temple officials decided to use tact instead of force to summon the apostles (5:26). The high priest interrogated them, wanting to know why they ignored the previous warnings they had received. Their answer was short and clear, and they followed it with a mini-sermon about the significance of Jesus and the Holy Spirit, and how the Jewish leaders had contributed to Jesus' death (5:29–32).

The response angered the council to the point where its members wanted to kill the apostles. The translation of the New English Bible is on target: "They were touched to the raw" (5:33). But a cooler head prevailed. Gamaliel, a highly respected rabbi, used logic, reason, and historical precedent to justify a policy of laissez-faire. The apostles claimed to be obeying God (5:29), but he advised his peers to wait and see if God was really behind this movement. After all, two previous movements had collapsed as quickly as they had arisen (5:35–39).

Demystifying Acts

Gamaliel appears in Acts with no introduction, but he was a significant person on the council. He was the grandson of the famous rabbi Hillel. Saul of Tarsus (the apostle Paul) was one of his students. He was a Pharisee with a reputation for scholarship, wisdom, and moderation. And he wasn't just scholarly; the people had a high regard for his opinion. He was a welcome model of reason and sanity in this emotionally charged situation.

Gamaliel's words swayed the Sanhedrin, and though spoken by a non-believer, the council proved to be prophetic for the whole book of Acts. He points out that if God is behind this movement, no one will be able to stop it. Sure enough, throughout Acts no one and nothing can stop the progress of the gospel, proving that this is indeed God's work. Yet, though it was swayed, the council didn't simply release the apostles this time.

Before letting them go—with additional orders not to talk about Jesus any more— the council had them flogged (5:40). But rather than being despondent from pain and shame, the apostles rejoiced that they had been deemed worthy of suffering in the same way that Jesus did. They had the honor of being dishonored, and the grace to be disgraced.

As for the orders of the Sanhedrin, silence was not an option. If anything, the apostles' experience only intensified their fervor to spread the good news about Jesus (5:41–42).

Take It Home

Sometimes committee work, or even fellowship within the church, can take on the tone of a business meeting, with varying opinions stated strongly and persuasively and little room for compromise. What can you learn from Gamaliel's advice (5:38–39), or from his example in general, to ensure that human argument doesn't short-circuit God's will during a hotly debated issue in the future?

ACTS 6:1–8:3

THE CHURCH'S FIRST CASUALTY

Setting Up the Section

To this point the commentary on the new and growing church has been overwhelmingly positive, even though problems are beginning to arise. The apostles have been imprisoned and flogged. Two members have died dramatic deaths as a result of lying to God. And this section describes another problem from within: discrimination. Yet the church does such a good job of resolving the problem that one of the people chosen to help attracts too much outside attention and becomes the church's first martyr.

📖 6:1–7

THE PROBLEM WITH SUCCESS

With the number of disciples steadily increasing in the church (6:1), problems were to be expected. But discrimination should not have been among them.

Demystifying Acts

"Grecian Jews" (NIV) or better, "Hellenistic Jews" (TNIV; *Hellenistai*), were Jews who had at one time lived outside of Palestine. They spoke Greek as their primary language and were culturally and socially distinct from the Hebraic Jews (*Hebraioi*). These latter had never left Palestine and spoke Aramaic as their native tongue. The tension between these two groups is understandable, but it prevented the complete unity of the church (6:1).

To say the apostles waited on tables (6:2) may sound condescending today when we think of the wait staff in a contemporary restaurant, but that was not the apostles' intent here. Their leadership role involved teaching and preaching, and they wanted to maintain their focus on what God was calling them to do. So they enlisted a group of other people who were called to minister in a more physical, material way. Yet the fact that the apostles sought out people known to be full of the Spirit and wisdom (6:3) indicated that the waiting-on-tables ministry was just as much a spiritual calling as teaching and preaching.

In addition to acknowledging the spiritual significance of this new ministry, the plan of the disciples was wise for a number of other reasons. They did not appoint a committee;

they appointed a ministry team and delegated the responsibility and authority to get the job done. In addition, they chose seven people to oversee the new program rather than a single person. There is great wisdom in the plurality of leadership in the church, with ministry exercised in community. Finally, the names of the people chosen were Greek (6:5). The church selected people who would be most understanding of the problem of discrimination, striving to be inclusive rather than exclusive.

The apostles' proposal pleased everyone, so the seven candidates were commissioned with prayer and laying on of hands (6:5–6). After the new ministers went to work, the church not only kept growing, but also began to see Jewish priests coming to believe in Jesus in large numbers (6:7).

The book of Acts will have more to say about Stephen and Philip, the first two of the seven listed (6:5). Philip reappears in Acts 8. Stephen's story follows immediately.

📖 6:8–15

THE BRIEF MINISTRY OF STEPHEN

Only one verse (6:8) is devoted to the wonderfully positive ministry of Stephen before we read of the conflicts he encountered. Yet his upright character becomes evident in contrast to the actions and statements of his accusers.

The Synagogue of the "Freedmen" (6:9), or Libertines, may have been composed of descendants of Jewish prisoners of war enslaved by the Roman general Pompey when he conquered Palestine in 63 BC. Later released, they formed a synagogue community of "freedmen." It is unclear whether Luke has in mind one synagogue, made up of Jews from various places (Cyrene, Alexandria, Cilicia, and Asia), or whether he is referring to two or more synagogues. In any case, these Jews opposed Stephen's preaching about Jesus.

The topic of their argument with Stephen is not mentioned, but they were no match for his wisdom. Yet rather than concede that he knew more than they did, they used the same tactic the Pharisees had used with Jesus: Get him to say something and then enlist false witnesses to twist his words (6:11).

Stephen's supposed offense was a double charge of blasphemy: speaking against the temple and the Law of Moses (6:13). The Law was God's Word, and the temple was God's house. So for Jews to speak out against either one was to speak against God Himself. Once more in Acts, the Sanhedrin was convened for a hearing about the new teachings of Christianity (6:12). Yet even before the trial began, everyone there noticed that Stephen's face was like that of an angel (6:15). Many believe that his face glowed with divine glory as Moses' had after he had spent time in the presence of God (Exodus 34:29–35).

📖 7:1–53

STEPHEN'S DEFENSE

The high priest (president and moderator of the Sanhedrin) began by asking if the charges against Stephen were true (7:1). In response, Stephen launched into a lengthy sermon that was, in fact, his answer to the question. In the panorama of God's dealings with His people, Stephen focused on four main epochs of Israel's history, each one with a major character.

Abraham (7:2–8)

It was thanks to Abraham's obedience to God that the Israelites got to Israel in the first place. He had left a comfortable home in Mesopotamia only because God told him to. He was later rewarded with land, a child of his own, and descendants too numerous to be counted. It was through Abraham that God's covenant of circumcision was established. God also shared with Abraham what would happen during the next phase of history—slavery in Egypt.

Joseph (7:9–19)

It was thanks to Joseph's obedience to God that the Israelites didn't starve during a seven-year famine. Joseph's brothers' hostility toward him had actually been God's method of placing Joseph in Egypt, where he was put in charge of Pharaoh's kingdom. It was at Pharaoh's invitation that Joseph's entire family moved to Egypt to survive the famine. But four hundred years later the family had grown into an immense force that threatened the Egyptian leaders who no longer remembered Joseph. Therefore, the members of the family of Israel (the Israelites) were enslaved.

Moses (7:20–43)

God had told Abraham that his descendants would become slaves in Egypt, but that He would punish the nation that enslaved them (7:6–7). It was thanks to Moses' (reluctant) obedience to God that the Israelites at last departed from Egypt and (after numerous trials and lapses of faith) finally made it to the promised land. Had Moses' parents obeyed Pharaoh's instructions, Moses would have been put to death as an infant. But through a series of God-directed events, he grew up as Pharaoh's grandson instead. He spent forty years in the palace, forty years in a lonely existence in the wilderness, and forty years leading his people. His final forty years were especially challenging because the people continually complained to him, wishing they were back in Egypt and constructed a golden calf as soon as Moses was gone for a while.

David and Solomon (7:44–50)

While in the wilderness, the Israelites had a portable tabernacle, created just as God instructed, that allowed the priests to operate and the people to worship and offer sacrifices. Joshua continued with it into the promised land. David wanted to build a permanent structure ("dwelling place" [7:46]) for God, but his request was denied. Instead, God allowed Solomon to construct the temple. But Solomon realized at the time, and Stephen reiterated in his speech, that God cannot be limited to any physical space—not even a temple dedicated in His name (1 Kings 8:27).

Why did Stephen single out these four periods of Israel's history? They were not random thoughts. The connecting feature of these four epochs is that in none of them was God's presence limited to any particular place. On the contrary, the God of the Old Testament was a living God, a God on the move who was always calling His people to fresh adventures and always accompanying them wherever they went. God does not live in buildings made by the hands of people.

Critical Observation

Peter and Paul would later build on Stephen's theme and explain that the Spirit of God now dwells in the hearts of believers, and together we are the living stones of God's house (Ephesians 2:19–22; 1 Peter 2:4–5).

Stephen appears to be one of the first Christians to understand, and certainly the first to declare it publicly, that God could never be contained in the buildings or boxes we try to put Him in. Heaven is God's throne and earth is His footstool. Stephen also understood that the patterns of the Old Covenant were passing away.

The false witnesses had accused Stephen of two blasphemies—that he spoke against the holy place (the temple) and that he spoke against the holy law (6:13). In response to both accusations, his defense was that nothing he said had been out of line with scripture. He showed that the Old Testament placed less emphasis on the temple and more emphasis on the Law than did his accusers.

At this point, Stephen the accused became the accuser. He used unflattering names to call out the members of the Sanhedrin and put them in the same category with their ancestors who had resisted the Holy Spirit and persecuted God's prophets (7:51). Although they placed such an emphasis on circumcision, their eyes and ears remained "uncircumcised"—just like those of the unbelieving Gentiles. And not only had they not obeyed the Law they claimed to hold so highly, they also had betrayed and murdered Jesus (7:52–53).

📖 7:54–60

THE DEATH OF STEPHEN

Stephen's words were not at all well received (7:54). The furious council members could hardly control themselves. It was then that Stephen saw a vision of Jesus and told them what he had observed (7:55–56). His use of the title "Son of Man" is significant. It had been how Jesus most often referred to Himself and subtly combined both the human and divine nature of His messianic role. (This is the final use of the term in the New Testament.) In addition, biblical references to Jesus at God's right hand refer to Him as seated (Psalm 110:1; Colossians 3:1; Hebrews 8:1; etc.). The fact that He is standing here, some speculate, is to receive Stephen into His presence.

The Sanhedrin was supposed to be a Supreme-Court-like body with strict rules and procedures. But here its members acted no better than a lynch mob (7:57–58). They didn't have the authority to carry out a death sentence, yet they dragged Stephen outside the city and began to stone him. It is here where we find the first biblical mention of a young man named Saul who would soon, due only to the grace of God, become the dynamic apostle Paul (7:58). Stonings could be messy, so Saul was tending to the coats of the participants—a role that indicates his endorsement of what was going on.

But in his final moments of what was intended to be agony, Stephen was still filled with the Holy Spirit (7:55) and responded very much the same way Jesus had during His crucifixion. Like Jesus, Stephen had been charged with blasphemy, and false witnesses were produced to testify against him. And Stephen's two final statements reflected two of his Lord's last words from the cross. First, he asked Jesus to receive his spirit, and then he prayed for forgiveness for those who were in the process of killing him (7:59–60). Finally, he fell asleep, a common biblical euphemism for death (7:60).

📄 8:1–3

PERSECUTION AS A WAY OF LIFE

The church was shocked by the martyrdom of Stephen and the violent opposition that followed, but with the benefit of hindsight we can see how in God's providence it was used to help fulfill the Great Commission. Stephen's death was the occasion of a great persecution that led to the scattering of the disciples out of Jerusalem and into Judea and Samaria (8:1). Yet wherever they went, they took the gospel with them.

Meanwhile, Saul quickly moved from tending coats into full-scale persecution of believers. He was both cruel and heartless, going from house to house and dragging off both men and women to be imprisoned—all in his desire to destroy the church.

Paul's story is dropped abruptly at this point, but will be picked up again in Acts 9.

Take It Home

Stephen was the first Christian martyr, but certainly not the last. Dying for one's beliefs is not a problem that has been left in the past. According to statisticians, more Christians died for their faith during the twentieth century than in all the previous centuries combined. These days we may hear more about suicide bombers dying for radical Islamic causes than about Christians dying around the world, but both are realities. The freedoms of the Western world may make martyrdom seem distant and unreal to us. So perhaps the harder question for the Western church is not, "Do you think you would be willing to die for your faith if it came down to it?" but instead, "Are you willing to live out your faith boldly and publicly?" On an individual level, are you making the most of the spiritual freedom you enjoy?

ACTS 8:4–40

FROM JERUSALEM TO SAMARIA TO ETHIOPIA

Setting Up the Section

Jesus had told His followers that they would be His witnesses in Jerusalem, Judea, and Samaria, and to the ends of the world (1:8). Until the stoning of Stephen, they had remained in Jerusalem with an idyllic unity and spirit of fellowship. In this section, however, persecution will drive them out of Jerusalem into the surrounding territories of Judea and Samaria.

📖 8:4–8

THE MINISTRY OF PHILIP, PART I

Change is seldom easy. It must have been difficult, if not a bit traumatic, for the church members in Jerusalem to disperse. Most descriptions so far in Acts have portrayed the church as an exciting and contagious place to be. Members ate in one another's homes. No one had any financial needs. Property was shared. Much time was devoted to prayer and learning from the disciples. There was power in the early church. Miracles took place, and new believers were added daily.

The few problems faced so far had been dealt with quickly, allowing the group to keep ministering and growing. The ministries of the newly designated Seven had started very well, especially the work of Stephen.

Then, with no warning, Stephen had been seized, carried before the Sanhedrin, and stoned to death. The crowd's hostile feelings toward Stephen extended into a great persecution against the church in Jerusalem. The apostles remained in Jerusalem and the church eventually survived there, but many members were scattered to new locations (8:1). They left the wonderful unity they had shared to settle elsewhere and begin new communities. Meanwhile, Saul was passionately seeking out and imprisoning all the believers he could find.

They might have been resistant to change, yet they preached about Jesus wherever they went and began to see positive things happening. Philip, another of the Seven, went to preach in Samaria. When he was no longer needed to disperse food to widows, Philip became an effective evangelist. Like Stephen, he was empowered to perform great miracles (6:8; 8:6). He drove out evil spirits and healed many paralyzed and crippled people, resulting in great joy.

THE GIFT THAT CAN'T BE BOUGHT

As it turned out, Philip's display of God's power was overshadowing the work of a sorcerer named Simon who had made a living in Samaria for a while (8:9). Simon's boast to be the Great Power (8:10) may have been a claim of divinity, or perhaps it was enough for him to claim an association with some unseen power. In either case, his ability to amaze the Samaritans with his magic came to an end when they saw Philip performing genuine miracles in the name of Jesus. Even Simon counted himself among the believers and was baptized with numerous other Samaritans. Yet Simon appeared to be more a follower of Philip, with an intense curiosity about the power he was using, than a follower of Christ (8:13).

But one great miracle had not yet been observed in Samaria. For some reason, the belief and baptism of the Samaritans were not accompanied by the receiving of the Holy Spirit, as all previous conversions had been. Peter and John had been sent from Jerusalem to observe for themselves the response of the Samaritans to Philip's preaching. When they arrived, they prayed for the Samaritans to receive the Holy Spirit, and the new believers did (8:14–17). Luke does not specify exactly what confirmed the presence of the Holy Spirit, yet it was very apparent because Simon the sorcerer witnessed something that impressed him. It is frequently assumed that the sign was speaking in tongues as it had been on the Day of Pentecost.

Peter had promised the gift of the Spirit to all who repented and were baptized (2:38–39), so why the delay in the arrival of the Holy Spirit in this one instance? The long history of tension (and even hatred) between the Jews and the Samaritans may help explain. Hostility had existed between the Jews and the Samaritans for centuries, and a schism had formed because of racial and theological differences. The mutual animosity was intense. For the Samaritans to believe in the same Savior and be baptized in the same Name as the Jews was an unprecedented event. The delay in the coming of the Holy Spirit allowed Peter and John to witness the event so they could return to the church in Jerusalem and confirm God's work among their former enemies. In addition, Philip's ministry as an evangelist was validated among the Samaritan people.

Critical Observation

It is rather ironic that John was one of the representatives sent to witness the coming of the Holy Spirit to the Samaritans. One of the last times he had been in Samaria, he had asked Jesus about calling down fire on the people (Luke 9:52–56). The very disciple who previously wanted God to pour out His judgment on the Samaritans was there to see God pour out His Spirit and His blessing instead.

Peter and John had laid their hands on the Samaritan believers prior to their receiving the Holy Spirit. Simon the sorcerer witnessed what happened and tried to bribe the two apostles to give him the same ability (8:18–19). Peter's response not only revealed the shallowness of Simon's previous "conversion," but also created great fear within the sorcerer (8:20–24). Judging from Simon's heart not right before God, wickedness, bitterness, and captivity to sin, it is doubtful that he had ever made a sincere decision to repent and follow Jesus. Even after Peter's harsh rebuke, Simon wouldn't pray to God directly but looked for someone else to pray for him (8:24). The word *simony* arose from this story, meaning the buying or selling of ecclesiastical pardons, offices, and such. Early church tradition also says that Simon originated the cult of Gnosticism and led believers astray with his false teachings.

In contrast to the reluctance of Simon was the enthusiasm of Peter and John. On their way back to Jerusalem, they preached the gospel in many other Samaritan villages (8:25). The love of Jesus was beginning to heal a rift that had existed for centuries.

📖 8:26–40

THE MINISTRY OF PHILIP, PART II

After such rousing success in Samaria, the angel's instructions to Philip don't seem to make much sense (8:26). Gaza is the most southerly of five Philistine cities near the Mediterranean coast. The road between Jerusalem and Gaza stretched through the desert for fifty or sixty miles. Why leave the crowds of eager-to-hear Samaritans to go into isolation in the wilderness? Yet Philip seemed to respond with no reservations.

Along the way he saw a chariot and was told by the Spirit to stay close to it (8:29). Inside was a man reading from the book of Isaiah. It was common practice in antiquity to speak aloud when reading. So Philip had the ideal opportunity to ask if the man in the chariot understood what he was reading. He had no idea.

It turned out that the man was an important official from Ethiopia, in charge of the queen's treasury. The reference to Ethiopia in this passage is not the contemporary country east of Sudan, but rather an area that would currently extend from southern Egypt into central Sudan. Candace (8:27) was actually a traditional title for the queen mother, who was responsible for performing the more mundane duties of the reigning king.

The queen's treasurer had traveled a great distance to worship in Jerusalem, but the fact that he was a eunuch may have prevented his inclusion in the ceremonies because Hebrew law forbade it (Deuteronomy 23:1). Perhaps he had gone all that way, only to be turned away from the temple and all the other worshipers.

If so, it is all the more significant that he was reading about someone else who was humiliated and without descendents (8:33). It was also all the more frustrating that he didn't really understand the scriptures. So Philip climbed up in the chariot with him and started with that very passage to tell him the good news about Jesus (8:31, 35). Jesus had no children, yet as our Messiah and Savior He created a whole new family of faith with His Father in heaven where there is room for us all.

When they traveled past some water, the Ethiopian asked to be baptized, and Philip complied (8:36–38). But as soon as the two came up out of the water, Philip disappeared under the power of the Spirit of the Lord. The Ethiopian never saw him again, but left rejoicing.

Demystifying Acts

Verse 37 is missing from many current Bible translations because it is not found in the original manuscripts and is thought to have been added later. It makes the Ethiopian's request to be baptized conditional on his belief, and provides his testimony: "I believe that Jesus Christ is the Son of God."

It appears that when the Ethiopian got back home, he started a family—not a physical one, but a spiritual one. The Christian church in Ethiopia sprang up and continued to grow, perhaps as a result of the Ethiopian's newfound understanding of the gospel, although there is no direct proof.

As for Philip, he turned up in Azotus (the Old Testament city of Ashdod), miles away from where he had been. He made his way north to Caesarea, preaching throughout various towns as he traveled (7:40). He appears to have settled in Caesarea (21:8).

Take It Home

The account of the belief and salvation of the Samaritans and their early inclusion into the church provides a good lesson for today's believers. Can you detect any people or groups who tend to be excluded from church involvement—either locally or worldwide? Do you think it's better for the church to remain somewhat segregated, or should God's people strive harder for total unity? What do you think it would take to resolve the conflicts and become more united, regardless of race, economy, political affiliation, etc.?

ACTS 9:1–31

THE SURPRISE CONVERSION OF SAUL

Setting Up the Section

After the arrival of the Holy Spirit, shortly after Jesus' ascension, the followers of Jesus were in for a lot of surprises. The apostles stopped cowering in seclusion and began to speak boldly in the streets and temple courts—even at risk of arrest and imprisonment. Priests and Samaritans were among those adding to the number of believers. But the biggest surprise yet is found in this section, where one of the foremost among Christian persecutors has a dramatic encounter with Jesus and becomes one of the foremost among New Testament evangelists.

ON THE ROAD TO DAMASCUS

Saul's experience on the road to Damascus is the most famous conversion in all of church history. Paul will later share his story with other people, which Luke also records, so the account is found three times in the book of Acts. But so far, each of the three mentions of Saul (7:58; 8:1, 3) has portrayed him as a relentless opponent of Christ and His church.

That hostile image continues in Acts 9:1–2. Saul had been involved, to an extent, with the stoning of Stephen (7:58). We don't know whether or not he actually participated in killings of other believers, but based on verse 1, that might be the case.

In any event, he had gone out of his way to secure official permission and paperwork needed to imprison any believers he found in Damascus. Believers weren't yet being called Christians. Jesus had referred to Himself as the way, the truth, and the life (John 14:6), so at this point the movement of His followers was sometimes called "the Way" (9:2). This term is found several times throughout Acts.

Critical Observation

The trip to Damascus was a commitment in itself. The city was about 150 miles from Jerusalem—a journey that would require almost a week. But a lot of Jewish people lived in Damascus, and the synagogues would be a good place to seek out adherents of the new Christian religion.

Saul wasn't alone. He had traveling companions, perhaps members of the temple police to help transport any believers he might find back to Jerusalem. Saul and his group were almost to Damascus when he saw a light from heaven and heard clearly the voice of Jesus (9:3–4). Saul fell to the ground and responded, and the voice confirmed that, indeed, He was Jesus. It's worthwhile to note that Jesus didn't accuse Saul of persecuting the church; it was Jesus Himself who was being persecuted. Saul would later come to understand the close interrelationship between Jesus and His followers, and would incorporate the concept into his Epistles.

Jesus told Saul to go on into Damascus and wait to be told what to do (9:6). The men with Saul heard a noise, but did not discern that it was a voice speaking to him. When he arose to comply, he discovered he was blind and had to be led by the others into the city. He was there three days, and unwilling to eat or drink anything. It was quite a humbling turn of events. Saul had come to Damascus to arrest anyone who believed in Jesus; instead he was arrested by Jesus, whose light shone not only in his eyes, but also in his heart. He had expected to enter the city with pride in his prowess as a self-confident opponent of Christ, but found himself humbled and blinded, a captive to the very One he had opposed.

SAUL IN DAMASCUS

Jesus was calling Saul to an exciting new ministry, but first He called a believer named Ananias for a short-term assignment (9:10–12). Saul had traveled to Damascus for the express purpose of imprisoning believers—which would perhaps result in their subsequent deaths. Ananias had full knowledge of Saul's mission (9:14), so it was no small matter for him to approach Saul to extend a favor and treat him as a believing brother. He expressed his concerns to the Lord, and was assured that Saul was a different person.

In Jesus' comments to Ananias, we learn a lot about Saul. His hometown is mentioned for the first time (9:11). Tarsus is still a city in Turkey, and having been in existence for more than six thousand years, may be the oldest city on earth. (Another contender for the title is Damascus.) It had a good reputation as an intellectual city. Tarsus is mentioned only five times in the Bible, each time in connection with Paul.

Demystifying Acts

Though it's not commonly heard today, *Ananias* was a common name in the Mideast during the first century. This passage tells of a disciple in Damascus by that name. Acts 5:1–11 told of the death of another Ananias and his wife, Sapphira. And later in Acts (23:1–5), Paul will defend himself before a high priest named Ananias.

Jesus' instructions to Ananias also explain that Saul would become His representative to the Gentiles and their kings, as well as his fellow Israelites (9:15). Later chapters in Acts will show Saul (Paul) before Roman rulers and various other groups of Gentiles. Ananias was also told of the suffering Saul would endure (9:16). Over the course of his life, Saul was beaten eight times for his faith. Once he was pelted with rocks and left for dead. On various occasions he spent a lot of time in prison. And tradition says that eventually Saul was beheaded in Rome by order of Caesar.

But none of these outward signs of belief had taken place in Saul's life as Ananias responded in great faith and went to the house where Saul was staying. Straight Street (9:11) shouldn't have been hard to find. Damascus is filled with short, crooked roads, but two parallel streets ran east to west to connect the city walls. Ananias even addressed Saul as "Brother Saul" (9:17), as he explained why he was there. After laying his hands on Saul, something like scales fell from Saul's eyes and he could see again. The first thing he did was go to be baptized. Then he ate for the first time in three days (9:18–19).

A subtle distinction is made between the appearance of Jesus to Ananias and His appearance to Saul. Ananias saw Jesus in a vision (9:10). But Saul had an encounter with the resurrected Jesus (9:17), which he confirms later in his writing (1 Corinthians 15:3–8).

Saul spent several days with the Damascus disciples. The reference to many days (9:23) was probably a three-year period. In retelling his story, Paul later adds the fact that he went to Arabia during this time—perhaps to study, meditate, pray, and discern God's will for his life (Galatians 1:13–18). During his time in Damascus, he immediately began to preach in the synagogues that Jesus is the Son of God (9:20). The antagonist of the believers had become a protagonist. The persecutor became a proclaimer. Right from the start, Saul was a powerful witness and defender of the faith. His sudden commitment to his newfound faith was confusing to people at first, of course. But when the Jews tried to challenge what he was saying, he bewildered them with his persuasive observations. No one could refute his arguments (9:21–22).

As days passed and Saul attracted more and more attention, the Jews in Damascus began to conspire to have him killed. The Roman governor was in on the plot as well (2 Corinthians 11:32–33). They set up a twenty-four-hour surveillance of the city gates and planned to catch him leaving the city, but he learned of their plot. The Damascus believers lowered him in a basket down the outside of the city wall during the night, after which he made it safely to Jerusalem (9:23–25).

📖 **9:26–31**

SAUL IN JERUSALEM

Back in Jerusalem, Saul was a man with no place to go. He, of course, wanted to unite with the believers there, but they didn't know what had happened to him in Damascus. He needed someone to reach out to him, as Ananias had done in Damascus. That person turned out to be Barnabas, the "Son of Encouragement," who had already been such an example of generosity in the early church (4:36–37). We aren't told that Barnabas received a vision or special divine instruction to provide the courage to meet with Saul. Perhaps he did it because he thought giving someone a chance for repentance and forgiveness was simply the right thing to do.

With Barnabas as his ally, Saul met with the church leaders (9:27). He recounted the events of his trip to Damascus and stayed with them. He also spoke boldly about Jesus throughout Jerusalem. And in very little time, he became embroiled in debates with the Jews there until they, too, conspired to kill him. When the Jerusalem believers discovered their plot, they sent Saul to Tarsus (9:30).

Saul had been perceived as such a monumental threat to the established Jewish way of life, that once he was removed from the geographic area the Jews didn't even bother to persecute the other believers. The church throughout the whole area—Judea, Galilee, and Samaria—had a period of peace. It continued to grow both in spiritual depth and in numbers (9:31).

Saul will be absent from Luke's narrative for the next few chapters, with Peter's ministry taking prominence. But then the account picks up with Saul again and continues throughout the rest of the book of Acts.

Take It Home

It's almost impossible to consider how the history of the church would have been different if Saul (Paul) had not played the part he did. Yet twice in the early stages of his faith, it was other people who played important roles in helping him find his place in the church. Ananias is only mentioned in this account and once more as Paul recounts his conversion (22:12). Barnabas is a bit better known, but not nearly as recognized as Paul. Yet the fearless service of Ananias and Barnabas should not go unnoticed. The church is always in need of those who will go out of their comfort zones to connect with people who both need to know more about Jesus and who have much to contribute. Do you know anyone who seems like a modern-day Ananias or Barnabas? Can you think of any opportunities you might have to reach out to someone, even if the prospect seems a bit frightening?

ACTS 9:32–11:30

INCLUSION OF THE "UNCLEAN"

Setting Up the Section

The early chapters of Acts show Peter as the primary leader of the church. He will soon fade from prominence as Saul (Paul) begins his ministry. And the previous section made clear that Saul was chosen to go to the Gentiles. However, in this section we discover that God also called Peter to a ministry that included Gentiles as well as Jews. Male or female, slave or free, Jew or Gentile—anyone who believes in Jesus can be included in His church.

📖 9:32–43

PETER HEALS AENEAS AND RAISES TABITHA

After Stephen's death, persecution had broken out against all the believers. Many left the city, but the apostles had determined to stay in Jerusalem (8:1). However, Saul's conversion had attracted much attention and prompted his departure for Tarsus, so the pressure was off of the other church leaders, and they enjoyed a respite from persecution.

Peter took the opportunity to get out of the city and engage in an itinerant ministry. He was probably offering encouragement to the various churches that had formed from the believers who had fled Jerusalem. Among his travels throughout the country he visited believers in Lydda (9:32), a town about twenty-five miles northwest of Jerusalem at the intersection of one highway from Egypt to Syria and another from Jerusalem to Joppa (on the coast). It was a decent-sized village according to the historian Josephus.

In Lydda, Peter came across a man named Aeneas who had been paralyzed for eight years and was currently bedridden. We aren't told of any preliminary conversation between the two. It appears that Peter simply declared Aeneas healed in the name of Jesus and told him to get up and walk, which Aeneas immediately did (9:34).

In many of Jesus' miracles, healing had been in response to a person's declaration of faith. Yet faith is not the power that brings about miracles. Faith is rather the preparation for the miracle—anticipation of what God will do not only in the person's body, but also in his or her spirit. There are instances in scripture, as in this one, where the person made no expression of faith prior to being healed. It appears that in certain cases healing initiates faith. On this occasion, all those in Lydda and Sharon (a fifty-mile stretch of fertile land along the coast of Palestine) who heard about the healing of Aeneas turned to the Lord (9:35).

Meanwhile, Peter was approached by two disciples from Joppa, urging him to go with them. Joppa was Judea's main seaport, only about twelve miles away. A faithful believer there had just died. Her name was Tabitha (Aramaic) or Dorcas (Greek). Both versions of the name mean "gazelle." Tabitha was a skilled seamstress who had a wonderful reputation for helping the poor and doing good, and many people were mourning her death (9:36, 39).

The Bible records three instances when Jesus raised someone from the dead, but none of His followers had ever attempted a miracle of this magnitude. It is possible that the believers in Joppa had sent for Peter only for his consolation and prayer support during this difficult time, although it seems that they were expressing the faith that he would perform a great miracle.

Peter had been present when Jesus had raised Jairus's daughter (Luke 8:51–56), and he followed much the same procedure here. He sent out all the mourners, then kneeled down and told the woman to get up. When she opened her eyes, he took her hand and helped her stand up. This miracle, like the healing of Aeneas, caused many people to believe in Jesus (9:42).

Peter then spent several days in Joppa, perhaps at the urging of the people there. The fact that he stayed in the home of a tanner (9:43) indicates a new level of inclusion. By most Jewish standards, someone who worked with dead animals would be ceremonially unclean and therefore looked down on. Peter's willingness to stay with Simon is a prelude to the story that follows.

📄 10:1–8

THE VISION OF CORNELIUS

Previous sections of Acts have hinted at a ministry to the Gentiles. The great response of the Samaritans to Philip's preaching (8:4–8, 14–17) was a beginning, even though the Samaritans had many beliefs similar to those of the Jews. The conversion of the Ethiopian eunuch was another positive sign of things to come. Now another noteworthy Gentile comes into the picture—a centurion named Cornelius.

The name was a very popular one in ancient Rome. In 82 BC a man named Cornelius Sulla freed ten thousand slaves, and as a token of appreciation they all took the name of their patron. It is quite possible that the Cornelius in this passage was a descendent of one of the freedmen of Cornelius Sulla.

We do know that this Cornelius was a centurion in what was known as the Italian Regiment (10:1). The Roman army was comprised of legions (about six thousand troops) divided into ten regiments. Centurions were responsible for commanding about one hundred soldiers within a regiment.

All biblical references to Roman centurions are positive. Cornelius is described as being a devout and God-fearing person who prayed and gave to people in need (10:2). The phrase *God-fearer* was a technical term that described someone who had essentially converted to Judaism except for one significant step: circumcision. Understandably, many adult men were reluctant to take this final step of conversion to the Jewish faith. But otherwise, it appears Cornelius sought to worship the one true God, accepted the monotheism and ethical standards of the Jews, and attended synagogue services.

As Cornelius was praying at 3:00 p.m., one of the traditional times for Jewish prayer (10:3), an angel came to him in a vision, called him by name, and told him to send people to Joppa and bring back Peter (10:3–6). As a centurion, Cornelius was accustomed to receiving and following orders, so he immediately dispatched two servants and a soldier (10:7–8).

Critical Observation

It is difficult to overstate the significance of what is happening here, as God is beginning to extend the invitation of salvation to the Gentiles. God had a unique purpose in choosing to bless the Jews—they were to be an example and a blessing to all the other families of the earth. Old Testament scriptures had pointed to a day when all nations would be included in the kingdom of God's Messiah. The tragedy was that the Israelites had twisted the doctrine of election into one of favoritism, and they became filled with racial pride and hatred toward others. They came to despise Gentiles to the point of calling them dogs. The traditions they developed over the centuries served to distance them from the Gentiles. Now, by bringing Peter and Cornelius together, God is beginning to unite these two vastly different groups.

📖 10:9–23a

THE VISION OF PETER

As Cornelius's men were making their way to the home of Simon the tanner to find Peter, the apostle was having a divine encounter of his own. At noon on the day after Cornelius had his vision, Peter was on the rooftop, praying while he waited for lunch to be prepared. His hunger played into the vision he received (10:9–10).

He saw a large sheet lowered from heaven that contained all kinds of animals, reptiles, and birds. Many, or perhaps all, were not "clean" as defined in the Law of Moses (and were very specifically prohibited in Leviticus 11), yet a voice called Peter by name and told him to kill and eat (10:13).

Peter's refusal to comply was emphatic (10:14). His hard-line stance was reminiscent of two previous occasions: once when Jesus had tried to tell the apostles of His impending death (Matthew 16:21–22) and again when Jesus tried to wash Peter's feet (John 13:6–8). It seems that Peter was still in the habit of trying to tell the Lord how things should be done in the kingdom. Even after a second and third command, Peter held fast. Then the sheet disappeared back into heaven (10:15–16).

Peter hardly had time to make sense of the vision before Cornelius's messengers arrived and called out for him. Before he could even answer, the Holy Spirit told him to accommodate them because they had been sent by the Spirit. It is interesting to note that the word translated "Do not hesitate" (10:20) can also mean, "Make no distinction." Peter was likely beginning to see the connection between his vision that had challenged the distinction between clean and unclean foods and the timely arrival of Gentile (unclean) visitors. So he went downstairs and introduced himself. The three men explained why they were there, and Peter invited them in as his guests (10:23).

The invitation was certainly a step in the right direction. For one thing, Peter had been waiting for lunch, and probably shared it with his three visitors. In addition, it was too late to begin the thirty-mile trip from Joppa back to Caesarea, so the three men needed overnight accommodations. Most Jews wouldn't consider allowing Gentiles under their roofs, much less overnight. God was beginning to break down some of the divisive barriers.

GENTILES ARE BAPTIZED INTO THE CHURCH

The next day Cornelius's three messengers led the way back to Caesarea, along with Peter and six believers from Joppa (11:12). The distance took more than a day to travel, so the group arrived four days after Cornelius had his vision (10:30).

Cornelius must have felt strongly that Peter would respond because he had gathered a large group of friends and relatives. As Peter entered, Cornelius met him at the door and fell at his feet in an act of worship. But Peter quickly made him get up, assuring the centurion that they were both equals (10:25–26).

Peter walked right into Cornelius's home (10:27), breaking down old taboos and setting an example both for the Gentiles there and the Jewish believers he had brought with him. By this time it was clear that he had come to understand his vision as a sign that the Gentiles were no longer to be considered unclean (10:28–29).

Cornelius succinctly explained the reason he had sent for Peter, and that he had brought together a group to listen to what God had commanded Peter to say (10:30–33). It is apparent that both Peter and Cornelius were not acting on their own instincts, but following what God had instructed them to do.

Peter began to speak to the crowd about Jesus' life and ministry, His death, and His resurrection. He emphasized the divine plan behind the events that had played out during Jesus' time on earth. Peter could offer not only the facts about Jesus, but also his personal verification as an eyewitness—both before and after Jesus' crucifixion (10:39, 41). And Peter's message provided the totality of the gospel. He concluded with an image of Jesus as the one appointed as God's judge of humanity, yet made it clear that forgiveness and salvation are available for anyone who believes in Him (10:42–43).

Demystifying Acts

In Luke's summary of Peter's sermon (10:34–43) we see the very heart of the gospel message. Theologians call this the *kerygma*, a Greek word that means "preaching" and represents the essential witness and affirmation of the New Testament preachers concerning the gospel of our Lord. The *kerygma* was the core message of the grace of God revealed in Jesus Christ.

Peter was still speaking when the truth of his words was confirmed by the arrival of the Holy Spirit on all who were listening. The Jewish believers were amazed to see Gentiles speaking in tongues and praising God—which demonstrated Peter's wisdom in bringing them to be witnesses (10:44–46).

The next step for those expressing faith in Jesus was baptism. Philip had baptized the Ethiopian eunuch in the solitude of the desert, and the Ethiopian may have been a Jewish proselyte. This would be the first time Gentiles were baptized to be included in the church along with Jewish believers. But apparently there was no objection, because Peter saw to their baptisms right away (10:47–48).

This was a memorable moment in the history of the church. The promise of the prophets centuries before was coming true. God's love, mercy, and grace were reaching everyone—not just the Hebrew nation. But it would take a while for the truth and significance of this event to sink in.

📖 11:1–18

PETER IN JERUSALEM

After staying a few days with Cornelius in Caesarea, Peter went back to Jerusalem. He immediately received criticism from the Jewish believers for visiting and eating with Gentiles (11:2–3). This accusation is somewhat reminiscent of the ones Jesus had regularly received from the religious leaders for eating with tax collectors and sinners.

In explanation, Peter started from the beginning and reviewed his vision, Cornelius's visit from the angel, the coming of the Holy Spirit to the Gentile believers, and the unanimous decision to baptize them (11:4–17). He repeatedly emphasized the work of God and the Holy Spirit as instrumental in bringing about the events.

Peter was persuasive, and his critics relented and praised God (11:18). As hard as it was to understand and acknowledge at the time, God was offering salvation even to the Gentiles. And if God was removing the distinctions between Jews and Gentiles, what right did Peter—or anyone else—have to harbor old prejudices? The dispute was settled, but only temporarily. It would take a long while and many additional debates to work through all the obstacles for allowing Gentiles the same rights and privileges of church membership that the Jews enjoyed.

📖 11:19–30

BARNABAS AND SAUL IN ANTIOCH

At this point Luke goes back to the persecution following the stoning of Stephen and follows a different storyline. He begins by telling about Philip's ministry, Saul's conversion, and Peter's outreach to the Gentiles—all essential to the history of the early church. But meanwhile, noteworthy events were taking place in Antioch of Syria.

Antioch was the third largest city in the Roman world, after Rome and Alexandria. It lay three hundred miles north of Jerusalem, about fifteen miles inland from the Mediterranean Sea. Its population (estimated to be five hundred thousand to eight hundred thousand) contained probably about one hundred thousand Jews along with a number of Gentile proselytes to Judaism. It was also a popular hedonistic destination, accused by the Roman satirist Juvenal of having a corrupting influence on Rome itself.

Yet it was here where some of the victims of the persecution in Jerusalem had settled and had taught the gospel. Many had spoken only to other Jews, but some had reached out to Gentiles as well, and both groups were beginning to see large numbers of people believing (11:21). The presentation of the gospel in the name of Lord Jesus (11:20) rather than Christ is due to the audience. The title "Christ" was equivalent to "Messiah," which would not have had significance to the Gentiles. Many of them, however, would have considered Caesar their "lord," and the teaching of the believers clarified that the title deserved to go only to Jesus.

News of the excitement and growth of the believers in Antioch reached all the way to the church members in Jerusalem. They responded by sending Barnabas to oversee the newly forming church. Here is yet another overwhelmingly positive description of Barnabas (4:36–37; 9:26–27): a good man, full of the Holy Spirit, and full of faith (11:24). As his nickname (Son of Encouragement) warranted, he encouraged the Antioch believers and rejoiced with them.

Tarsus, where Saul was staying (9:30), was about ninety miles away, yet Barnabas went to invite him to Antioch as well. The two were ideal for working among Gentiles, and they spent an entire year with the believers in Antioch (11:26). Tradition indicates that Luke was from Antioch, so it is possible that he was among the new converts who learned of the truth of Jesus from the lips of Barnabas and Saul during this time.

It was in Antioch where believers in Jesus were first called Christians (11:26). The distinction of belonging to Christ's party, or being Christ followers, as the word *Christian* implies, would begin to distinguish the group. Until this point, Christianity had been perceived as an offshoot of Judaism. But now that Gentiles were joining the church, it was clear that was not the case. However, a reference to *Christian* occurs only three times in the New Testament (Acts 11:26; 26:28; 1 Peter 4:16).

The Jews believed the spirit of prophecy had been suspended after the Old Testament writing prophets, and was to be renewed again in the coming messianic age. So early Christians not only acknowledged Jesus as a prophet (3:22; 7:37), but also recognized prophecy as a gift of the Holy Spirit (1 Corinthians 12:28). And prophets operated throughout the early church. The group in this passage (11:26–27) predicted a famine that struck during the reign of Claudius (AD 41–54). Agabus (11:28) would later warn Paul of impending danger (21:10–11).

The genuine faith of the believers in Antioch was evident from their willingness to give to the church in Jerusalem (11:29–30). The Jerusalem church had generously shared its leaders to assist the growth of those in Antioch. Now the Antioch Christians were supporting the Jerusalem church financially.

This is the first biblical mention of the role of "elders" (11:30). The word can mean simply older men, though in this context it seems to refer to church officers. They would be the ones responsible for distributing the gift that had been delivered to them. Jewish synagogues employed elders, and it seems that the position was adopted by the Christian church as well.

Take It Home

Cornelius and Peter were very different people. Yet as they each responded to God's direction, they got together and both learned more about God as a result. Do you know someone who has a very different view of God than you do? If so, do you make the most of opportunities to interact and learn more about his or her opinions of spiritual things? You might not agree with most, if any, of the specifics. But sometimes the very act of discussing matters of faith will be a catalyst for spiritual growth for one, if not both, of you.

ACTS 12:1–24

PETER'S PRISON BREAK

Persecution to Please the Crowds	12:1–3
Peter's Arrest and Prison Escape	12:4–19a
The Death of Herod	12:19b–24

Setting Up the Section

Aside from the death of Stephen and a bit of persecution from Jewish authorities, Luke's history of the early church has been very positive so far in the book of Acts. However, the conclusion of the previous chapter hinted at a famine and some monetary need in Jerusalem (11:27–30). This section continues to report increasing problems for the church—in this case, intensified persecution. And while God continues to provide for some of the believers in miraculous ways, others are beginning to be imprisoned and even killed for their beliefs.

📖 12:1–3

PERSECUTION TO PLEASE THE CROWDS

It is debated whether Luke presents the material in this section thematically or chronologically. King Herod Agrippa I (12:1) was the grandson of Herod the Great and a nephew of the Herod (Antipas) who had killed John the Baptist. He ruled Judea from a headquarters in Jerusalem from AD 41 to 44, the year he died.

The famine mentioned at the end of the previous section (11:27–28) occurred in AD 46. So it is possible that Luke wasn't writing chronologically. Or if Barnabas and Saul were in Jerusalem before the death of Herod *and* during the famine, it would have required two visits—a reasonable possibility for a pair who were on the road so frequently.

Herod had Jewish ties and always tried to sustain a good relationship with those in charge of the Jewish people. As the Jewish believers fell out of favor with the established authorities, Herod found he could impress those in control by mistreating the Christians. He began arresting church members and had James (the brother of John and one of the

Twelve) put to death (12:2). The arrests were due to no other reason than the believers' association with the church. This persecution was fueled by a political motive rather than a religious one.

The Feast of Unleavened Bread (12:3), or Passover, was one of three annual religious festivals that Jewish males were expected to attend, so the population of Jerusalem would swell with those men loyal to their history and traditions. When Herod saw that the death of James pleased the people, he arrested and imprisoned Peter. By now most people knew that Peter was the leading apostle in the church, and that he had been associating with Gentiles. He was the perfect target in Herod's ongoing thirst for popularity.

Critical Observation

Technically, Passover was the meal celebrated to commemorate the exodus of the Israelites from Egypt and God's sparing of the firstborn in all the homes with blood on the doors (Exodus 12). But that specific celebration was followed immediately by the Feast of Unleavened Bread, when all yeast and leavening agents were removed from homes during a week-long celebration. As the two events were commemorated together year after year, they became essentially one in the minds of the people. *Passover* was the popular term for the dual celebrations.

📖 12:4–19a

PETER'S ARREST AND PRISON ESCAPE

This is the third instance Luke records of Peter being imprisoned. The first time he and John only spent a single night in jail; in the second incident he and all the other apostles were miraculously released during the night and were found the next day, preaching in the temple courts (4:3; 5:17–26).

Perhaps Herod had heard of Peter's propensity to escape from prison. The precaution seemed extreme to assign sixteen guards to a single prisoner. But the four squads of four soldiers should have provided ample round-the-clock attention. Peter's likely place of incarceration was the Fortress of Antonia, a Roman stronghold that stood against the north wall of the temple enclosure. A Roman guard usually chained his left hand to a prisoner's right hand, but Peter was chained to guards with *both* hands (12:6).

Herod's plan was to keep Peter in prison until the eight-day celebration of Passover and the Feast of Unleavened Bread was over, and then he would bring him out for a public trial. Since James had recently been killed, it might seem likely that Peter would be concerned for his life. But in spite of the stressful situation, the guards, and the chains, he was sleeping soundly. Peter had a habit of sleeping when he should have been praying (Luke 9:32; 22:45), but in this case Peter's ability to sleep seems to reflect a lack of fear or worry. Perhaps he had confidence in Jesus' previous prediction that he would grow to be an old man (John 21:18). Additionally, we are told that the church was earnestly praying on Peter's behalf (12:5).

What happened next was so unlikely that Peter didn't know if it was actually happening or if he was having another vision (12:9). An angel appeared and a bright light shone in the cell. Still, the angel had to strike Peter to wake him up. Peter did as the angel instructed (12:7–8). The chains fell off his wrists, the various prison doors opened as they came to them, and Peter soon found himself alone and free on the street outside the prison (12:8–10). The reality of the situation suddenly struck him, so he began thinking of a safe place he could go (12:11).

He may have known that other believers were praying for him at the home of Mary, the mother of John Mark (12:12). Peter's inability to get inside at first is comic in its true-to-life appeal (12:13–18). Even though committed church members were earnestly praying for Peter's release, they found it hard to believe when it actually happened. The servant girl was too excited to open the door, and the other believers were too skeptical to go see for themselves. Meanwhile, Peter kept knocking until someone finally let him in.

Demystifying Acts

John Mark was a cousin of Barnabas who would later accompany Paul and Barnabas on their first missionary journey. He and Paul would have a falling out, but it would later be resolved and the two would become close friends. Mark also wrote the Gospel that bears his name. Tradition says he also was Peter's interpreter in Rome and established the church in Alexandria, Egypt.

The assumption that the figure at the door was Peter's angel (12:15) reflects the belief (based partially on Jesus' words in Matthew 18:10) that guardian angels oversee God's people and could take on the appearance of the person being protected. Another explanation is that angel might have been a reference to a human being dispatched by Peter with a message (the same Greek word can mean "angel" or "messenger"). Or a third possibility was that Herod had already killed Peter, and the apostle's spirit had shown itself to the believers.

Since James, the brother of John, had already been killed (12:2), the James referred to in verse 17 was almost certainly the brother of Jesus—a child of Mary and Joseph. James was becoming prominent in the early church in Jerusalem and will appear again later in Acts.

After Peter's previous release from jail, he had been instructed to go to the temple courts and teach. This time, however, the political climate was much different. His life was in danger. Saul had left the area to spend time in Tarsus, and Peter was leaving, too (12:17). We know from later biblical references that, at some point in his life, Peter probably visited Corinth, Rome, and Antioch.

The next morning, Herod discovered Peter was gone. He held the guards responsible, probably assuming the only way Peter could have escaped was through their cooperation with him or through negligence. Either way, their sentence was death (12:18–19).

THE DEATH OF HEROD

The sudden mention of Herod's decision to leave Jerusalem (12:19) may possibly be attributed to his desire to save face after losing a key prisoner. He decided to visit some of his subjects on the Mediterranean coast who were eager to regain his favor because their food supply depended on him (12:20).

Luke's version of this account is quite concise. The Jewish historian Josephus elaborates considerably more. It seems that Herod stood in the outdoor theater on a festival day, attired in a silver robe that gleamed in the sunshine. The people, eager to flatter him, went so far as to call him a god, and Herod said nothing to correct them. He was then immediately struck with stomach pains and had to be carried out of the theater. According to Josephus, he died five days later.

People have speculated as to the exact diagnosis of the disease that killed Herod, saying it might have been appendicitis that led to peritonitis complicated by roundworms, or possibly a cyst caused by a tapeworm. Luke simply makes it clear that Herod's miserable death was a judgment of God (12:23).

Herod had tried to hinder the growth of the church. Suddenly, he was gone and the Word of God was continually increasing and spreading (12:24). From this point on, it would be spread with more intention.

Take It Home

A logical question that arises from this section is why bad things happen to some people and not others. Why did James die at the hands of King Herod while Peter was freed as the result of an incredible miracle? In this case it seems clear that we must leave such things up to a sovereign God. We certainly can't make a case that Peter was a better person than James, or that James had done anything to warrant death. After all, Peter's time was coming (John 21:18–19). What are some similar questions you tend to struggle with? Do you get frustrated when you can't determine answers, or are you able to leave everything in God's hands and trust that He is in control no matter what happens?

ACTS 12:25–13:52

THE GOSPEL MOVES OUTWARD

Setting Up the Section

Up to this point, any contact between the believers in Jesus and the Gentile community has been quite one-sided. In each case, the contact was clearly God-directed, where Jewish believers were approached by curious Gentiles. But in this section, that will change. The church at Antioch begins to see the opportunity of approaching the Gentiles with the good news of the gospel. So its leaders designate a pair of proven disciples to travel, preach, and build up churches that have begun in various faraway places.

📄 **12:25–13:3**

THE CALL OF BARNABAS AND SAUL

Barnabas and Saul had spent a year in Antioch (11:26) prior to delivering a financial gift from believers there to the church in Jerusalem (11:30). When they returned to Antioch, they took John Mark with them (12:12). Mark was a cousin of Barnabas (Colossians 4:10).

In this section of Acts, Barnabas seems to be the prominent figure. When he and Saul are mentioned, his name comes first, as it does in the list of prophets and teachers at the Antioch church (13:1). Their names suggest a broad mix of people in the Antioch church: *Simeon* was a Jewish name, and *Niger* suggested a dark-skinned person, possibly from Africa. Niger and Lucius were Roman names, and Manaen's associate (Herod the tetrarch) was Herod Antipas—the man responsible for the beheading of John the Baptist.

It was this group of leaders who discerned God's direction to set aside Barnabas and Saul for a special calling. Apparently little time was wasted. As soon as they finished fasting and praying, they sent them off (13:3).

This commissioning of Barnabas and Saul marks a turning point in Acts. Until now, the church's contact with Gentiles has been almost incidental. When Gentiles got involved in some way, the Jewish believers dealt with it. But here, under the leading of the Holy Spirit, they sent two dedicated church members into predominantly Gentile territory. Barnabas and Saul will still have Jewish audiences as well as Gentile ones, but in most cases from this point forward it will be the Gentiles who are more responsive to their message.

MINISTRY IN CYPRUS

The Holy Spirit led them first to Cyprus, perhaps because Barnabas had ties to the island. Cyprus was a significant location situated on a major shipping route. It was also a province of Rome, and the Senate had assigned a proconsul to govern there. The news about Jesus had already reached Cyprus from people fleeing persecution in Jerusalem, but it had gone out to only the Jewish population there (11:19).

As Barnabas and Saul entered a new community, they would usually go to the synagogue. The people assembled there—both Jews and God-fearing Gentiles—would have a decent knowledge of spiritual truth, which made a good foundation for the presentation of the gospel message. In addition, traveling philosophers or religious figures were frequently invited to speak. The presence of more than one synagogue at Salamis indicates a large Jewish population (13:5).

Paphos (13:6) was the provincial capital on the western coast of the island. It was there where the Roman proconsul, a man named Sergius Paulus, heard about Barnabas and Saul and sent for them.

When the gospel had previously gone out to the Samaritan community, Luke had recorded an unusual confrontation between a local magician and Peter and John (8:9–24). A similar encounter took place in Cyprus. The Roman proconsul had an attendant named Bar-Jesus, who claimed to be a Jewish prophet but was in reality a sorcerer (which is what his nickname, Elymas, meant). When the sorcerer tried to sway the proconsul from the truth of what Barnabas and Saul were teaching, Saul took the lead and passed God's judgment of temporary blindness on the man. It was an appropriate attention-getter for someone who tried to blind others to the truth of God's Word. (Saul knew from experience that temporary blindness could lead to clear spiritual vision [9:1–19].) In addition, the clearly evident power of God convinced Sergius Paulus to believe the truths he was hearing that amazed him so (13:12).

This was another first for Christianity—the presentation of the gospel to someone in authority in Roman aristocracy. The conversion of the proconsul also legitimized a direct ministry to the Gentiles.

Demystifying Acts

It is at this point in Acts that Luke begins to refer to "Saul" as "Paul," and to give him the place of prominence in the group. Both names were probably given to Paul by his parents at birth, a common practice for Jews living among Gentiles. *Paul* (meaning "little") was his Roman name, while Saul was his Jewish name. Paul likely began to use his Roman name when his ministry shifted decisively toward the Gentiles.

MINISTRY IN PISIDIAN ANTIOCH

After spending time in an area familiar to Barnabas, the travelers sailed north to Pamphylia, not far from Cilicia, Paul's home province. At this point John Mark left the other two to return to Jerusalem (13:13). His reason for leaving is not stated. He was young and may have been homesick or fearful of illness or other dangers of travel. Or because of his strong ties to the Jerusalem church, he might not have been completely comfortable with the attention being given to the Gentiles. If so, he would not be the only Jewish believer to express discontent in the weeks and months to come. But whatever the reason for Mark's leaving, it would later cause a rift between Paul and Barnabas (15:36–41).

Pisidian Antioch (13:14) is not to be confused with the Antioch that had sent Paul and Barnabas on this journey, or with another Antioch in nearby Phrygia. The popularity of the name is due to a ruler in 281 BC who had both a father and a son named Antiochus, and founded sixteen cities named in honor of them.

The one hundred-mile journey from the seaport of Perga (13:13) would have taken Paul and Barnabas from sea level to an elevation of 3,600 feet. Bandits roamed the roads, and later Paul would say he was in ill health when he arrived here (Galatians 4:13–14). Yet they went to the local synagogue as usual and were invited to speak (13:15).

What follows is the longest of Paul's sermons (though no doubt in condensed form) to nonbelievers in Acts (13:16–41). The content is very similar to previous messages presented by Peter (2:14–39) and Stephen (7:2–53), providing a broad overview of Israel's history and concluding with the fact that Jesus was the fulfillment of all that had been promised.

Paul's reference to 450 years (13:20) was likely the time span of four hundred years spent by the Israelites in Egypt, forty years spent in the wilderness, and about another decade to conquer and settle in the promised land.

Critical Observation

Paul's clarification that John the Baptist had not been the Messiah (13:24–25) hints of a problem the early church may have faced. Some believe that certain disciples of John the Baptist had moved out of Palestine, teaching that John had been the Messiah. Later passages in Acts (18:24–25; 19:1–7) seem to indicate that some people believed the baptism of John the Baptist was all that was necessary for salvation.

Paul acknowledged the reverence the people held for King David, and said that God had raised up Jesus in much the same way He had raised up David as king (13:33). But in regard to Jesus, Paul also speaks of how God raised Him to emphasize Jesus' victory over death and the grave (13:30, 34, 37).

Paul's closing statements regarding forgiveness, belief, and justification (13:38–39) are explained more fully in his letters to the Romans and the Galatians. His Epistle to the Galatians was written to the people in this area—very likely many who responded to this message in the synagogue. He concluded his sermon with an appropriate quotation from the book of Habakkuk (Habakkuk 1:5; Acts 13:41).

The response to Paul's sermon was quite positive. He and Barnabas were invited to speak again the following week. In the meantime, numerous listeners sought them out to learn more (13:42–43). An enormous crowd turned out to hear them the following Sabbath, which created jealousy among the Jews and caused them to begin badmouthing Paul (13:44–45).

Paul and Barnabas boldly rebuked the Jewish lack of faith and turned their focus primarily to the Gentiles (13:46). The Gentile believers were honored to be included in God's plan, but the Jewish resistance only increased as the jealous ones solicited support from prominent people in the community. As a result, Paul and Barnabas were persecuted and forced to leave the area. They simply shook the dust off their feet and moved on, leaving behind a number of disciples filled with joy and the Holy Spirit (13:52). This event is a key turning point and pattern-setter in Acts. The Jews, for the most part, reject the gospel, so Paul turns to the Gentiles, who will respond positively. This pattern will be repeated again and again until its climax in Acts 28.

Take It Home

Paul and Barnabas (and John Mark, to begin with) were stepping out into new and unfamiliar territory to share their faith with others. Have you ever had a similar experience? If so, which of the three do you best relate to: (1) Paul, who dealt with sickness and opposition to speak boldly to those willing to hear; (2) Barnabas, who seemed quite content to take a secondary position; or (3) John Mark, who retreated to a more familiar setting to continue his ministry?

ACTS 14:1–28

COMPLETION OF THE FIRST MISSIONARY JOURNEY

Setting Up the Section

As Paul and Barnabas take the gospel into areas where it has not been heard, they continue to encounter a wide variety of problems. They have met resistance that will graduate into full-scale violent persecution in places. Yet the message they present and their ability to convey their ideas are so persuasive that the crowds sometimes go overboard in enthusiasm, creating an entirely different kind of problem. In this section, they complete their first journey and return to the church in Antioch.

📖 14:1–7

MINISTRY IN ICONIUM

A noted Roman road (the Via Sebaste) ran from the port city of Ephesus westward to the Euphrates River. At Pisidian Antioch (the most recent stop of Paul and Barnabas) it branched into two roads. One went north through mountainous terrain to the Roman colony of Comana, about 122 miles away, and the other moved southeast across rolling country, past snow-capped mountains, and through the Greek city of Iconium, about eighty miles from Pisidian Antioch, and then ended another twenty-four miles later at the Roman colony of Lystra. So Paul and Barnabas were literally at a fork in the road, and they chose the southeastern route that would take them to people in three very different types of cities in the southern area of the Roman province of Galatia.

Their next stop, Iconium (14:1), sat in a high plateau surrounded by fertile plains and green forests, with mountains to the north and east. As usual, Paul and Barnabas went first to the synagogue and spoke. But the people's reaction was strongly divided. Many people believed and responded—both Jews and Gentiles. But, as in Pisidian Antioch, the Jews who refused to believe caused trouble. This time they tried to influence the Gentiles to join them in resisting Paul and Barnabas.

But God was with His representatives and enabled them to perform great miracles as they stayed in the city and spoke boldly for Him (14:3). They continued to win over many people, but others sided with the Jewish antagonists. When Paul and Barnabas discovered a plot to stone them, they finally moved on, preaching wherever they went (14:5–7).

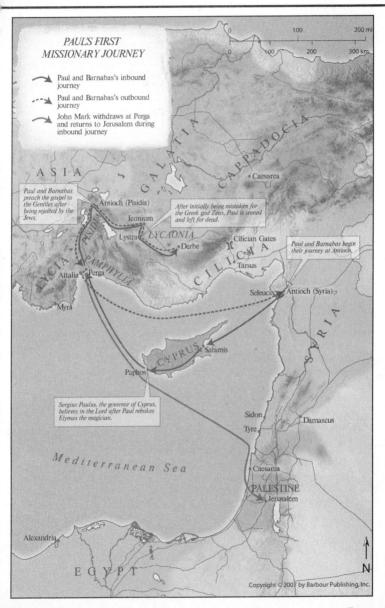

PAUL'S FIRST MISSIONARY JOURNEY

→ Paul and Barnabas's inbound journey

- - → Paul and Barnabas's outbound journey

→ John Mark withdraws at Perga and returns to Jerusalem during inbound journey

Paul and Barnabas preach the gospel to the Gentiles after being rejected by the Jews.

After initially being mistaken for the Greek god Zeus, Paul is stoned and left for dead.

Paul and Barnabas begin their journey at Antioch.

Sergius Paulus, the governor of Cyprus, believes in the Lord after Paul rebukes Elymas the magician.

ASIA · GALATIA · CAPPADOCIA · Caesarea · Antioch (Pisidia) · Iconium · PISIDIA · Lystra · LYCAONIA · Derbe · Cilician Gates · CILICIA · Tarsus · LYCIA · PAMPHYLIA · Attalia · Perga · Myra · Seleucia · Antioch (Syria) · SYRIA · CYPRUS · Salamis · Paphos · Sidon · Damascus · Tyre · Caesarea · PALESTINE · Jerusalem · Mediterranean Sea · Alexandria · EGYPT

Copyright © 2007 by Barbour Publishing, Inc.

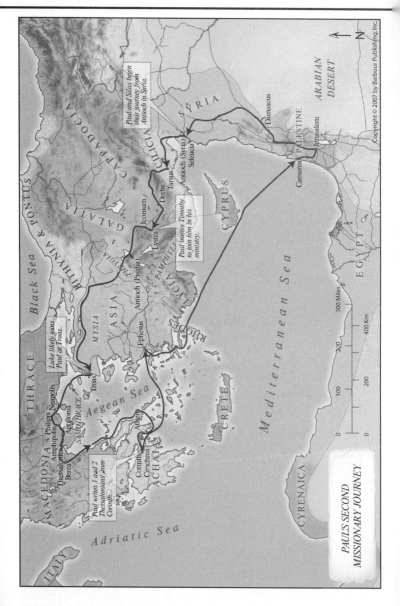

Paul and Silas begin their journey from Antioch in Syria.

Paul invites Timothy to join him in his ministry.

Luke likely joins Paul at Troas.

Paul writes 1 and 2 Thessalonians from Corinth.

Copyright © 2007 by Barbour Publishing, Inc.

PAUL'S SECOND MISSIONARY JOURNEY

MINISTRY IN LYSTRA

No mention is made of a synagogue in Lystra, which suggests a prominently Gentile population. So Paul preached to a crowd that formed. One among them was a crippled man who had never walked, but Paul saw he had the faith to be healed and commanded him to stand. The man then jumped up and began to walk. This miracle, early in the ministry of Paul, was very similar to one early in the ministry of Peter (3:1–10).

But in this case, without benefit of Old Testament scripture or knowledge of the true God, the people of Lystra believed the Greek gods were walking among them. Hermes (the Roman god Mercury) was supposedly the messenger god, so the people thought Paul must have been the human embodiment of him. They thought Barnabas was Zeus (the Roman Jupiter). They were shouting to one another with excitement, but spoke in a native language that Paul and Barnabas didn't understand. There was a temple to Zeus in Lystra, and only when the priest approached with bulls and wreaths (that would be placed on the sacrificial animals), preparing to offer sacrifices to them, did the two apostles realize what was going on.

Paul and Barnabas did everything in their power to dissuade the people from sacrificing to them. They tore their clothes to indicate extreme grief and distress (14:14). They assured the crowd that they were both just fellow human beings (14:15). They explained that all the good things that occurred were the result of a living God (14:15–17). And still, it was all they could do to calm the people.

Yet the situation quickly went from one extreme to the other. A group of Jews who had opposed Paul in Antioch and Iconium showed up and enlisted support from the people in Lystra. Before long, Paul's stoning that had been planned in Iconium was carried out in Lystra. It was no judicial execution of judgment; it was a lynching. They left Paul for dead. Some people speculate that he did actually die and came back to life, though no evidence exists to prove this theory. But equally miraculous is the fact that he was able to get up and return to the city after such an experience (14:19–20). The next morning Paul and Barnabas left for Derbe, a journey of about sixty miles.

Demystifying Acts

Paul refers to this stoning in 2 Corinthians 11:25 (see 2 Timothy 3:10–11). It may have been the occasion when he was caught up to the third heaven and witnessed amazing things he was not permitted to talk about (2 Corinthians 12:2–6).

📖 14:21–28

MINISTRY IN DERBE AND THE RETURN HOME

Only one verse is devoted to the work of Paul and Barnabas in Derbe (14:21). But after the opposition, persecution, and confusion they had just faced in Iconium and Lystra, it was probably encouraging to preach and see a large number of people become disciples of Jesus.

Paul and Barnabas had gotten within 150 miles or so of Tarsus, Paul's hometown. But he had recently spent time there, so they turned around and retraced their route, strengthening and encouraging the believers as they returned (14:21–26). By this time Paul was speaking from experience when he told them, "that they must enter into the Kingdom of God through many tribulations" (14:22 NLT). It certainly must have taken a great amount of faith and courage to go back through the same cities that had sent hostile delegations to cause them trouble and pain, and surely the believers realized the dedication demonstrated by Paul and Barnabas.

In addition to providing encouragement, Paul and Barnabas addressed the needs of the new churches by appointing elders in each place (14:23). Paul would later declare that elders shouldn't be new converts (1 Timothy 3:6), so he may have chosen believers who had previously served in the Jewish synagogues and would have had a good working knowledge of scripture.

On their arrival back in Antioch (in Syria), they reported to the people who had commissioned them. They had been gone the better part of two years. Their focus was on God's work and how He had opened a door of faith for the Gentiles (14:27–28). Though not stressed at this point, they reported that God's salvation is by faith—not by adapting to Jewish customs or performing any other kind of works. This would soon become a major issue in the church.

Paul and Barnabas stayed a long time in Antioch and were probably glad for the opportunity to rest. Paul wrote his letter to the Galatians from Antioch at about this time.

Take It Home

The behavior of the people in Lystra was extreme, yet somewhat reflective of certain people's opinions in the contemporary church. One moment they had a too-high opinion of Paul and Barnabas as gods; the next they were literally throwing stones at Paul. Have you ever known someone who held a religious figure to an impossibly high standard, only to be immensely let down when the person didn't (couldn't) live up to expectations? What were the circumstances? What was the result? How might the problem have been prevented?

Setting Up the Section

Acts 15 begins the second half of the book. It also stands as a pivotal passage in the history of the church. Until this point, the believers in the new church were primarily Jewish, although Gentiles were being converted. But the church had a decision to make. Was it okay to simply express one's belief in Jesus and be included in full fellowship? Or shouldn't Gentiles be expected to adhere to the same high standards as the Jewish believers? Was circumcision and keeping the Law of Moses necessary for salvation? And just as noteworthy as what was decided was how the church leaders arrived at their decision.

📖 15:1–4

THE ISSUE AT HAND

By the time the council in Jerusalem convened, Gentiles had been joining the church for about ten years and were welcomed simply by baptism. The movement began with Cornelius, the God-fearing centurion, and his friends and family whom Peter had baptized in Caesarea (10:44–48). Next came the great number of people in Syrian Antioch who believed when unnamed missionaries began speaking to Greeks (11:20). Barnabas had been sent to confirm the salvation of the Gentiles, and he had recruited Paul to help train the new believers. The church in Antioch had then sent out Paul and Barnabas to travel and preach to people in predominantly Gentile territories, and they returned with news that God had "opened the door of faith to the Gentiles" (14:27).

What had begun as a trickle of Gentile conversions was fast becoming a torrent.

The Jewish believers had little difficulty accepting the Gentiles because many Old Testament passages predicted their inclusion. Yet they were beginning to question exactly how God intended to incorporate the Gentiles into the believing community. It was one thing for the leaders of the Jerusalem church to give their approval to the conversion of Gentiles in general, but could they also approve of conversion without circumcision, faith in Jesus without complete adherence to the Law and traditions, or commitment to the Messiah without inclusion in Judaism?

The first issue that came to the fore was circumcision. The debate began in Antioch, when a group from Judea arrived and started teaching that circumcision was essential for salvation (15:1). This group may have come from the party of the Pharisees (15:5) and might have been the group Paul referred to in Galatians 2:11. Paul and Barnabas, of course, couldn't have disagreed more with their opinion.

It was quickly decided that a delegation including Paul, Barnabas, and a number of others would go from Antioch to Jerusalem to discuss the matter with the apostles and elders. Along the way they spread the word of how Gentiles were becoming believers, and the news made the Jewish believers glad. The apostles and elders in Jerusalem were also glad to see them and to hear of their experiences (15:4).

📖 15:5–21

DISCUSSING THE ISSUE

The Jewish Christians who were Pharisees already had their minds made up. Their representatives insisted that Gentile believers get circumcised and be instructed to obey the Law of Moses (15:5). (The group promoting these teachings would eventually become known as the Judaizers.) Their stance was not surprising. In essentially every encounter the Pharisees had with Jesus, they were holding out for more stringent obedience not only to God's written Word, but also the hundreds of extrabiblical traditions they had developed over the centuries. When Jesus presented a much less legalistic perception of God, they usually were offended and incensed.

Demystifying Acts

The council at Jerusalem had to determine whether Christianity was simply a reform movement within Judaism, or whether Jesus' life, death, and resurrection had initiated a whole new age of salvation. Some of the participants argued that Gentiles must adhere to the same laws and traditions as Judaism in order to find favor with God. But others were beginning to see that the gospel of Jesus was the good news of God's love for the whole world, and that salvation came through faith alone in Jesus Christ and His death on the cross.

The Pharisees' statement evoked a lot of discussion among the church leaders (15:6). In effect, they were suggesting that Moses needed to complete something Jesus had begun, and that the Law should supplement the gospel. But the people who had firsthand experience with the Gentiles knew that was not the case. They each took a turn speaking.

Peter related the story of his encounter with Cornelius and how he had seen that God made no distinction between Jews and Gentiles (15:9). He pointed out that since the grace of God was the source of salvation for the Gentiles, it was also all that was necessary for the Jews as well (15:11). To subject believers to other requirements was tantamount to putting a yoke on them (15:10).

Paul and Barnabas related the signs and wonders they had witnessed God perform among the Gentiles in the various places they had been. The emphasis was not on their efforts, but God's work (15:12).

Last to speak was James, one of the brothers of Jesus who came to faith after the Lord's resurrection. He came to be known as James the Just because of his piety, and was the leader of the "mother church" in Jerusalem. The Jewish roots were still strong in the Jerusalem church, and if anyone was to back the proposal of the Pharisees, it would probably be James. But James referred to the scriptures (Amos 9:11–12) to confirm the experience that the other speakers had described (15:13–18). The inclusion of the Gentiles in the church was not a divine afterthought; the prophets had foretold it. The corresponding evidence between scripture and personal experience was, for James, conclusive.

Critical Observation

During this period of biblical history when miraculous signs and wonders were taking place on a regular basis, God chose to reveal His will to the council in Jerusalem by means of experience, scripture, and reason. The personal experience of Peter, Paul, and Barnabas was a reminder of God's work in history. Then there was an appeal to scripture, God's revealed Word and the only infallible rule in matters of faith in practice. And finally, there was an appeal to reason. In this case there was no prophetic utterance or writing on the wall. The checks and balances of experience, scripture, and reason continue to be the most common way that God reveals His will to His people.

Still, James had a pastor's heart. He knew if Jews and Gentiles were to come together in the church, they would need to be sensitive to one another's feelings. Many Gentile practices were highly offensive to Jewish sensibilities. So James suggested that a letter be written, asking Gentiles to follow a few basic guidelines (15:20)—not because they were "deal breakers" in regard to salvation, but because the elimination of such practices would go a long way in appeasing their Jewish brothers and sisters.

📄 15:22–35

ADDRESSING THE ISSUE

A letter was drafted to go out to Gentile converts. The message was clear and direct, yet tactfully inoffensive (15:23–29). The council members made a number of points. First, they distanced themselves from the Judaizers—the group who had been teaching the necessity of circumcision as a requirement for salvation. Second, they named specifically chosen delegates of the council who would personally verify what was being communicated in writing. Judas and Silas would not only explain the content of the letter, but also minister personally to the Gentile Christians. And third, the council members shared their unanimous decision not to require anything of the Gentile converts other than a few requested cultural abstentions that would have been particularly repulsive to Jewish Christians (15:28–29).

The council could have simply sent out the letter, but it realized the importance of personal contact, and had it hand delivered by personal emissaries. Judging from the names, Judas (Barsabbas) would have been a Hebrew-speaking Jew. Silas (*Sylvanus* in Latin) was Greek-speaking and a Roman citizen (16:36–37). By sending Judas and Silas back to Antioch with Paul and Barnabas, the two would not only verify the decision of the council to the pro-circumcision group (who wouldn't have agreed with it) but would also explain the letter, interpret its meaning, and secure the agreement of the recipients.

Upon the messengers' arrival in Antioch, the believers there gathered to hear the letter read (15:30–31). They were pleased with its positive message. Judas and Silas stayed for a while to strengthen and encourage them, and then returned to Jerusalem. Paul and Barnabas stayed to continue teaching and preaching (15:33–35).

Take It Home

Essentially, the Jewish Christians who were Pharisees were suggesting that faith in Jesus Christ in itself was not enough for salvation. They wanted to add circumcision and obedience to the Mosaic laws. And across the centuries, there have been numerous people who wanted to make the gospel a "Jesus plus" kind of equation. You can be saved if you believe in Jesus. . .plus lead a good life, or give up all your bad habits, or attend church regularly, or give more to the church. And it's not that such additions are necessarily *bad* things, but they aren't requirements for salvation. If you had been at the council of Jerusalem, which of the speakers would you have most related with? Can you see similar issues in the church today, or would you say the contemporary church is relatively free of such influences?

ACTS 15:36–16:40

A SECOND JOURNEY, A DIFFERENT PARTNER

An Irresolvable Dispute	15:36–41
A New Partner, a New Recruit	16:1–5
A New Direction	16:6–15
A Jailer Finds Freedom	16:16–40

Setting Up the Section

Little by little the church has been becoming more accepting of the inclusion of Gentile believers. Paul and Barnabas, still in Antioch where many such converts lived, both had a heart for going out into Gentile territory and spreading the good news about Jesus. So when a disagreement kept them from traveling together, they paired up with other people and doubled their outreach. Paul and his new traveling companion, Silas, prepare to revisit the churches previously ministered to, and they end up widening the scope of their ministry considerably.

🖹 15:36–41

AN IRRESOLVABLE DISPUTE

Paul and Barnabas had been a devoted and productive team. After Paul's sudden conversion, it was Barnabas who had first approached him in the Jerusalem church and brought him into fellowship. When Barnabas was sent to observe the church in Antioch and saw it in need of gifted teachers, he went to Tarsus to get Paul to help lead. They had traveled together on a missionary trip that covered roughly seven hundred miles on land and five hundred miles on the sea. So now that the controversy over the matter of circumcision was settled (15:1–35), they discussed taking another trip to return to the communities they had originally visited.

Yet in spite of everything they had been through together, a problem arose, and they were unable to agree on a resolution. For some reason (never stated), John Mark had left them shortly after beginning the first trip. Apparently Barnabas thought that Mark had learned his lesson from his previous failure, and wanted to invite him on this second trip. But Paul felt Mark had deserted them and didn't want him to go. Paul and Barnabas got into such a disagreement that they went their separate ways (15:39).

Luke makes no judgment about who was right or wrong. But the result was a doubling of outreach. Barnabas took Mark (his young cousin) with him and went to Cyprus—an area of familiarity where they would probably face little opposition. Paul paired up with Silas, one of the two representatives of the Jerusalem church who had returned with him to Antioch (15:22). After a short stay, Silas had gone back to Jerusalem. But the fact that he was again in Antioch (15:40) may indicate his interest in the church there. Paul and Silas headed north to Syria and Cilicia, encouraging the churches wherever they went.

Demystifying Acts

Luke records the strong disagreement between Paul and Barnabas, declines to take sides, and then leaves the matter unsettled. But the rest of the story can be determined from other biblical sources. Certainly Paul's opinion was valid: Their ministry was too important to bring along a relative who wasn't committed. But Barnabas, the "Son of Encouragement," knew that people frequently need a second chance. So later we see that Mark had become a valuable asset to Peter (1 Peter 5:13), and many believe that Peter was the source of Mark's Gospel. Mark's ongoing faithfulness even won Paul over eventually (Colossians 4:10; Philemon 24). And in the final days of his life, Paul sent for Mark because he was an attribute to his ministry (2 Timothy 4:11).

16:1–5

A NEW PARTNER, A NEW RECRUIT

Paul and Barnabas had previously sailed to Cyprus, then sailed north, and had approached the cities of Iconium, Lystra, and Derbe from the west. But with Silas, Paul took a land route that took them first through Tarsus, and then into the other cities from the east.

In Lystra was a young believer named Timothy, whose mother was Jewish and father was Gentile (16:1). His mother and grandmother were both exemplary believers (2 Timothy 1:5) who certainly influenced his faith, and it is possible that Timothy had responded to Paul's message on the apostle's previous trip through Lystra. Over a decade later, when Paul wrote to him, people were still considering Timothy too young to be a minister (1 Timothy 4:12), so at this point he must have been quite an outstanding youth. Everyone who knew Timothy spoke highly of him, and Paul invited him along on the journey.

Paul and Silas were delivering news of the decision of the Jerusalem Council—that believing Gentiles didn't need to be circumcised before joining the church (16:4). Yet Paul had Timothy circumcised before taking him along (16:3). We aren't told why Timothy hadn't already been circumcised, yet it was likely in deference to his father's Gentile culture. But in working with Jewish believers, it would appear callous and even sacrilegious for the son of a Jewish mother to be uncircumcised. So for the good of the ministry, and not as a matter of legalism, Timothy was circumcised. (In a similar circumstance with Titus, a Gentile believer, circumcision itself was the issue. Paul refused to have Titus circumcised [Galatians 2:1–5].) As the trio went from town to town, the churches grew both spiritually and numerically.

📖 16:6–15

A NEW DIRECTION

Paul, Silas, and Timothy soon found themselves in new territory as they set out across Galatia (modern Turkey), headed westward toward the Aegean Sea. They might have turned south, but were told by the Holy Spirit not to enter Asia. When they considered going north through Bithynia, they were also prohibited. So they found themselves in Troas, a seaport on the Aegean Sea (16:8).

Critical Observation

The doctrine of the Trinity has not yet been addressed, but the persons of the Godhead are used interchangeably throughout the book of Acts. For example, in the Ananias and Sapphira story (5:1–11), lying to the Holy Spirit was equated with lying to God (see verses 3, 4, 9). And here we see guidance provided by the Holy Spirit (16:6) as well as the Spirit of Jesus (16:7).

Receiving only negative guidance can be frustrating, yet Paul and his companions were patient and faithful. In Troas Paul was given positive guidance through a vision that made it clear that they should proceed to Macedonia, even farther west (16:9–10). In Troas they also picked up another companion. The writing shifts from third person to first person, indicating that Luke joins the group. Yet he doesn't join the party as a mere observer; he feels called by God to preach the gospel with the others as well (16:10).

From Troas the group sailed to Philippi, a Roman colony in what is now Greece. Luke's description of Philippi (16:12) seems a bit more glowing than that of other places, suggesting that he grew up there and perhaps attended its noted medical school. They stayed a few days in Philippi. There is no mention of a synagogue, so the Jewish community must have been very small. But on the Sabbath, when the group went to find a place to pray, they found a group of women by the river and started a conversation with them.

One of those present was a business woman named Lydia, a seller of purple cloth—something only the wealthy could afford to buy (16:14). She was a Gentile who worshiped God to the extent that she understood Him, but her understanding was greatly increased as Paul spoke and God opened her heart. She was immediately baptized along with her household, which could have included servants and children. And she convinced Paul and his group to stay at her house (16:15), which also indicates that she was a woman of means to have such space available. Lydia is the first known convert on the European continent, and her home may have become the first house church in Philippi.

A JAILER FINDS FREEDOM

Another time in Philippi when Paul and the group were on their way to pray, they passed some men with a slave girl. (Verse 17 is the last use of first person for a while, indicating that Luke stayed in Philippi while the others in the group moved on.) The young girl made a lot of money for her owners by predicting the future through a spirit that possessed her (16:16). It was also not uncommon for opium to be used to promote clairvoyance, so the girl might have been a drug addict. Upon meeting Paul's group, she started following him around day after day, proclaiming who they were and what they were doing (16:17–18). Paul finally had enough and commanded that the spirit leave her.

When it did, her owners were incensed. Rather than being glad that the girl was no longer troubled by the spirit, they only saw that their source of easy income was gone. Instead of admitting it was a money issue, they accused Paul and Silas of promoting Jewish customs that weren't acceptable for Romans (16:20–21). In response, the surrounding crowd joined the attack as Paul and Silas were stripped, beaten, and securely imprisoned (16:23–24).

Peter had been fast asleep in a similar situation (12:6), but in this case Paul and Silas were singing hymns at midnight, which drew the attention of the other prisoners. Then an earthquake shook the foundations of the prison, not harming anyone, but flinging open all the doors and loosening all the chains holding the prisoners (16:25–26).

When the jailer awoke to discover what had happened, he was going to kill himself because he knew the Roman authorities would do as much or worse (16:27). (Herod had previously ordered Peter's guards killed [12:19].) But Paul stopped him with the surprising news that no one had escaped. (The reason for their reluctance to flee is not recorded. Perhaps the prisoners recognized the work of God in connection with the hymns and the miraculous nature of the earthquake.)

The jailer was no longer the authority figure. He fell trembling before Paul and Silas, freed them, and then asked what he needed to do to be saved (16:30). Their succinct answer: Believe in the Lord Jesus (16:31). But they went on to explain the gospel to the jailer and his family, who all believed (16:32–34). After the jailer washed the wounds of Paul and Silas, they baptized the man and his household.

In the morning, word was sent from the city officials to let Paul and Silas go, but they wouldn't leave until the magistrates came themselves to release them (16:37). This was the first they had mentioned that they were both Roman citizens, which alarmed the officials. Roman citizens had rights and should not have been beaten—especially before a trial. But Paul and Silas were probably more concerned about the propriety of the situation. They had just come to Philippi with news of Jesus, and had been treated as common criminals. By demanding an official release, their innocence would be a matter of record.

Their request was accommodated, although the magistrates did ask them to leave the city (16:39). So they made one more stop at Lydia's house to encourage the believers, and then moved on (16:40).

Take It Home

The dispute between Paul and Barnabas (15:36–41) offers an important lesson in conflict management. Too often we may feel that total unity is always the sign of God's presence and blessing. But here, two very faithful, dedicated, and conscientious believers had a difference of opinion. They each did what they felt was right. And in time, they each realized how God had worked through both of them. Can you think of any similar situations in your own life, or in the workings of your church, where a strong disagreement was a potentially damaging problem? What can be done in such circumstances to continue to function as a united body even when not everyone is in total agreement?

ACTS 17:1–34

MOVING THROUGH GREECE

Ministry in Thessalonica	17:1–9
Ministry in Berea	17:10–15
Ministry in Athens	17:16–34

Setting Up the Section

After Paul and Silas paired up to go back to the churches that Paul and Barnabas had previously visited, God's Spirit then directed them to travel through new territory with the good news of Jesus. Along the way they have been joined by Timothy, who is still with them, and Luke, who has remained in Philippi. This leg of the journey will take them south again, through Thessalonica, Berea, and Athens—and they get quite a different reception in each location.

📖 17:1–9

MINISTRY IN THESSALONICA

After being asked to leave Philippi, Paul and Silas moved on and passed through two other prominent cities before deciding to stop in Thessalonica, about one hundred miles away (17:1). The mention of a synagogue in Thessalonica (17:2) may indicate the absence of one in the other towns, explaining why they passed through those locations before stopping. And even though they had just been beaten and imprisoned in Philippi, they didn't alter their usual routine. When they arrived in Thessalonica, they went to the synagogue and spoke to the people assembled there. The response must have been encouraging because they had the opportunity to speak on three consecutive Sabbaths (17:2). And based on other indications (Philippians 4:14–16; 1 Thessalonians 2:8–9), they spent much longer than two or three weeks there.

The appeal of the gospel was widespread. Those responding to Paul's teaching were some of the Jews, a large number of Gentiles, and a considerable number of prominent women in the city (17:4). However, as had been the problem previously, the Jewish leaders grew jealous and took action.

In this instance, they went to the marketplace and incited a mob to go after Paul and Silas. When they couldn't find them at Jason's house where (apparently) they had been staying, they took Jason and some other believers as well. Little is said about Jason, although Paul had a relative of that name (Romans 16:21). Perhaps Jason knew more than he was telling about Paul and Silas but, if so, did not let the crowd know. The mob grabbed Jason and some other believers and charged them with treason before the city officials (17:7). The charge was serious, but apparently the evidence was scant, and Paul and Silas could not be found. So Jason and the others only had to post bond and were released (17:9).

📖 17:10–15

MINISTRY IN BEREA

By nightfall the believers in Thessalonica had reconnected with Paul and Silas and seen them on their way to Berea, about fifty miles southwest of Thessalonica. Berea had a large population, but was of little importance historically or politically.

Yet in a spiritual sense, Berea was one of the more outstanding cities Paul visited. He and Silas went to the Jewish synagogue, as was their custom. But while the Jews of Thessalonica had quickly become jealous and antagonistic, the Jews of Berea were different. They didn't take what Paul was teaching at face value, nor did they hear his new gospel and dismiss it with little thought. Instead, every time Paul said something, they pored over what had been written in their scriptures to see if he was speaking the truth. And as a result, many of the Jews and Gentiles believed—both men and women (17:11–12).

The positive atmosphere was short-lived, however, because the agitators from Thessalonica heard that Paul was in Berea and followed him there to stir up trouble (17:13). Rather than allowing the situation to become a public spectacle as it had previously, some of the believers immediately escorted Paul to Athens—about three hundred miles away, and possibly a sea voyage. Since Paul was apparently the main target of the agitators, Silas and Timothy were able to remain in Berea for a while to help the church get started. They arranged to follow Paul to Athens soon.

📖 17:16–34

MINISTRY IN ATHENS

Alone in Athens, Paul quickly grew dismayed as he saw all the idols. The city was five hundred years past its Golden Age, but remained a center of culture and intellect. Many of the temples and statues that Paul saw are still there today, now admired for their artistic rather than spiritual impact.

With the wide variety of religious beliefs present in Athens, there was a segment of Jewish believers and God-fearing Gentiles, whom Paul addressed in the synagogue. But Athens had another place where people gathered: the marketplace (*agora*). It took Paul little time to meet various philosophers there and discuss their views. When they found his presentation of the gospel hard to grasp, they invited him to speak to the Areopagus, both a location ("hill of Ares") and the name of a court that dealt with matters of morals and the rights and restrictions of people who lectured in public.

This was a prime opportunity for Paul because the Athenians were eager to hear new and different ideas (17:19–21). And Paul found a novel approach to present the gospel. He had seen an altar inscribed with the words To an Unknown God (17:23). This was because they worshiped many gods, and the people were afraid of overlooking one and suffering his wrath. Paul explained that he knew the God they didn't—the God who made the world and everything in it, the Lord of heaven and earth. Paul's God did not live in temples or need anything from humans. He was the Creator who took a personal interest in the lives of those He created (17:24–26).

Demystifying Acts

Epicureans were followers of Epicurus, a Greek philosopher (341–270 BC). He taught that nothing exists but matter and space, so the chief purpose of humankind should be to achieve happiness and pleasure. For a philosopher, that joy was gained through intellectual challenge and growth, but his followers over the years had found pleasure through physical, sensual fulfillment. So what had begun as a philosophy of the highest standards had quickly acquired a bad reputation.

Stoics believed that the true essence of life was the capacity to understand the rational order veiled by natural phenomena. Freedom and joy were the result of detaching from the outer world and mastering one's reactions to his environment. Stoicism didn't allow for sympathy, pardon, or genuine expression of feeling. Famous Stoics included Zeno, Seneca, Cicero, and Marcus Aurelius.

To emphasize his point that God was more personal than all the idols strewn around Athens, Paul quoted Greek literature that his hearers would have been familiar with. Verse 25 had indirectly quoted Epimenides, a poet from Crete who had written, "For in Him we live, and move, and have our being." (Paul quotes him again in Titus 1:12.) Then, in verse 28, Paul quotes a poet from Cilicia (his homeland) named Aratus.

Critical Observation

Even though Paul's listeners were open to new ideas, the Areopagus did not tolerate an anything-goes atmosphere. Socrates had been sentenced to death by poisoning for promoting strange ideas in Athens, so Paul was not entirely free from danger in this setting.

Paul's point was that it is somewhat ironic that humans, as the created offspring of God, try to create gods of stone or precious metal. In fact, the acknowledgement of that fact should lead to repentance (17:29–31). When Paul brought up the topic of resurrection, he started getting resistance from some of his listeners. But he also had the attention of some of the others who wanted to hear more and eventually became believers (17:32–34).

However, no evidence exists that a church was formed in Athens as a result of Paul's visit. Even though a number of people in Athens believed, Paul's later reference to the first converts in this area (1 Corinthians 16:15) was to those in Corinth—his next stop.

Take It Home

Many modern Christians could learn from the first-century Jews of Berea. Rather than take someone's word for something—even someone as trustworthy and insightful as the apostle Paul—they searched the scriptures to verify what he was saying. Do you think most people do the same thing today? Or do they go to church to be told what to believe? To what extent do you tend to verify the "truths" you are taught from the Bible?

ACTS 18:1–22

WRAPPING UP THE SECOND MISSIONARY JOURNEY

Ministry in Corinth	18:1–8
First a Promise, Then a Test	18:9–17
Home Again	18:18–22

Setting Up the Section

Paul and Silas have set out on a second missionary journey, picking up Timothy along the way. But after being pursued from city to city by some troublemakers who would do Paul harm, he had gone ahead of the others into Athens while they stayed a while with the believers in Berea. Paul spoke to a group of philosophers in Athens, but didn't get a particularly enthusiastic reception. So he moves on to the next town: Corinth.

📖 18:1–8

MINISTRY IN CORINTH

Athens is the more familiar city to most modern ears, but in Paul's day Corinth had surpassed it in significance. The Roman military had attacked and destroyed major portions of Corinth in 146 BC, after its citizens had participated in an anti-Roman uprising, and it had remained in ruins for a century. But in 46 BC, Julius Caesar passed through and saw its potential as a Roman colony, so the city was rebuilt. By the time Paul went through, it was probably the wealthiest city in Greece—a major multicultural urban center with a population of 750,000 people.

One thing that made Corinth so popular was its location. The southern portion of Greece would be an island were it not for a narrow five-mile strip that connects the southern portion to the northern part. Sailing around the entire southern part of Greece was hazardous because of heavy winds and rough seas. It had proved more reliable to unload large ships on one side of the isthmus and have porters carry the cargo to the other side. Smaller ships would be dragged fully loaded on wooden rollers across the five-mile stretch. And Corinth lay right in the center of that isthmus, profiting from east and west seafaring traffic, as well as from the travelers going back and forth to the southern section of the peninsula.

In addition to the financial wealth of Corinth, it had a wealth of religious options as well—most of them pagan. A noted temple to Aphrodite, the Greek goddess of love, was there. Prostitution was so rampant in the city that the Greek word meaning "Corinthian girl" came to be a slang term for a promiscuous woman. Corinth was also a center of homosexuality with a temple to Apollo, the epitome of male beauty. Nude statues and friezes in various suggestive poses paid tribute to this god of music, song, and poetry. In addition, the Corinthians could visit temples to Asclepius (the Greek god of healing), Isis (the Egyptian goddess of seafarers), and her Greek counterpart, Poseidon.

There was also a synagogue, so Paul went to it on every Sabbath to reason with the Jews and Gentiles who gathered there (18:4). In the meantime, he had met a couple named Aquila and Priscilla with whom he shared a trade, so he stayed with them. They were in Corinth due to anti-Jewish persecution in Rome (18:2).

Critical Observation

It was a custom in New Testament times to teach every Jewish boy a trade. Jesus had been trained as a carpenter. Paul learned the craft of tent making, which involved working with leather, hair, and wool. It may be that it was Paul's shared trade with Aquila and Priscilla that brought them together at first—not necessarily a shared belief in Jesus (although that would later become evident).

Luke says nothing of Silas and Timothy having met Paul in Athens, as had been their plan (17:15). But apparently they had done so and had been sent out again, because while Paul was in Corinth they were both returning from Macedonia (18:5). It is likely they brought a financial gift from the churches because at that point Paul began a full-time ministry of preaching and teaching, attempting to help the Jewish population see the significance of Jesus.

But it reached a point where Jewish resistance became so strong that Paul gave up on them. Shaking out his clothes (18:6) was akin to shaking the dust off one's feet, as Jesus had previously instructed His disciples to do when they encountered resistance. Their time would be better spent moving on to someone who did want to hear rather than continuing a fruitless debate with someone whose mind was already made up (Luke 9:5; 10:10–11).

Paul didn't have to go far to find new opportunities to speak. Right next door to the synagogue was the home of a believer where he could teach. In addition, the synagogue leader and his entire household became believers, which influenced a number of other Corinthians as well (18:7–8).

📖 18:9–17

FIRST A PROMISE, THEN A TEST

It seems that Paul was facing more opposition than Luke describes here, because the vision he received appears to be in regard to specific threatening circumstances (18:9–10). But its message was consoling in a number of ways: (1) God was with Paul to allow him to keep speaking; (2) no one would attack or harm him in Corinth; and (3) many other believers were in Corinth. So Paul stayed a year and a half. He must have appreciated the opportunity to remain in one place for a while and build relationships rather than move on to another town as quickly as he had been doing. In addition, he might have used Corinth as a base from which he could visit and speak in neighboring districts during that time.

One incident of resistance to Paul while in Corinth is recorded. A group of Jewish people made a cohesive attack to get him in trouble with the Roman authorities. They hauled him into court and accused him of attempting to institute a new and unauthorized religion (18:12–13). Paul was about to defend himself, but didn't even get to speak. Instead, the proconsul, a man named Gallio (who happened to be the brother of the Roman philosopher, Seneca), rebuked the Jewish group and drove them out of court.

Members of the crowd then turned on the leader of the synagogue and began to beat him, which didn't even faze Gallio (18:17). It is unclear whether the attackers were Gentiles who resented the motives and actions of the Jews, or whether the Jews attacked their own synagogue leader because he did a poor job of representing them in court. The synagogue ruler was named Sosthenes, which was also the name of a later associate of Paul (1 Corinthians 1:1). Perhaps the synagogue leader became a convert after this experience.

Although Gallio's ruling essentially allowed Paul to continue his ministry unencumbered, it doesn't seem that Gallio personally became a believer. He later committed suicide.

📖 18:18–22

HOME AGAIN

When Paul finally left Corinth, Priscilla and Aquila went with him (18:18). Priscilla's name is mentioned first, which is not typical and may indicate that she was the more prominent leader or teacher. Before leaving, Paul got a haircut in connection with a vow. The reason and specifics are not recorded.

Demystifying Acts

Occasionally a vow was taken and the person would immediately shave his head in response to an immediate crisis such as a serious illness. More common, however, was the Nazirite vow (Numbers 6:1–21), a temporary time of special devotion to God during which the person would let his hair grow and abstain from certain foods. Perhaps Paul's vow was in connection with his ministry in Corinth, which lasted a year and a half (Acts 18:11). Cutting his hair was the sign that he had concluded his commitment.

Paul stopped briefly in Ephesus, went to the synagogue, and had a good response. The Jewish people there wanted him to stay longer, but he wanted to move on. However, he promised to return if it was God's will (indeed, he would be back soon for a lengthy stay), and he left Aquila and Priscilla there (18:19). Paul appeared to be in a hurry to get back to Jerusalem, perhaps for Passover or some other significant event. The statement that "he went up and greeted the church" (18:22 NASB) suggests it was the church at Jerusalem, which required an ascent in the hills to get there. Then he went down to the church in Antioch (18:22).

And with that, Paul concluded his second missionary journey. Luke devotes little attention to how things were on the home front or how long Paul stayed before starting out again. In fact, the very next verse says that after spending some time in Antioch, Paul set out again on what would become his third missionary trip (18:23).

Take It Home

When you think of initiating conversations about your faith or looking for those who might be interested in the gospel, do you ever consider the people in your workplace? When alone in a strange new city, Paul found a natural bond with fellow tentmakers. Perhaps Aquila and Priscilla were already believers as well, but we don't know for sure. It might have been that the "shop talk" came first and led to more spiritual matters. As you interact with neighbors or coworkers during the next few weeks, keep your eyes and ears open for opportunities to allow the Holy Spirit to work and take your conversations to a more meaningful spiritual level.

ACTS 18:23–19:41

THE THIRD MISSIONARY JOURNEY BEGINS

Setting Up the Section

Paul has spent a number of years traveling from place to place, preaching the gospel and establishing and building up churches. He made one journey with Barnabas and a second with Silas. In this section he sets out on his third trip, and his emphasis is in Ephesus, a city where he was unable to spend much time previously.

📖 18:23–28

INTRODUCING APOLLOS

Luke's abrupt summary of Paul's second journey (18:18–22) and start of his third one (18:23) seems to be intentional. His focus, therefore, remains on the city of Ephesus. That's where Paul had a positive response from the people at the end of his second trip. That's where he left Aquila and Priscilla while he returned to Jerusalem. That's where he is heading—and will spend almost all of his time—on this third journey. And it's also where we first find Apollos (18:24).

Apollos was a Jewish believer who knew the scriptures very well and had been taught about Jesus. He was a bold speaker in the synagogue, yet he had only experienced the water baptism of John the Baptist to express repentance for sin and evidently didn't yet understand the work or power of the Holy Spirit (18:25–26). So Aquila and Priscilla helped him understand more fully the truths of Christianity. Before long he was eager and ready to move on to Achaia (the territory surrounding Corinth [now southern Greece]) to minister to the believers there. He left with the support and endorsement of the Ephesian church, and was effective there in proving that Jesus is God's Messiah (18:27–28).

📖 19:1–20

CLARIFYING THE TRUTH IN EPHESUS

Not long after Apollos left Ephesus, Paul arrived (19:1). He found other disciples who, like Apollos, had not experienced a full Christian conversion. They were believers, to be sure, but had never even heard of the Holy Spirit (19:1–2). Paul began with what they were familiar with—the baptism of John the Baptist, explaining that John had pointed the way to One coming after him, Jesus. Then Paul baptized them in the name of Jesus. As he did, the Holy Spirit came upon them and they started speaking in tongues and prophesying (19:4–7).

Critical Observation

Ephesus was the capital of Asia Minor in what is modern-day southwest Turkey. It ranked in importance only behind Rome, Athens, and Alexandria. Thanks to a thriving port, it had become the chief link for communications and commerce between Rome and the East. The city contained one of the largest libraries in the ancient world and was a center of learning. But, like Corinth, it was known for pagan worship. Its temple to Diana (Artemis)—about four times the size of the Parthenon in Athens and said by numerous historians to be one of the most beautiful buildings ever built—was one of the seven wonders of the ancient world.

Paul spent three months speaking out in the synagogue, but some of the members stubbornly refused to believe and started publicly disparaging the gospel (19:8–9). So Paul left with those who believed him and moved his ministry to a local lecture hall for the next two years—the longest stay anywhere in his ministry. Word spread about his teachings until everyone in Asia had heard the gospel (19:10).

In addition, the authentic power of God was becoming evident in contrast to other sources of power. Ephesus had developed a reputation for being the magic capital of the world. So God did amazing things through Paul's ministry to validate his teachings. Handkerchiefs and other articles Paul had touched could be carried to sick or possessed people, and they would be healed (19:11–12).

In another graphic example, a group of Jewish exorcists (the seven sons of Sceva) had been going around evoking the name of Jesus to try to cast out evil spirits. Perhaps they wanted to emulate Paul's ability because they used his name as well (19:13), but their efforts backfired when one particular spirit challenged them. The possessed man single-handedly overpowered the whole group and left the exorcists bleeding and naked (19:13–16).

The failure of this group of exorcists was a boost to the church, as the name of Jesus gained more reverence. New believers publicly confessed their previous evil deeds. A group of former sorcery practitioners brought its scrolls and burned them—no small act of contrition considering the combined value added up to fifty thousand silver coins, each one worth about what a laborer would earn for a day's work. So the Word of God spread not only geographically, but grew more influential and respected as well (19:17–20).

🔖 19:21–41

CHRISTIANITY VS. COMMERCE

At this point Paul decided (and perhaps felt led) to make his way to Rome (19:21). He would spend a little more time in Ephesus and then take a roundabout route to Jerusalem in order to visit young churches and take up a collection for the believers in Jerusalem who were struggling financially. He sent two associates ahead of him to Macedonia. Erastus was another of Paul's fellow ministers (19:22; 2 Timothy 4:20).

Demystifying Acts

Luke's reporting at this point is focused primarily on Paul, who by this time has a number of assistants in various places. Paul will later mention many of them in his letters, but Luke doesn't acknowledge them all in Acts. For example, Luke mentioned Silas nine times between Acts 15:40 and 18:5, but not at all after that even though Silas remained active in ministry. Paul also had much to say about Titus, but Luke doesn't mention him at all.

Paul was accustomed to facing resistance to his teachings from skeptics and proponents of other beliefs, but in Ephesus he encountered opposition from merchants. Paul's preaching had been so effective that the metalworkers who made idols of the goddess Artemis (Diana) were experiencing a significant decline in income. One of the highlights in the temple of Artemis was an object that was said to have fallen from heaven (19:35). Some believe it may have been a meteorite that resembled a woman with many breasts. (A popular image of Artemis was as a multibreasted fertility goddess.) But fewer and fewer souvenirs were being sold as people believed in Jesus in response to Paul's messages (19:23-26).

So Demetrius, one of the local silversmiths, called a meeting and united his fellow craftsmen. Under the guise of loyalty to Artemis, they soon had incited the entire city. A mob mentality ensued. For two hours, crowds shouted in unison, "Great is Artemis of the Ephesians!" (19:34).

Archaeologists have discovered that the theater in Ephesus seated twenty-five thousand people, so the crowd could have been enormous (19:29). Yet most of the people didn't even know what was going on (19:32). Some were seizing anyone associated with Paul that they could find (19:29). And when someone tried to quiet the people and establish order, they refused to let him talk because he was a Jew (19:34). Many people still didn't differentiate between Judaism and Christianity, but both were detrimental to the sellers of idols.

Evidently Paul was somewhere else in Ephesus. He wanted to go address the crowd, but was restrained by fellow believers who realized the great danger he would be in (19:30). Even the city officials who knew Paul begged him not to appear in front of the crowd (19:31), which shows that Christianity was becoming more of a public influence.

Finally, the city clerk, a position much like a contemporary mayor, subdued the crowd and pointed out that the Christians had done nothing malicious or worthy of mistreatment (19:35-38). He knew Demetrius and the other craftsmen had been behind the pandemonium, and explained how they could legally take appropriate steps to seek the justice they desired (19:38-39). He also warned that Rome could impose penalties or restrictions on the city if its citizens were prone to riot (19:40). And with the situation finally diffused, he sent everyone home.

Paul left the city soon afterward. He would later write of fighting wild beasts at Ephesus (1 Corinthians 15:32). Perhaps this was the incident he had in mind.

Take It Home

Two incidents from this passage make a powerful contrast that is relevant for today's believers. One is the willingness of the former sorcerers, who put their faith in Jesus, to repent and eliminate their occult resources at great personal expense. The other is the attitude of the silversmiths, who resisted the gospel and used a religious guise to attempt to ensure their financial security. Christians can find themselves embroiled in economic dilemmas in a number of ways. Have you (or someone you know) ever had to make a decision to obey God that required a financial sacrifice? (For example, leaving a lucrative job because it required moral sacrifices, refusing to sell or promote certain items that might impair someone's spiritual growth, etc.) What were the results of the decision? How did you (or the person) feel afterward?

ACTS 20:1-38

A FORLORN FAREWELL

Setting Up the Section

Paul is on his third missionary journey, and has never spent as much time in one place as he has in Ephesus. But his desire to collect an offering for the church in Jerusalem and start out for Rome has led to his decision to leave. This time his parting is particularly sad because he realized he might never see the Ephesians again. Yet God continues to do great things through Paul's ministry.

📖 20:1–6

MINISTRY IN MACEDONIA AND GREECE

The uproar in verse 1 refers to the riot incited by Demetrius the silversmith and fellow craftsmen because Paul's teachings were causing them to lose money on idol sales (19:23–41). But that's not what prompted Paul's departure; he had already resolved to leave. Timothy and Erastus were already in Macedonia (19:21–22), so Paul set out in that direction.

As should be evident by now, Paul rarely traveled alone. Luke lists several of his companions on this leg of his journey (20:4). They represented the different regions of Macedonia that were taking part in the collection to be delivered to the believers in Jerusalem, who were suffering from a famine in the Middle East. The churches didn't just send money; they sent people to help as well.

In his travels, Paul demonstrated flexibility and sensitivity to the leading of the Holy Spirit. Some scholars believe the three months he spent in Greece (20:3) was winter in

Corinth, and while waiting until ships would sail again, Paul wrote his Epistle to the Romans. Yet at the end of that waiting period, he opted not to sail because he learned of a plot against him. On a ship, it would have been too easy for his enemies to kill him and toss his body overboard, so he decided instead to backtrack through Macedonia. He never resisted suffering when it advanced the promotion of the gospel, but he also used common sense in addition to being sensitive to the leading of God.

In his interaction with the young churches, Paul advocated and demonstrated much encouragement (20:2). They were facing a lot of challenges and obstacles, and Paul could certainly be direct when they got off track. But he also knew the power of encouragement in motivating people to keep going through trying times. The Greek word translated "encouragement" includes aspects of entreaty, exhortation, comfort, and consolation.

At this point in Paul's travels it seems that Luke again joined his group. The story picks up again with a first-person account (20:5–6).

📄 20:7–12

AN ALL-NIGHT SERMON. . .AND ITS CONSEQUENCES

In connection with Paul's seven-day stay in Troas (20:6–7), Luke provides the first clear biblical reference of how Christians met for worship on Sunday rather than Saturday (the Sabbath). The Sunday gatherings were to commemorate Jesus' resurrection that took place on Easter Sunday.

Paul was planning to leave the next day and was spending the evening in fellowship with the other believers. They began by breaking bread (20:7), a reference to a regular celebration of the early church called the *agape* feast ("love feast")—basically a potluck dinner that concluded with the celebration of the Lord's Supper. For some of the poorer members of the church, it may have been the only decent meal they had all week.

Afterward, Paul had much to say, and he was still speaking when midnight arrived. A young man named Eutychus was seated on a high window ledge, perhaps trying to get some fresh air due to the many lamps burning (20:8) and what would almost certainly have been the warmth of a crowded room. As Paul kept talking, Eutychus fell fast asleep, dropped from the third floor, and died when he landed on the ground below. Since Luke was there, the death would have been confirmed.

Paul went to see and threw himself on the body, wrapping his arms around the young man—reminiscent of the Old Testament prophets Elijah (1 Kings 17:21) and Elisha (2 Kings 4:34–35). Just as Peter's faith in the power of God had brought Tabitha back to life (Acts 9:40), Paul's faith restored life to Eutychus.

Paul went back to preaching and continued until dawn. The friends of Eutychus took him home and felt immense comfort (20:11–12).

Critical Observation

The name *Eutychus* means "fortunate." It was a relatively common name among slaves who had been freed, though probably few lived up to the name as well as the young man in this account.

GOOD-BYE TO EPHESUS

Apparently Paul wanted to spend every minute possible in Troas. He sent his companions ahead by ship, knowing that he could take a shortcut across land to catch up with them at Assos. After several days of sailing, they arrived at Miletus. Ephesus was nearby, but Paul had determined not to return there. He had spent almost three years with the Ephesians, and a visit would have taken more time than he had to spend. (He wanted to get to Jerusalem by Pentecost [20:16].) Also, his recent run-in with the guild of silversmiths might have led to legal complications that would have tied him up as well. So rather than going again to Ephesus, he had the elders of the church meet him in Miletus (20:17–18).

At this point comes the only sermon in Acts directed exclusively to Christians (20:18–35). Paul's words to the Ephesian elders are both encouraging and cautionary. Groups of antagonists were out to smear Paul's good name (17:5–9), so he began by defending the sincerity of his motives and reminding them of his personal ministry in Ephesus (20:21). Paul's reference to teaching "from house to house" (20:20) may refer to house churches, many of which probably included one of the elders who had come to see him off.

He continued by sharing his current plans with them (20:22–27). He didn't know for certain what would happen, but he was realistically expecting prison and hardships (20:23). He viewed his ministry the same way a runner sees a race. In spite of any obstacles and difficulties he might face, his goal was to finish the race and complete the task he had been given (20:24).

Paul didn't anticipate ever visiting Ephesus again (20:25), although it seems that he did. (He later refers to events that appear to have taken place after the ones recorded in Acts [Timothy 1:3–4].) So before he left, he wanted to reassure the Ephesian elders of his own innocence and integrity.

Then he challenged them to the same commitment in their own ministries (20:28–31). They were shepherds entrusted by the Holy Spirit with the flock of God. Paul wisely advised the church leaders to watch over themselves as well as their congregations (20:28). After Paul had gone, the flock would come under attack from wolves (20:29)—people who would distort the truth and attempt to lead them astray. Some of the leaders of the early church would indeed fall away from the faith (2 Timothy 4:9–10), so Paul warned them to always be on their guard (20:31).

Finally, Paul reminded the elders of his love, a love borne out in his actions (20:32–35). Both his encouragement and his admonition were rooted in his affection for the Ephesian church. Paul had worked with his hands (20:34) to ensure that the work of God continued.

Demystifying Acts

While speaking to the elders of Ephesus, Paul attributes a quote to Jesus: "It is more blessed to give than to receive" (20:35). It has become a familiar saying and one very closely associated with the Bible. Yet this is the only place it appears. It is found nowhere in the Gospels.

Paul and his traveling companions had to tear themselves away from their Ephesian brothers in order to prepare to sail the next day (21:1). After his farewell speech, Paul prayed for the group, and there wasn't a dry eye among them (20:36–37). Most upsetting was their concern that they might never see Paul again. And as will soon be seen, they had good cause to be concerned.

Take It Home

Try to put yourself in Paul's place by recalling an instance when you had spent a lot of time and devoted a lot of emotional energy to a group of people, and then had to leave for some reason. What kind of farewell did you have? How did people express their emotions prior to your leaving? Have you kept up with them, or did the bonds of friendship diminish after you left?

ACTS 21:1–26

EXPECTING TROUBLE, BUT MOVING AHEAD

Sailing Back to Jerusalem	21:1–9
Advance Warning	21:10–16
Rebutting a Rumor	21:17–26

Setting Up the Section

The majority of the content of Acts 13–20 has been about Paul and his companions' journeys in taking the gospel out of Jerusalem and Antioch into other parts of the world. In this section he heads back toward Jerusalem after his third trip. Although he has faced various hardships throughout his travels, he is warned specifically of trouble ahead if he continues. Yet he is not deterred.

📄 21:1–9

SAILING BACK TO JERUSALEM

Never one to shrink from danger, Paul endured much physical abuse and challenge as he proclaimed the truth of Jesus Christ in numerous new and different places. Yet as he neared the end of his third missionary journey, the signs became more and more ominous.

His clear intent was to first get to Jerusalem, after which he had to go to Rome (19:21). He was aware of repeated warnings from the Holy Spirit that hardships and prison were continual possibilities (20:22–23). He didn't expect to return to the area he had just left (20:25), and his departure left everyone in a state of anxiety and grief (20:36–38). Yet he continued on a direct path to get back to Jerusalem by the day of Pentecost (20:16; 21:1–3).

Demystifying Acts

In addition to Luke's skilled eye as a doctor, he also seems to have had a fondness and appreciation for seafaring. Detailed passages of sea travel have been sprinkled throughout his writing and continue in this passage (note all the references to "we"), and will extend to the very end of Acts.

The stop in Tyre (21:3) put Paul on the mainland, not far from Jerusalem. He found a number of believers there and stayed with them for a few days while the ship unloaded its cargo. And again, the Holy Spirit warned through these believers that he would face trouble in Jerusalem (21:4).

Paul had been through the area of Phoenicia at least once before (15:3), although this is the first mention of his visit to Tyre. Yet after only a week, the church members had a difficult time saying good-bye. A large group of families escorted him out of town and prayed for him before sending him on his way (21:5–6).

The ship's next stop was at Ptolemais, where Paul and his group were able to connect with yet another assembly of believers (21:7). As they got closer to Jerusalem, they were probably finding more and more Christian groups that had sprung up about twenty-five years previously, when persecution in Jerusalem had forced believers out into other communities. But this was only an overnight stop, and they continued the next day to Caesarea.

In Caesarea, Paul and his companions were hosted by a name familiar to some of them: Philip (21:8). Like Stephen, Philip was one of the Seven who had been designated to help the apostles shortly after the coming of the Holy Spirit at Pentecost (6:1–7). Philip had been the first to take the gospel cross-culturally into the region of Samaria (8:5–7, 12). He was the one who had helped the Ethiopian eunuch to understand and believe in Jesus, baptizing him and sending him back to Africa with the truth of the good news (8:26–40). Now, some twenty-five years later, Philip was connected with a group of believers in Caesarea—and not only him, but his four virgin daughters as well, who were all prophetesses (21:9).

📖 21:10–16

ADVANCE WARNING

But it was another prophet who was more prominent during Paul's stay with Philip. A man named Agabus (who has also previously appeared in Acts [11:28]) had come out to meet them. Paul had been warned by other prophets against returning to Jerusalem. Agabus had the same message, but used a more emphatic means of communicating it. His symbolic binding of Paul (21:11), combined with his dire warning, left the group anxious and tearful. But Paul was more upset with their heartbreaking response than with the anticipation of potential trouble in Jerusalem (21:13). One thing that made Paul such a devoted and persistent messenger for God was his willingness not only to suffer, but also to die if it came to that.

One reason for the high emotion was that Jerusalem was their next stop—only about sixty-five miles ahead. But when the group could not persuade Paul to change his plans, it was willing for God's will to be done (21:14). Perhaps Paul was so determined because he was bringing back the money that had been collected from the other churches (that were in primarily Gentile territory). By doing so, he would be emphasizing the unity of the worldwide church, which was very important to him.

Critical Observation

Some people question the leading of the Holy Spirit in this account. On numerous occasions, prophets had warned Paul of impending danger if he went to Jerusalem (21:4, 10–12). Yet Paul was responding to the Spirit in his desire to go (19:21; 20:22–23). Some people believe Paul was so determined to get to Jerusalem that he missed God's will and should have listened to the messengers God put in his path. Others feel the prophets merely confirmed what Paul already knew from the Holy Spirit. Those in the latter group believe the lesson is that just because something appears to be difficult doesn't mean it isn't the will of God.

After a few days in Caesarea (21:10), Paul's group moved on and stayed overnight in the house of a man named Mnason (21:16). He had been a disciple for a long while and was from Cyprus, as was Barnabas. Their next stop would be Jerusalem.

📄 21:17–26

REBUTTING A RUMOR

Paul refers to his delivery of the financial gift from the other churches in various epistles (Romans 15:25–27; 1 Corinthians 16:1–4; 2 Corinthians 8–9). Luke makes no mention of it here, and later acknowledges it only briefly as he records Paul's account of this moment (24:17). Luke's ongoing focus has been on the spread of the gospel and the growth of the church from Jerusalem outward, so his emphasis here is Paul's report to the church in Jerusalem. In addition, the "we" references conclude in verse 18, suggesting that Luke either moved on or changed the tense to emphasize Paul's ministry.

Upon Paul's arrival in Jerusalem, he found much to be the same as when he had last been there. James, the brother of Jesus, was still the leader of the Jerusalem church (15:13; 21:18). Paul's report of the work of God among the Gentiles encouraged them all. The Jerusalem church had good news as well: Thousands of zealous Jewish converts had been added to their number (21:20).

But one major concern had arisen during Paul's absence. Rumors had spread that not only had Paul taken the gospel to the Gentiles, but also that he was telling them to reject Jewish customs and circumcision—which, of course, wasn't true (21:21). There was nothing wrong with such traditions; it was just that they had nothing to do with salvation. Now that Paul was back in town, the church leaders wanted to settle the matter.

An ideal opportunity arose when four men of the church were preparing to conclude a vow they had made to God. Paul had recently done the same thing in Corinth (18:18). (See Acts 18:18–22 inset concerning Nazirite vows.) So the elders recommended that Paul join the four men in their rites of purification. In addition, he would pay for their offerings that were prescribed by Mosaic Law. Each man would bring two lambs, one ram, a grain offering, a drink offering, and a basket of unleavened cakes and wafers (Numbers 6:13–15). After each man's offering was presented to God by the priest, the man would shave his head and his hair would be placed in the fire of the fellowship offering (Numbers 6:16–18).

Paul had no problem accommodating the request, and joined the men in their purification the next day (21:26). The ceremony was one that was entirely voluntary and did nothing to compromise his Christian convictions. Yet his willingness to comply was proof that he wasn't promoting the cessation of Jewish rights and traditions.

In addition, the Jerusalem elders reiterated the previous decision of the council (15:20, 29) that Gentiles hold to certain restrictions: abstaining from food sacrificed to idols, from partaking of blood, from eating the meat of strangled animals, and from sexual immorality (21:25). Both Paul and the other church leaders continued to hold firm to their commitment to salvation by grace, yet allowed both Jews and Gentiles leeway in following their own traditions to promote greater unity in the church.

Take It Home

This passage, perhaps as much as any other so far, has shown Paul's strong determination to continue his ministry for God even in the face of opposition and persecution. (Prophesies of the trouble he would face will be fulfilled in the next section.) Are you inspired by such devotion, or do you tend to disagree with Paul's decision? If you were the one who had been warned by a number of godly people that trouble was in store if you went one direction, would you do it anyway? Or would you choose an alternative course of action? Why?

ACTS 21:27–22:29

TROUBLE IN JERUSALEM (AS PREDICTED)

Same Problem, New City	21:27–32
Paul's Arrest and Defense	21:33–22:21
The Rights of the Accused	22:22–29

Setting Up the Section

In this section, Paul finally arrives in Jerusalem after his third journey. From the moment he planned to come, he was aware that it would be a perilous and threatening trip for him. His first few days were nothing but positive as he shared his exploits with the elders of the church and heard how God had been active in Jerusalem as well. But it didn't take long for trouble to start, and it would be a long while before he would get the matter settled.

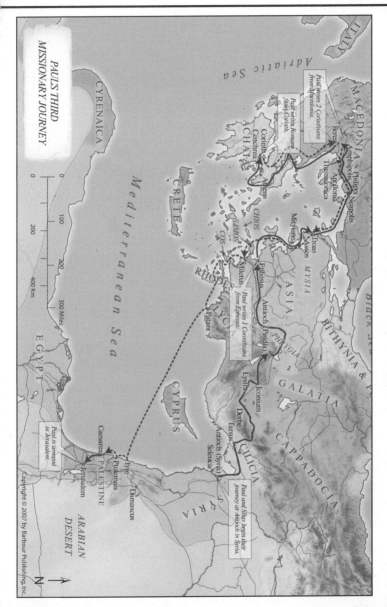

PAUL'S THIRD
MISSIONARY JOURNEY

CYRENAICA

Mediterranean Sea

EGYPT

CRETE

CYPRUS

ITALY

Adriatic Sea

MACEDONIA

ACHAIA

Paul writes 2 Corinthians
from Macedonia.

Paul writes Romans
from Corinth.

Corinth
Cenchrea
Athens
Thessalonica
Berea
Apollonia
Amphipolis
Neapolis
Philippi

Assos
Troas
Mitylene

MYSIA

CHIOS
SAMOS
COS
RHODES

Miletus
Ephesus

Paul writes 1 Corinthians
from Ephesus.

Patara

ASIA

Antioch
(Pisidia)

PHRYGIA

Lystra
Iconium

Derbe

GALATIA

Tarsus

CILICIA

Antioch (Syria)
Seleucia

CAPPADOCIA

BITHYNIA & P

Black Se

Paul and Silas begin their
journey at Antioch in Syria.

Caesarea
Ptolemais
Tyre

PALESTINE

Jerusalem
Damascus

SYRIA

Paul is arrested
in Jerusalem.

ARABIAN
DESERT

N

0   100   200   300 Miles
0 100 200 300 400 Km

Copyright © 2007 by Barbour Publishing, Inc.

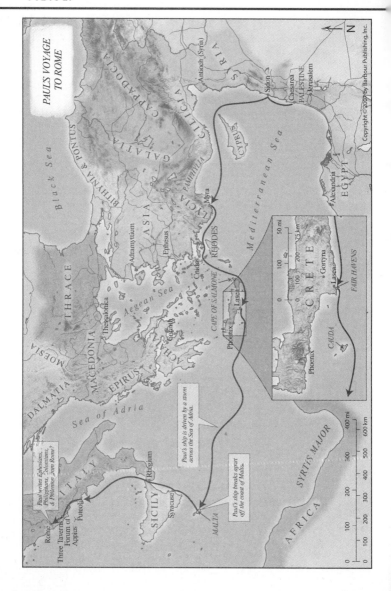

PAUL'S VOYAGE TO ROME

Paul writes Ephesians, Philippians, Colossians, & Philemon from Rome?

Paul's ship is driven by a storm across the Sea of Adria.

Paul's ship breaks apart off the coast of Malta.

Copyright © 2007 by Barbour Publishing, Inc.

SAME PROBLEM, NEW CITY

Shortly after Paul's arrival in Jerusalem, he had been invited to participate in a Jewish purification ceremony to quash some rumors that he was preaching that all Jewish customs should be abandoned (21:21–26). He was glad to do so, and was planning to devote seven days to it (21:27).

But before he could complete the allotted time, he was seen at the temple by a group of Jews from Asia. He was accustomed to being followed from town to town by disgruntled, nonbelieving Jews who simply wanted to create trouble for him and stir up additional opposition to his teaching. Now they had found him in Jerusalem, and they resorted to the same strategy.

They didn't have their facts straight, but it didn't matter. They saw someone they knew from Ephesus, a Gentile man named Trophimus, and accused Paul of taking Gentiles into areas of the temple where only Jews were allowed (21:27–29). Their accusations were entirely unfounded, yet were enough to rile the crowd. They dragged Paul out of the temple, intending to kill him.

PAUL'S ARREST AND DEFENSE

The scene was so potentially violent that the Roman commander in charge (a man named Claudius Lysias, according to Acts 23:26) hurried out with sufficient forces to stop those who were beating Paul (21:30–34). He first arrested Paul and placed him in a kind of protective custody, bound with two chains, most likely between two guards (21:33). He then tried to determine from the crowd who Paul was and the nature of his offense, but his efforts were futile due to inconsistent answers and ongoing pandemonium. The mob was still trying to get to Paul, and the soldiers had to actually carry him into the barracks and away from the chanting crowd (21:35–36).

Paul asked the commander for a favor, speaking in Greek, which surprised the Roman leader. Until that moment, the commander thought he might have captured a terrorist—an Egyptian who spoke no Greek—who was on the loose. So Paul's words took Lysias aback (21:37–38).

Critical Observation

In AD 54 an Egyptian man had posed as a prophet and attracted thousands of Jewish followers. He led them to the Mount of Olives, telling them he was about to command the walls of Jerusalem to fall, after which they could storm in and overpower the Romans. But the Romans saw what was happening, confronted the group of rebels, and killed some of them. The Egyptian had escaped, but his supporters were still disgruntled. Lysias may have assumed Paul was that man and the mob was meting out its own justice.

Still, he granted Paul's request to speak to the crowd. Surprisingly, the crowd got quiet. . .and even quieter when Paul addressed them in Aramaic, the most familiar language of the local people (21:40–22:2).

The crowd's complaint was that Paul wasn't "Jewish" enough, so he presented his life story with an emphasis on his Jewish upbringing. He was born a Jew in Tarsus, but had spent much time in Jerusalem. He had been tutored by Gamaliel, the most eminent rabbi of the time, who had died just five years earlier. (Gamaliel's wisdom was demonstrated in Acts 5:33–40.)

In addition, Paul had been as zealous as anyone in wanting to quash the spread of "the Way" (Christianity). He did everything within his power to imprison and kill believers (22:4–5). The hostile crowd surely was with him up to that point.

Next Paul shared with them his experience on the road to Damascus (9:1–19; 22:6–16). He told them about the bright light from heaven, the voice of Jesus that only he could hear, and the instructions to go into Damascus to wait to be told what to do. Paul's description of Ananias was exemplary: "a devout observer of the law" (22:12 NIV). It was Ananias who had confirmed that Paul would be a witness to all men—which would have included the Gentiles (22:15; see 9:15).

At that point Paul had been baptized. (It wasn't the water baptism that had washed his sins away [22:16], although repentance and baptism are almost always closely linked in the New Testament. Paul had already submitted to Jesus and received the Holy Spirit [9:6, 17–19]; his baptism was an outward verification of the inner change that had occurred.)

So far the hostile crowd was still listening to him (22:22), but the next portion of his testimony would incite it once more. He again emphasized his prior mistreatment of believers, confessing his part in the death of Stephen (22:19–20). Still, the Lord had told him that he would not be accepted by his Jewish peers. As a result, he was sent to the Gentiles (22:21). These instructions had come during a supernatural vision that took place in the very temple Paul was accused of having defiled.

📖 22:22–29

THE RIGHTS OF THE ACCUSED

Paul's explanation was completely truthful and sincere. He wasn't anti-Jerusalem. He had indeed tried to teach in Jerusalem until a contingent of Grecian Jews attempted to kill him, and the other believers had sent him to Tarsus (9:28–30). Yet the crowd refused to listen to his message that Jews and Gentiles were equal and could come to God on identical terms. For those views, the people still wanted him dead and made their wishes known in no uncertain terms (22:22).

Again, the Roman commander ordered Paul indoors. His plan was to submit Paul to a brutal flogging and force him to say more about why the crowd was so irate. This was no small punishment. The scourge consisted of strips of leather fastened to a wooden handle. Embedded in the leather were pieces of metal or bone. Sometimes a scourging crippled a person for life. Occasionally the victim died as a result.

But while the centurion in charge was preparing Paul to be whipped, Paul made a legal appeal (22:25). No one had asked, but Paul was a Roman citizen with rights that were about to be violated. Those rights were well respected by Roman officials, so the centurion went immediately to the commander, who went to Paul for confirmation (22:26–27).

Demystifying Acts

Essentially, Roman citizenship was the right to be treated as equal to the citizens of Rome. Roman citizens were spared humiliating punishments such as crucifixion or scourging, and they had more right to appeal official decisions than did noncitizens. Some people were born into citizenship, as was Paul (22:28). The status of "Roman citizen" could be purchased. Or sometimes a magnanimous emperor would bestow citizenship on individuals, cities, or even an entire province.

Paul affirmed that, yes, he had been born a citizen (22:28). Most likely, his father or some relative farther back had been designated a Roman citizen and had passed the status along to Paul. The Roman commander, on the other hand, had paid a lot of money to acquire citizenship.

The plans to have Paul whipped were immediately canceled. The commander was alarmed because he had almost committed a grievous injustice. He still wanted to find out why Paul had been such a target for the Jews, but now it would be done by means of a trial rather than the use of force.

Take It Home

In this passage we see the importance of being able to tell one's story of spiritual conversion and growth. While it didn't get Paul out of trouble in this case, a hostile crowd settled down to hear what he had to say. In addition, we see that we don't need to know all the answers to difficult theological issues. We simply need to be able to verbalize the things we have seen, heard, and know from personal experience to be true. Sometimes a story of personal experience will be much better received from someone than a sermon or Bible quotation. Personal stories can open doors, preparing a heart for other truths of God. When was the last time you told your story? As you go through the week, look for new opportunities to share with others what God has done for you.

ACTS 22:30–23:35

PAUL'S TRIAL BEGINS

Setting Up the Section

After the completion of his third missionary journey, Paul has returned to Jerusalem. He had been participating in a purification ceremony when he was dragged from the temple by an angry group of Jews who thought his work with the Gentiles involved advocating the rejection of all Jewish customs and traditions. The mob tried to kill him, but was stopped by Roman authorities. In this section, the Romans call together the Sanhedrin to help them figure out exactly what is going on.

📖 22:30–23:11

DISORDER IN THE COURT

After planning to flog Paul, the Roman commander, Claudius Lysias, had narrowly avoided trouble when Paul announced that he was a Roman citizen (22:25–29). Paul was spared a scourging, but Lysias still hadn't determined why Paul was the target of such a large and hostile mob. He ordered the Jewish Sanhedrin to assemble and interrogate Paul (22:30).

Many of the members of the Sanhedrin didn't think much better of Paul than those in the angry crowd, including the high priest, Ananias. As soon as Paul had spoken his first sentence, Ananias commanded that he be struck in the mouth (23:2).

Critical Observation

Ananias ruled as high priest from AD 48–59. He was a brutal and scheming man, known for greed and the use of violence. He embezzled money and gave large bribes to the Roman authorities. He was detested by many Jews because he supported Rome. When the war with Rome broke out in AD 66, Ananias's house was burned by Jewish nationalists, and he was forced to take shelter at the palace of Herod the Great in the northern part of Jerusalem. He was eventually found hiding in an aqueduct on the palace grounds and killed.

Ananias was acting in the role of a judge. Paul was quick to point out that *he* was being held to the standards of Jewish law, yet his judge was breaking the law by ordering violence within the court, and his comments included some name calling (23:3). Immediately he was rebuked by those nearby for insulting the high priest (23:4).

Paul quickly explained that he didn't realize that the order had come from the high priest. Some believe Paul had trouble seeing, in which case his poor vision might have prevented him from recognizing Ananias as the high priest. Besides, Paul had been out of Jerusalem for a while and the position of high priest changed quite often. Others feel his reply may have been somewhat sarcastic, and that Paul refused to recognize the authority of anyone who would use the office of high priest to promote unwarranted hostility. But his rapid shift from calling Ananias a "whitewashed wall" (23:3) to his appeal to the group as "brothers" (23:5) suggests sincerity. Whatever his motive, he apologized and submitted to the legal protocol (Exodus 22:28).

Yet Ananias's action must have alerted Paul that he had little chance of receiving a fair trial, so he took the offensive. He knew the Sanhedrin was comprised of a number of Jewish sects, two of the main ones being the Pharisees and the Sadducees. The Pharisees had a high regard for oral tradition; the Sadducees only respected the written law. The Pharisees believed in predestination; the Sadducees believed in free will. The Pharisees believed in the existence of angels and evil spirits; the Sadducees didn't. And the Pharisees believed in the resurrection of the dead, while the Sadducees denied resurrection.

When Paul took a stand for resurrection, he knew he would divide the group. He was right. His statement (23:6) sent the whole council into an uproar. The Pharisees suddenly began taking his side while the Sadducees argued all the more. The conflict intensified to the point where the Roman commander again had to retrieve Paul by force and take him back to the barracks for his own safety (23:10).

After being a target of hostility for two different mobs on two consecutive days, Paul might have felt very disheartened. But the next night he received affirmation from Jesus through a supernatural revelation, encouraging him to keep going. He would indeed be traveling on to Rome, as he had hoped (23:11). Paul didn't see many visions in his ministry, and must have appreciated this unusual blessing that strengthened his weakened spirit.

23:12–35

THE PLOT TO MURDER PAUL

Paul didn't realize it at the time, but he needed some supernatural support. The next morning a group of more than forty Jewish men took an oath not to eat or drink until Paul was dead (23:12–13). This group enlisted the help of the chief priests and elders. The plan was to have Paul summoned back to court. The conspirators would lie in wait, perhaps along some narrow street where Paul could easily be intercepted and killed.

But the right pair of ears happened to overhear the plot. At this point we discover that Paul had a sister and nephew in Jerusalem (23:16), and the young man found out about the ambush planned against Paul. He told Paul, Paul alerted the Roman commander, and Paul's nephew was warned to keep quiet about what he knew.

Demystifying Acts

Luke, who provides so many interesting details in his Gospel and the book of Acts, tells us essentially nothing about Paul's relatives. If he had a sister in Jerusalem, why didn't Paul stay with her? Maybe they weren't believers, yet if not, why take a risk to help Paul? Did they have a connection with the Jewish leadership that allowed them to know so many details of the plot against Paul? And how did a young man gain access to the Roman barracks so easily? We are given the facts but no further explanation.

Remembering that Paul was a Roman citizen, the commander acted immediately. He dispatched two centurions and a detachment of two hundred soldiers, along with seventy horsemen and two hundred spearmen. Even if it encountered the forty assassins, a Roman contingent of 470 soldiers should have had no trouble defeating them. Yet the soldiers weren't looking for a fight. They left at 9:00 p.m., escorting Paul during the night toward Caesarea (a two-day journey) where he would be much safer (23:23).

Paul was being delivered to Antonius Felix, the ruling governor of Judea (23:24). The Roman commander sent a letter to be delivered along with Paul, which would have been expected. Since the message was being sent from one political leader to a superior, Lysias subtly glosses over some of the details of the events he describes. For example, he didn't rescue Paul *because* he was a Roman citizen (23:27). As a matter of fact, he had been preparing to torture Paul during interrogation when he happened to find out about Paul's citizenship (22:23–29).

Still, the letter served to help Paul because Lysias expressed his opinion that Paul was not guilty of any serious crime. There may have been some disagreement about Jewish law, but Paul certainly didn't deserve death or imprisonment (23:29). Lysias also informed Felix that he would be sending Paul's accusers to present their case before him (23:30).

The night travel must have been strenuous for the party escorting Paul. The soldiers traversed thirty-five miles the first night, much of it across difficult terrain—including a long stretch that would have been ideal for an ambush. But after arriving safely in Antipatris, the remaining distance to Caesarea (twenty-seven miles) was far less threatening. So the foot soldiers returned to Jerusalem while the cavalry continued ahead with Paul (23:31–32).

The journey took place without incident. The letter and the prisoner were delivered to Felix, who agreed to hear the case. Paul was held in the palace of Herod until his accusers arrived to prosecute the case (23:35). Unaware of it at the time, this was one of Paul's more pleasant stays. He would be in other prisons in the days to come.

Take It Home

Consider the anger and frustration the Jews felt because they were under Roman control. Yet it becomes more evident in this passage of Acts (and previous ones) that God is actually the One in control. If Paul's Jewish antagonists had had their way, they would have killed him (21:31). But God used a Roman centurion, a Roman commander, 470 Roman soldiers, and a Roman governor to ensure that Paul was spared and would continue to stand for Him. Have you recently felt, like Paul, that people or forces were out to get you? If so, how can the acknowledgement of God's sovereignty help you endure? Is it possible that God might provide for you, using some unexpected people or methods?

PAUL'S TRIAL BEFORE FELIX

Setting Up the Section

In this section, Paul must defend himself before the Roman governor of Judea, Felix. But things could be worse. The Roman commander in Jerusalem has already taken Paul into protective custody to prevent zealous Jewish traditionalists from killing him. And when an elaborate plot was discovered that involved more than forty assassins sworn to murder Paul in Jerusalem, the Romans initiated a change of venue by leaving during the night to escort him to Caesarea. He is being held in the palace of Herod, awaiting his trial.

📖 24:1–9

THE CASE FOR THE PROSECUTION

Felix, the governor, had agreed to oversee Paul's trial, and had sent for Paul's accusers. It was a two-day journey from Caesarea to Jerusalem, so it took five days for the messenger to be dispatched and the group to arrive. In the meantime, Paul was kept under guard.

Felix knew something of Hebrew culture and traditions from his third wife, Drusilla (24:24). She was the daughter of Herod Agrippa I and sister of Agrippa II. Felix had seduced her away from another king, a fact that will later become significant.

When the Jewish entourage arrived, the group included the high priest (Ananias), a number of Jewish elders, and their lawyer (or orator) who was named Tertullus (24:1). They met with Felix and listed their charges against Paul before he was called in.

After Paul was summoned, the trial began. Tertullus opened with what is known as a *captatio benevolentiae*, a flowery and flattering statement meant to capture the good-will of the judge (24:2–4). He noted Felix's penchant for peace and his reforms, and promised to be brief so as not to weary the busy governor.

Critical Observation

For anyone who heard the description of Antonius Felix as presented by the spokesperson for Paul's opponents, it would seem that he was a wise and beloved leader. That would be far from the truth. Born a Greek subject named Antonius Claudius, he was eventually freed by the emperor Claudius at which time he acquired the name *Felix* ("happy"). He found favor with both Claudius and then Nero, but he was a tyrannical and selfish leader. Far from being a man of peace as portrayed in Acts 24:2, he had squelched several insurrections, using harsh brutality.

As Tertullus turned his attention to the charges against Paul, he was direct and succinct. He alleged that Paul: (1) was a troublemaker who created riots among the Jews throughout the world; (2) was a leader in the Nazarene sect (Christianity); and (3) had intended to desecrate the temple (24:5-6).

Although it may seem that this was a matter for the Jewish courts, each of the charges touched on concerns of the Roman Empire. The Romans demanded order in their territories and would not tolerate anyone going around stirring up riots. They also had a tolerance of Judaism, but now the Jews were trying to distance themselves from the Nazarene sect. It was becoming clear that Christianity was more than just a branch of Judaism, and its leaders might be committing treason against the empire. And even the goings on within the temple needed to be coordinated with the Romans. So far the Jews had been given the right to execute any Gentiles found in the areas where they were not permitted. Yet it was a Roman commander who prevented them from carrying out that sentence on Paul.

Tertullus invited Felix to interrogate Paul himself. And, of course, the Jewish elders who had come with him were backing up everything he said (24:8-9).

📄 **24:10-21**

PAUL'S REBUTTAL

At this point, Felix motioned for Paul to speak (24:10).

Paul also began with a captatio benevolentiae, but his was considerably more modest and moderate than Tertullus's (24:10). Then he went right to refuting the accusations of the prosecution, one by one.

First, he emphasized that he was not a troublemaker, and that at no time had he attempted to instigate an insurrection. He had gone to Jerusalem as a pilgrim to worship, not as an agitator to cause a riot (24:11-12). He had cut his visits with other churches short in order to be in Jerusalem for the Feast of Pentecost.

Second, Paul stressed the similarities between what his prosecutors believed and what he believed (24:14-16). He pointed out that they worshiped the same God, had the same forefathers, believed in the same scriptures, and maintained the same hope that God would resurrect both the righteous and the wicked. The sect that his opponents accused him of leading was actually a faith quite similar to their own.

Finally, Paul had done nothing that could be construed as defiling the temple (24:17-18). Not only was he not connected to any kind of crowd or disturbance, but he was also ceremonially clean. It wasn't until the Jewish troublemakers from Asia showed up that there was a riot. *They* were the ones who had come into the temple and started the whole melee.

And speaking of those people, if they had a charge against Paul, they should have been present to say so. In lieu of that, the people who *were* there should have cited a specific crime he had committed when he had been standing before the Sanhedrin.

As it came time for Felix to make his ruling, he found himself in a political tight spot. He wanted to curry favor with the Jewish authorities, but he didn't have a legal basis to do so. Lysias, the Roman commander in Jerusalem, had found no fault in Paul. The Jewish

Sanhedrin had been unable to convict him of any crime. And Tertullus had certainly not substantiated his charges.

Yet Felix wasn't yet willing to release Paul, probably because there wasn't anything in it for him (24:26). If Paul had been the average prisoner, he would have offered a bribe and been out in no time. And perhaps Felix had paid special attention to Paul's testimony about delivering gifts and presenting offerings (24:17). But Paul was not about to pay for his own release. So Felix used a stall tactic by saying he would wait to decide until after the arrival of Lysias, the commander in Jerusalem who had written the letter to Felix (24:22). Yet there is no indication that Felix ever sent for Lysias.

In the meantime, however, Felix didn't seem to consider Paul any kind of threat and allowed him a minimum-security environment. Paul was still supervised by a centurion, yet had a degree of freedom and opportunities for friends to visit (24:23).

During Paul's imprisonment, Felix would stop by from time to time. He was still hoping for a bribe (24:26), yet Paul used some of those opportunities to talk about Jesus. Not long after Paul's trial, Felix and his wife, Drusilla, summoned Paul to listen to what he had to say about Jesus. Felix had been governor of Judea for six years and certainly must have been aware of the spread of "the Way" throughout his territory. Paul's words, however, were alarming to Felix who was not known for being either righteous or self-controlled (24:25). He was sitting there beside a woman he had stolen away from another married man, so Felix became afraid as Paul connected such behavior with God's judgment.

Demystifying Acts

Luke doesn't explain the details of the transition between Felix and Festus (24:27). Felix was recalled to Rome after an outbreak of mob violence in Caesarea during which he had allowed Roman troops to kill thousands of Jews and loot the homes of the wealthy. The Jews complained to Rome, and Felix was dismissed from his position as governor. He likely would have been executed had it not been for the influence of his brother, Pallus.

Felix hurriedly dismissed Paul after this first private discussion (24:25). He sent for Paul frequently for subsequent discussions, but kept Paul incarcerated for two years before he was finally forced to step down (24:27). It was the mistreatment of his Jewish subjects that led to his loss of position, and Paul's release would have only created more dissension among them. Festus, who replaced Felix as governor, would prove to be a much better leader.

Take It Home

Paul was probably one of the most knowledgeable, well-trained, and effective speakers of his time. He had spent years by this time telling others—both Jews and Gentiles—about his faith in Jesus and the scriptural evidence that backed his beliefs. And while he inspired many people to believe, there were many others who didn't. Paul spoke to Felix on numerous occasions, and appeared to have his attention and respect. But Felix never acted on what Paul was telling him. How do you feel when you speak out or use your gifts for God, and you don't get the response you hope for? Are you quick to give up? Or, like Paul, do you keep going until you find someone willing to respond?

ACTS 25:1–26:32

A SECOND TRIAL IN CAESAREA

Setting Up the Section

For two years, Paul has been under arrest in Caesarea, the victim of the bureaucracy of the Roman Empire. Charged by a group of Jews in Jerusalem and the target of an assassination plot, he had been brought to Caesarea for trial. The case against him had been weak, yet the governor (Felix) would not pardon him, attempting to endear himself to his Jewish constituents. Felix has just lost his position, leaving his successor, Festus, the problem of what to do with Paul.

📖 25:1–12

FESTUS TRIES PAUL

We know relatively little about Porcius Festus, the successor of Governor Felix in Judea. He lived only two years after his appointment, yet is remembered as being wiser, more reasonable, and more effective than his predecessor.

It didn't take long for Festus to get around to the business of governing. Three days after arriving at his palace, he made the sixty-five-mile, two-day trip to Jerusalem. It was the displeasure of the Jewish people that had led to the dismissal of his predecessor, so Festus showed wisdom in immediately consulting with the Jewish leaders.

At the same time, he was no pushover. The Jews knew they had no real case against Paul, so they begged to have him returned to Jerusalem, secretly planning to kill him along the way (25:3). Festus denied their request, but agreed to a retrial in Caesarea if they still wanted to press charges. They had little choice but to comply.

Festus spent over a week in Jerusalem (25:6), but held Paul's trial as soon as he got back. It was essentially a repeat of the previous prosecution by Tertullus (24:1–9). The Jewish prosecutors made many serious accusations concerning Paul, but couldn't prove any of them. They had accusers, but no witnesses. And all Paul could do was again deny that he had done anything wrong in regard to either Jewish or Roman law (25:8).

As a new governor, Festus didn't want to start his term in office by provoking the Jews if it could be helped. But like Felix, he had no evidence on which to convict Paul (25:9). At this point he did what may seem unusual to a modern court: He consulted the accused. He suggested that Paul might want to return to Jerusalem to be tried. His sensitivity to Paul was likely in recognition of Paul's rights as a Roman citizen.

Festus's attempt to placate the Jews didn't work because Paul knew he would be better off in a Roman civil court than a Jewish religious one. Paul emphatically stated that he would not resist the death penalty if anyone could prove anything against him. But since they couldn't, he would take advantage of his right as a Roman citizen and appeal to a higher court. His next stop would be in Rome before the emperor or his representatives. Even though the current emperor (or Caesar) was Nero, he had not yet developed the reputation of unpredictable leadership and oppression of Christians.

Paul's appeal to Caesar (25:11) must have been a great relief for Festus. Not only would it get Paul out of Festus's jurisdiction in Caesarea, but it also meant he did not have to make a decision that would antagonize the Jews.

📖 25:13–22

FESTUS AND AGRIPPA

Not long afterward, Festus had a visitor: Marcus Julius Agrippa II. He was a descendant of Herod the Great and the person Rome had appointed king over the territory northeast of Judea. Agrippa was accompanied by his sister, Bernice (25:13), who was also his consort. They had tried to squelch rumors of an incestuous relationship by having Bernice marry Polemo II, the king of Cilicia, but she soon returned to Agrippa.

Critical Observation

Herod the Great and his successors are integral antagonists in the New Testament story. The original Herod was the one who had slaughtered the young males of Bethlehem in an attempt to eliminate Jesus as an infant (Matthew 2:16). His son, Herod Antipas, made an impulsive promise at a birthday party that led to his beheading of John the Baptist (Mark 6:17–28) and was the Herod involved with Jesus' trial (Luke 23:8–11). Herod the Great's grandson, Herod Agrippa I, killed James the apostle and had similar plans for Peter (Acts 12:2–4). The Acts 25 passage introduces Agrippa II, son of Herod Agrippa I and the fourth (and final) generation of Herods in scripture. Agrippa II was the last of the family dynasty, and the least odious of the Herods.

The couple was in Caesarea for an extended stay, to welcome Festus to the neighborhood (25:14). They lived in the adjoining province, in Caesarea Philippi. It was protocol for Roman rulers to welcome newcomers and build relationships, and Festus was glad for the interaction with Agrippa. He knew the king was knowledgeable about Jewish culture and customs. Frankly, he didn't understand all that was involved in the Jewish elders' accusations against Paul, and he was glad for the opportunity for a consultation.

It is interesting that Luke provided Festus's outsider perception of everything that had been going on (25:14–21). The governor's account appears honest and straightforward, yet the religious significance had escaped him. He was confused about a dead man named Jesus who Paul claimed was living (25:19), and he had no idea how to respond. Yet his story intrigued Agrippa, who requested the opportunity to hear Paul himself (25:22). Festus agreed to set something up for the next day.

But far from simply having Paul released for a conversation with Agrippa, Festus went out of his way to create an event for his visitors. Everyone of any status in his court and in the city of Caesarea was invited. Agrippa and Bernice entered the room in a formal and courtly manner (25:23). For such an occasion, they would have been wearing their purple robes of royalty and their gold crowns. Festus, too, had a ceremonial uniform, including a scarlet robe. When the officials were all seated, Paul was summoned.

What a contrast he must have made in the great assembly. Paul is thought to have been short and balding. He likely had scars from the beatings and stoning he had already received in his many travels. And he was still wearing the handcuffs by which he would be chained to his guard(s) (26:29).

Festus opened the proceedings by explaining why Paul was being brought before the crowd. It wasn't an official trial, yet he would have to write up the facts of Paul's case to be sent along with him to Rome. Festus was looking for advice from the group—especially Agrippa. Yet Festus also made clear his personal opinion that Paul had done nothing worthy of death—in spite of what Paul's Jewish prosecutors had claimed (25:24–25).

📖 26:1–32

PAUL AND AGRIPPA

Festus yielded the floor to Agrippa, who gave Paul permission to speak. This was a dramatic moment. For four generations, the Herod family had obstructed the work of God through Jesus, John the Baptist, James the apostle, and now Paul. Yet here God's Word is still being boldly proclaimed before the current Herodian leader. This is also the moment when the words of Jesus to His disciples, and later specifically to Paul though Ananias, were first fulfilled about being brought before governors and kings (Matthew 10:18; Acts 9:15).

Paul had been assured, both from Jesus and from Festus (23:11; 25:12) that he would eventually be heard in Rome. Therefore, he had no pressing need to defend himself and could use this opportunity instead to promote the gospel and attempt to sway the opinions of some of the leaders of the Roman Empire.

What follows is the longest of Paul's five defenses that Luke records in Acts. Paul even asked for Agrippa's patience before he began, knowing that he would not be brief (26:3). And just as Paul's defense before Felix had reflected his awareness that there were many Jews in his audience, in this case he tailors his speech for the Gentiles who are listening.

Paul's introductory remarks were complimentary, but not flattering (26:2-3). Agrippa was indeed familiar with Jewish customs. Among other things, it was his job to oversee the treasury of the temple and to appoint the high priest. Paul was glad to talk to an authority who knew more about Judaism than Festus, and Festus was glad for Agrippa's help in assessing Paul.

Next Paul spoke of his roots in Judaism (26:4-8). From his childhood he had been devoted to his beliefs, and had eventually become a Pharisee—as dedicated and meticulous as anyone. Yet he felt his faith in Jesus was not in opposition to his Jewish training; rather, Jesus was the fulfillment of what the Jews had been anticipating for centuries (26:6-7). And Jesus' claim to Messiah was based on His resurrection from the dead (26:8). (At this point, Paul expanded his audience, rather than continuing to speak solely to Agrippa.)

Paul followed his exemplary background with a frank confession of his initial fervor to eradicate Christianity before it became a threat to his Jewish upbringing (26:9-11). At the time he didn't believe that Jesus had risen or was the Messiah, and he was near-fanatical in opposing those who did. His reference to casting votes against them (26:10) is usually thought to be a figure of speech rather than literal. It is conceivable that Paul might have been a member of the Sanhedrin at some point, but there is no evidence that he was.

Still, he was as intent as anyone else on targeting those who believed in Jesus, which is what made his conversion story so powerful (26:12-18). This is the third time Luke included the same account (9:1-9; 22:6-11), although in this version he provided a bit of new information. For one thing, Paul mentions that the voice of Jesus he heard was speaking Aramaic (26:14). And in the same verse he cites a Greek proverb about kicking against the goads. Paul included this bit of information while talking to his Gentile audience; it wouldn't have been as meaningful to his fellow Jews. Also significant to his Roman listeners should have been the fact that a voice came from heaven to correct his actions. Additionally, his mission to the Gentiles would include presenting a message of forgiveness of sins and acceptance by God (26:17-18).

Demystifying Acts

A *goad* was a pointed stick used to drive large animals. Whether or not the animals wanted to go in that direction, it did them no good to resist the sharpened goad. "Kicking against the goads" had become a familiar phrase in the Greek world to signify someone who opposed a god or gods. Paul later uses another Greek idiom, "Done in a corner" (26:26).

Everything Paul had said so far was to explain to his high-ranking listeners why he had been arrested. He was simply doing what he had been called to do (26:19-23). It had nothing to do with treason or rebellion. And even though the Jews had seized him and tried to kill him, what he was saying was nothing that hadn't already been prophesied in their scriptures. But thanks to God, he was still alive and able to speak to the assembly.

It was when Paul stressed that Jesus had been the first to rise from the dead for the benefit of both the Jews and Gentiles (26:23) that his discourse was interrupted, beginning a most unorthodox altercation between the bench and the witness stand. First it was Festus who apparently couldn't restrain himself any longer and accused Paul of insanity (26:24). He willingly acknowledged Paul's vast knowledge, but feared Paul's intense study had driven him crazy. Festus's Gentile outlook of life and death allowed no possibility for resurrection.

But Paul calmly denied the accusation of insanity. Rather than taking it personally, he pointed out that everything he was saying was a matter of common knowledge. His assertions were not only true, but also reasonable (26:25). The ministry, death, and resurrection of Jesus had been public and were open to verification. In addition, anyone who believed what the Old Testament prophets had written and compared their prophecies with the historical facts concerning Jesus of Nazareth must acknowledge the truth of Christianity.

Paul knew Agrippa was aware of both Jewish history and the current events concerning Jesus, and asked him directly for his input. Paul's question seems simple enough (26:27). Yet Agrippa was anticipating Paul's follow-up question. If Agrippa admitted to believing in the writings of the prophets, he would surely be asked if he agreed that Jesus had fulfilled those predictions. And he wasn't ready to make such a statement that would lose the support of the majority of the Jews, or let Paul get the better of him in this formal assembly, for that matter.

So Agrippa deflected the attention placed on him with a question of his own (26:28). It is not unreasonable to suppose that his comment was a lighthearted attempt to provide a break in the proceedings. Perhaps Paul's response had a similar tone (26:29). He was clearly serious about his prayers for Agrippa as well as everyone else present and his desire for all of them to be like him. But his final words, "except for these chains," could conceivably have been delivered with a smile.

Whatever the tone of the delivery, Agrippa stood at that point and the assembly was concluded (26:30). Agrippa, Bernice, and Festus hadn't even gotten out of the room before they had agreed that Paul had done nothing for which he should die—or even be imprisoned (26:31). In addition, Agrippa would have released him on the spot if Paul hadn't already made an official appeal to the emperor (26:32).

Agrippa's closing comment confirms the previous results of Paul's trials. Paul had not been found guilty of any crime by the Jewish Sanhedrin (23:9), the Roman commander in Jerusalem (23:29), or two successive Roman governors in Caesarea (24:22–27; 25:25). Now, the king over the territory, a high-ranking Roman authority with long-standing close connections to the Jewish people, could find no fault with Paul. Yet Paul still had another trial to withstand, this one before Caesar himself.

At least Paul would be out of his two-year palace captivity during his transfer to Rome. He had a lengthy voyage ahead of him, and it would not all be smooth sailing.

Take It Home

One significant thing worth noting from this passage is Paul's lack of intimidation. In previous chapters of Acts it has been clear that he has not been intimidated by threats of violence or harm; he has continued in spite of everything that has happened to him. But today's Christians—those in the West, at least—may not relate very well to such physical persecution. Contemporary believers may identify more with this passage where Paul might have been intimidated by status, yet wasn't. He could walk into a room filled with the most important people in his community and his world, share his personal testimony with them, and invite them to consider becoming believers themselves. How would you do in such a setting? Would you be reluctant to be so bold among dignitaries? Or do you think you would respond much like Paul did?

ACTS 27:1–44

PROBLEMS ON THE WAY TO ROME

Sailing West	27:1–12
Into a Hurricane	27:13–26
Shipwrecked, but Ashore	27:27–44

Setting Up the Section

Paul, the prominent figure in the book of Acts, has spent the last two years under guard in Caesarea, waiting for the governor to try him. Felix never got around to it because he was hoping for a bribe. But when Festus, the new governor, arrived, Paul immediately received his trial. Festus didn't fully understand the intricacies of the case and would not make a decision. In response, Paul appealed his case to a higher court—before Caesar himself. If he hadn't done that, he would have been released (26:32). But Paul was eager to go to Rome, and begins his journey in this passage.

📖 27:1–12

SAILING WEST

When Paul first started thinking seriously about going to Rome (19:21), he probably hadn't counted on first spending two years under house arrest and then moving on to Rome as a prisoner. Yet regardless of the conditions, Jesus' promise to him (23:11) was at last being fulfilled.

Luke didn't mention any of Paul's associates who might have come by to see him during his two-year imprisonment, though he had the freedom to receive visitors (24:23). Yet as soon as Paul prepared to sail toward Rome, the book of Acts reverts back to first person (27:1). The last first-person reference was used shortly before Paul's arrest that eventually landed him in Caesarea (21:18), so perhaps Luke had been nearby this whole time.

Little is known about the Imperial Regiment (27:1), as was true about the Italian Regiment mentioned in Acts 10:1. But Julius, the centurion assigned to oversee Paul, would have been responsible for one-sixth of the regiment.

Aristarchus was a believer who had been with Paul both just before his arrest (19:29) and now (27:2), so he, too, may have attended to Paul's needs for the previous two years. He would later be associated with Paul in Rome (Colossians 4:10), so it seems that Paul had friends with him during this long voyage. He was also allowed to get off the ship and visit fellow believers at Sidon, their first stop (27:3). Perhaps Paul's Roman citizenship gave him certain privileges that other prisoners didn't receive.

Prevailing winds in the Mediterranean during fall are usually from the west (27:4), the direction the ship was headed, so sailing was slow. Rather than continuing to follow the coastline, the centurion decided to change ships and attempt to put out to sea. Paul and the other travelers were placed on an Egyptian grain ship (27:6, 38), but their progress wasn't much better. After many days they finally made it to the island of Crete and a harbor called Fair Havens (27:7–8).

Then they had a decision to make. The Day of Atonement was already past (27:9). In AD 59, the year that Paul set out for Rome, the date would have been October 5. The Romans preferred not to sail after mid-September, and any attempts after the first of November were considered suicidal. Everyone agreed that it would be foolish to attempt to make it to Italy. But Fair Havens wasn't a good harbor, and there were no sizable towns around where the crew could pass the winter, so many wanted to sail to Phoenix, a location forty miles farther west.

Paul warned the others that to continue would mean disaster (27:10). But the centurion, who was responsible for the final decision, was swayed by the opinion of the majority, and they moved on.

📖 27:13–26

INTO A HURRICANE

It appeared to be a good decision at first. A gentle wind blew from the south, helping them along. But soon a raging wind came out of the northeast, blowing the ship away from shore (27:14).

Critical Observation

Ancient ships did not have benefit of sextant nor compass, depending instead on astronomical indications and landmarks on shore. In cloudy weather, sailors were at a loss for determining direction (27:20).

A granary ship could be as large as one hundred forty feet long by thirty-six feet wide and thirty-three feet tall, but it wasn't designed for handling storms. The bow and stern were the same width, and it had no rudder, being steered instead by two large paddles coming from each side of the stern. A single mast with a large square sail made it impossible to make progress into the wind, and placed a strain on the ship during high winds.

Fearing that the ship might break apart, the crew took five precautionary measures to save the vessel when they had a few moments of relative calm near the island of Cauda: (1) They managed to haul the lifeboat onto the deck, as it had probably been taking on water (27:16–17); (2) they passed cables transversely beneath the ship and tightened them with winches to hold the ship together like a tied-up package (27:17); (3) they lowered the sea anchor to serve as a brake as they drifted (27:17); (4) they jettisoned much of the cargo to lighten the ship (27:18); and (5) after three days, they tossed out all the ship's nonessential tackle (27:19).

They had no idea where they were, but feared the sandbars of Syrtis (27:17), which were off the coast of northern Africa and had grounded a number of ships. Even after doing everything they knew to do, most had given up any hope of surviving (27:20). There was still food available, yet the sailors weren't eating (27:21).

After many days of enduring the turbulent seas, Paul stood and addressed the others. His opening comment might sound a bit like "I told you so" (27:21), but his intent was likely to convince them of the truth of what he was about to tell them. He explained that an angel had appeared to him, told him not to be afraid, and assured him that God would spare the lives of everyone on board because of Paul (27:23–24). Paul challenged everyone to persevere and have faith that everything would be all right. They would run aground (27:26) and the ship would be destroyed, but all the people would survive (27:22).

📄 27:27–44

SHIPWRECKED, BUT ASHORE

It is no wonder morale was low. Imagine being at sea with 275 other people (27:37) and being tossed by ferocious weather for two entire weeks with no control over where you were going (27:27). It was enough to drive seasoned sailors to despair. And when they realized they were coming upon land (27:27), still with no control, some prayed for daylight while others tried to sneak away in the lifeboat (27:29–30). Paul saw what was going on, alerted the centurion, and the soldiers scuttled the lifeboat.

It wasn't yet dawn, but Paul again tried to lift everyone's spirits. He took some practical steps to prepare them for what was to come. He urged them to eat, he again promised that no one would lose a single hair from his head, and he thanked God publicly (27:34–35). The others were encouraged, ate all they wanted, and then threw all the remaining grain into the sea to again attempt to lighten the boat. They were planning to make it to shore soon, and wanted the ship to sit as high in the water as possible.

By then it was daylight, and they saw a sandy beach on an unidentified stretch of land. Their plan was to run the ship right up onto the shore, but it hit a sandbar they had not seen (27:39–41). As a result, the bow was stuck fast in the sand while the stern was smashed into pieces by the pounding waves.

Demystifying Acts

The stranded ship on the sandbar placed the Roman soldiers in a dilemma. It was an easy swim to shore, and if a prisoner were to escape from their custody the Roman Empire required that the guard be killed. Not wanting to place their own lives in risk, the soldiers were preparing to kill the prisoners (27:42). But by this time, the centurion in charge seemed to trust Paul, and forbade his soldiers from harming anyone.

The centurion instructed those who could swim to make their way to shore first. The others found pieces of the battered ship and used them to float to shore. And just as Paul had promised, everyone arrived safely on the land, which they soon discovered to be the island of Malta.

Take It Home

Just as Jesus had calmed storms and controlled the winds and waves for His disciples on the Sea of Galilee, He saw Paul safely through this threatening sea voyage. We should not fail to notice the angel's promise to Paul: "God has graciously given you the lives of all who sail with you" (27:24 NIV). Paul's situation was probably not a one-time incident when God's protection of His people also spared others around them. Can you recall any instances when nonbelievers might have benefited because of the presence of a righteous person making godly decisions? Can you think of any times when your own decisions have had positive effects on many others?

ACTS 28:1–31

ROME AT LAST

Winter in Malta	28:1–10
From Malta to Rome	28:11–16
Ministry in Rome	28:17–31

Setting Up the Section

Paul's numerous missionary trips had created within him the desire to one day reach Rome and preach there. After a number of legal trials and two years of imprisonment while waiting, he had at last set out on his way—but still as a prisoner. In addition, his ship had encountered a violent storm and wrecked just off the shore of Malta. But he had Jesus' promise that he would arrive in Rome, and in this closing section of Acts he finally gets there.

WINTER IN MALTA

Malta meant "refuge," and lived up to its name for Paul and his fellow shipwreck victims. They found themselves about five hundred miles west of Crete, where they had last put out to sea, and they were only about fifty-eight miles away from the island of Sicily, which was just off the southwest corner of the Italian mainland.

The word for "islanders" (28:2) also means "barbarians," but not in the sense the word is usually used today. In Paul's time it was a term used to indicate anyone who didn't speak Greek. It is evident from Luke's description of the Maltese people that they were far from barbaric.

Indeed, they extended unusual kindness toward the stranded sailors, building a fire on shore to get them warm and dry (28:2). Paul pitched in to help gather wood, and as he was placing it on the fire a poisonous snake amid the brush became startled and struck his arm (28:3). The islanders, who would have known the danger of being bitten by that particular species of serpent, supposed that Paul had been a murderer intended to perish in the sea, yet had somehow escaped (28:4). They watched a long time for the effects of the poison, and when Paul showed no ill effects at all they assumed he must be divine (28:6).

Dike (pronounced Dí-*kay*) was the Greek goddess of justice, frequently portrayed as holding a staff and balance. It was belief in Dike that helped the Maltese natives explain why bad things happened to certain people. Yet their mythology didn't hold true for Paul, and they didn't automatically assume a god (or God) might be protecting Paul. So the only thing that made sense to them was to believe that Paul was a god himself.

Paul continued to mystify the islanders. He and a group (including Luke) were invited to the home of the chief official on Malta. The man's father was in bed with a serious illness. Even in modern times, Malta fever was prevalent in the area, with symptoms lasting an average of four months—and sometimes as long as two or three years. The source was eventually identified as a microorganism in the milk of Maltese goats, and a vaccine was developed. But Paul had no vaccine, and instead laid his hands on the man and prayed for him (28:8). When the official's father was immediately healed, the other sick people on the island flocked to Paul and were also cured (28:9).

Critical Observation

Throughout the book of Acts, Paul displays healing power. Yet in his epistles we discover he had some kind of ailment (a thorn in his flesh [2 Corinthians 12:7–10]) that was never removed. Like Jesus, he used God's power for the benefit of others. But when it came to his own physical problems, he went to God in prayer and submitted to His will.

Paul and the others had to wait out the winter on Malta. But three months later, when they were again ready to sail, the grateful people provided them with all the supplies they needed (28:10).

FROM MALTA TO ROME

Sailing in the Mediterranean would have picked up again around mid-February, which fits the three-month span of time spent on Malta (28:11). Another ship was in a nearby port—probably another grain ship since it, too, was Egyptian. Its figurehead was of Castor and Pollux, sons of Zeus and the twins portrayed in the constellation Gemini. They were thought to protect sailors, and the sighting of Gemini in the night sky was considered a good omen. But the men who had been traveling with Paul knew something of the God who could really protect those at sea.

Arrangements were made, most likely by the centurion, for Paul's group to be transported to Italy on this Alexandrian ship. The first stop was a three-day layover in Syracuse (28:12), a major city on the eastern coast of Sicily. From there they continued north to Rhegium (now Reggio di Calabria), on the "toe" of the Italian mainland, just east of Sicily. A favorable wind the next day carried them 180 miles farther north to Puteoli (now Pozzuoli), a large port protected by the Bay of Naples. A group of believers invited Paul to spend a week with them before going on to Rome, still seventy-five miles away. Evidently, the centurion responsible for Paul had developed enough respect for him to allow him certain privileges rather than moving straight ahead to Rome.

Demystifying Acts

It should be understood that Paul wasn't going to Rome to introduce the gospel, but to deepen the comprehension of the believers there. Puteoli and other communities had a large Jewish population, many of whom had surely traveled to Jerusalem and witnessed the coming of the Holy Spirit years ago. So groups of Christians had already sprung up in various locations (28:14–15). In addition, Paul had written his Epistle to the Romans three years prior to his arrival. So the believers in the area already had a decent understanding of the significance of Jesus' death and resurrection.

After everything Paul had gone through to get to Rome to preach, his entry into Rome is understated (28:14). News of his approach had preceded him. Believers from Rome came flocking to meet him and got as far as the Three Taverns (a way station thirty-three miles outside of Rome) and the Forum of Appius (forty-three miles from Rome). They would have traveled the famed Appian Way, one of the great Roman roads named after Appias Claudius.

The meeting of Paul by the Roman citizens (28:15) is more formal than it may seem. The Greek word used is the same that would apply to an official city delegation going out to greet a general or king. Paul was treated as one of the great heroes of the faith. He was encouraged, not at the attention he received, but at the very sight of believers representing Jesus Christ in the heart of the Roman Empire (28:15). It must have also been encouraging to be granted a large degree of freedom while awaiting his trial in Rome. Although he was always under guard, he was allowed to live by himself (28:16).

MINISTRY IN ROME

One of the first things Paul did during his two-year stay (28:30) was to meet with the Jewish leaders in Rome, perhaps to preempt any problems like those he had faced in other cities. The outspoken segment of Jews who had opposed him in Jerusalem would be likely to arrive after finding out he was in Rome. He quickly summarized what had happened to him and why he had come (28:17–20).

The local Jews said they hadn't heard any bad reports about Paul (28:21). Perhaps they were being tactful because communication between Rome and Jerusalem was usually good, and it had been almost two and a half years since the riot for which he was arrested. (He had been in prison in Caesarea for two years and in transit from Caesarea to Rome for at least three and a half months.) Yet they were curious about Christianity and eager to hear Paul's explanation (28:22).

A meeting was arranged, and a great number of people turned out to hear Paul, who spent the entire day teaching and encouraging them to believe in Jesus. True to the pattern in previous cities, some did believe and others refused to (28:23–24). As those Jews who rejected the gospel were leaving, Paul quoted Isaiah 6:9–10, a prophecy that the Jewish people would close their eyes and ears to (28:26–27). (Jesus had cited the same quotation in reference to His ministry [Mark 4:12].) Paul's last encounter with the Jews thus follows the common pattern throughout Acts. While some responded favorably, most rejected the message, and Paul turned to the Gentiles. They would believe.

It wasn't Luke's intent to write the biography of Paul. Rather, he had recorded the spread of the gospel from Jerusalem to Samaria to the ends of the earth, and from its Jewish roots to the Gentile world (Acts 1:8). As he concludes with the gospel reaching Rome, it may be frustrating that he leaves Paul still under arrest and awaiting trial for two full years. But Luke's central theme comes through loud and clear. Despite his imprisonment, Paul is able to receive visitors and continues to proclaim the kingdom of God "boldly and without hindrance" (28:31). Though Paul is in chains, the gospel cannot be chained and continues to advance despite opposition!

POSTSCRIPT

It was during this two-year period that Paul wrote his Prison Epistles: Philippians, Ephesians, Colossians, and Philemon. Most scholars believe Paul was subsequently exonerated in Rome and released. He took a fourth missionary journey (based on comments in his Epistles) and may even have gone to Spain. But he later found himself in Rome again, this time in a dank prison expecting to die (2 Timothy 2:9; 4:6–8). Tradition says he was beheaded in Rome at the command of Emperor Nero.

Take It Home

Looking back on the ministry of Paul after everything he has been through, his conversion story becomes even more powerful. Luke included it three times in the book of Acts (9:1–19; 22:6–21; 26:12–18). The before-and-after story of Paul is perhaps one of the most dramatic imaginable. Consider your own life before and after becoming a believer. What are some of the biggest differences you have noticed? Do you have a sense of where God may be leading you at this point in your spiritual journey?

ROMANS

INTRODUCTION TO
ROMANS

It is easy to forget that the Epistle to the Romans is a letter and not a theological treatise. It is so often used in doctrinal studies and pursuits that we may miss the heartfelt passion that the author, Paul, had for his readers, many of whom he had never met. It isn't the first of Paul's letters chronologically, though it is placed first among his Epistles in the New Testament.

AUTHOR

Paul is the writer of this Epistle. Skeptics have challenged the authenticity of some of Paul's other Epistles, but Romans has never seriously been questioned.

PURPOSE

Paul considered himself an apostle to the Gentiles (11:13), yet he had never been to Rome, the center of the secular Roman Empire. He was planning a visit on his way to Spain (15:23–24, 28), and was writing in anticipation of his arrival. Yet his Epistle is far more than a casual letter. He laid out a fresh and clear explanation of God's plan of salvation for both Jews and Gentiles—one that has continued to inspire and motivate Bible readers for centuries.

OCCASION

Paul was probably writing from Corinth on his third missionary journey, preparing to return to Jerusalem with a financial gift he had collected from the churches in Greece (15:25–29). But he was already making plans for a fourth missionary journey and hoped to include Rome. So while in Corinth (or near there), he wrote his Epistle to inform the church of his plans. As it turned out, he would arrive in Rome as a prisoner (Acts 28:16), but was given a lot of freedom to minister and eventually was released.

THEMES

The themes that permeate the Epistle to the Romans are righteousness from God and justification by faith. Through faith in Jesus Christ, God's righteousness is imparted to human beings. It was how Abraham was justified before God prior to the giving of the Mosaic Law. And it was how Gentiles were able to come to God without being required to be circumcised or observe all the Jewish dietary restrictions and feast days.

HISTORICAL CONTEXT

We know little about the origins of the church in Rome. It is likely that Jewish pilgrims in Jerusalem had become believers on the Day of Pentecost, returned home, and started the church. When Paul finally got to visit (during the early portion of Nero's reign), a group of believers traveled many miles to meet him along the way and escort him back to Rome (Acts 28:14–16).

CONTRIBUTION TO THE BIBLE

The book of Romans has been called the Constitution of the Bible. The privileges and freedoms it describes are good news not only for the Gentiles, who came to God with little knowledge and no traditions, but also for the Jews, who had drifted away from the genuine worship of God and had rejected Jesus. God's love, mercy, and grace are abundant enough for everyone to experience His forgiveness. The realization that people are justified by faith alone has been an eye-opening and life-changing reality for Martin Luther, John Wesley, and other church leaders.

OUTLINE

ROMANS 1:1–32

ACTING ON WHAT WE BELIEVE

Setting Up the Section

Paul wrote his letter to the Romans before ever visiting Rome, yet his heartfelt concern for the believers there is clearly evident throughout this Epistle. After a short salutation and brief personal comments, Paul begins what has become a masterpiece on the topic of righteousness. In this section, he emphasizes the absence of righteousness in humankind, which he will later contrast to the righteousness of God.

📄 **1:1–7**

SALUTATION TO THE CHURCH IN ROME

Paul consistently begins his letters by identifying himself, as he does in this Epistle (1:1). He had been called by Jesus to be an apostle—someone sent out bearing the authority of another. After Paul's conversion, it didn't take long for him to consider himself a servant (literally, a slave) of Jesus. He had placed himself completely at Jesus' disposal, listening for and responding to his Master's commands. And since it was Jesus who was in control of Paul's life, that's whom he immediately began to write about.

Critical Observation

For the first-century readers to whom Paul was writing, the concept of servanthood was not necessarily drudgery. To be the Lord's servant was an honor. The nation of Israel as a whole was referred to this way (Isaiah 43:10) as was Moses (Joshua 14:7), King David (Psalm 89:3) and the great prophet Elijah (2 Kings 10:10).

The gospel Paul describes had not just appeared; it had been promised long ago in the Old Testament scriptures (1:2). The prophets had foretold the ministry and death of Jesus. Yet many people had missed the significance of His life and death. Among the prophecies was the prediction that the Messiah would not only be the Son of God (1:4), but also a descendant of David (1:3). He was fully human and fully divine, begotten by God, but born of a woman as well. Jesus was not just a great teacher, leader, and healer; He was declared to be the Son of God through the power of His resurrection from the dead (1:4).

In verse 5, Paul mentions two characteristics—grace and apostleship—that he attributes to himself, though he uses the editorial "we." Apostleship is not something available to all believers, but rather a unique calling. What *is* available to all believers is the calling to belong to Christ (1:6). Believers form a family of brothers and sisters who are provided for by a heavenly Father. The call to be saints (1:7) means to be set apart from the secular world. It is something not only desirable, but also achievable for all Christians.

📄 **1:8–17**

PAUL'S DEEP DESIRES

After Paul's salutation, he first expresses thankfulness for the Christians in Rome (1:8). Paul is grateful that they have already developed a reputation for faithfulness. His reference to all the world means *his* world—the Roman Empire. And although their faith inspires his gratitude, he doesn't thank them, but rather he thanks God. For Paul, thankfulness and prayer are directly connected (1:9–10).

Paul is also praying for the opportunity to visit Rome (1:10). He feels a deep longing to get there (1:11). It is his desire to share his spiritual gifts with the people there, and that he and they will be mutually encouraged as they interact (1:11–12). The ministry of believers to one another is a give-and-take relationship. Paul desires encouragement just as much as the Christians in Rome need to receive it from him. His desire to visit had just been intensified by having had to wait so long (1:13).

Paul follows with three strong personal statements about his desire to preach in Rome. He is obligated, eager, and not ashamed (1:14–17).

Paul isn't ashamed of the gospel because it is the source of both the power of God (1:16) and righteousness from God (1:17). The word he uses for "believing in the gospel" (1:16) means more than simply intellectual assent. It refers to having confidence and placing one's trust in something.

📄 **1:18–32**

THE WRATH OF GOD

God's wrath is not a popular subject among many people—even believers. Yet just as people are right to become angry in certain circumstances (sexual abuse of children, rape, betrayal of a confidence, widespread slaughter, etc.), so it should make sense that God, too, becomes angry in response to these and other sins. Yet God's wrath is not like human anger, which is frequently petty, controlled by emotion, and given to whims. Rather, God's wrath is always holy and just—a natural expression of His holiness and justice.

Paul lists the reason for God's wrath as the suppression of the truth. God's involvement with humankind should be evident by His creation, if nothing else (1:19-20). While immoral people have a bent toward things that are destructive, those who suppress the truth are perhaps the worst of the bunch. After knowing truth, but resisting it, these individuals grow more comfortable with immorality, or they try to justify or deny their inappropriate actions (as they have since Adam and Eve).

God is the source of truth and righteousness, so all alternatives (foolishness and idols) are shallow substitutes (1:21-23). God's wrath targets the various sins, not the people. Yet when people stubbornly refuse to repent, God will eventually allow their sinful desires to run rampant (1:24-25).

The list Paul provides of sinful desires and shameful lusts (1:26–32) is quite detailed, including homosexuality, envy, murder, deceit, gossip, arrogance, and much more. Such actions are not committed in ignorance, but in willful defiance (1:32).

God's wrath against sin is what allows Him to permit such things to occur. As He lets people go their own way, they see the results of sin all around them. Yet He is still there for all who place their faith in Him.

Paul will have more to say about God's wrath in the next sections, including what can be done to avoid it altogether.

Take It Home

Review Paul's list of sinful actions (1:24–32) and mentally list the ones for which you have been guilty. Be sure to adapt the list to modern times. For example, idolatry may no longer be defined by a statue of Baal in your den, but rather by a big-screen TV during college football season. Would you consider any of the behaviors on Paul's list to be "little" sins? Do you think their inclusion on this list allows you to continue to consider them "little"?

ROMANS 2:1–29

GOD HAS NO FAVORITES

Setting Up the Section

Paul has just presented a somewhat scathing description of the behavior of humans when they reject God and live according to their sinful desires and natural lusts (1:24–32). It isn't a pretty picture. And neither is his next description of people who feel they have their lives together enough to pass judgment on others. Paul is about to point out that no one—Jew or Gentile—is righteous and law-abiding enough to avoid God's wrath on his or her own merit.

2:1–16

JUDGMENT AND THE LAW

In the previous section, Paul wrote about how people refused to recognize God based primarily on nature and His creation. Here he begins to reflect on how people also reject God by ignoring His special revelation through scripture.

It sounds as if Paul has someone in mind as he begins (2:1). But he had not yet visited Rome to meet the people in the church there. Instead, he uses a literary device (the diatribe style) in which the writer addresses an imaginary pupil or rival and makes his point by making bold statements and asking questions.

Paul's point is that anyone who passes judgment on others is actually condemning himself or herself as well (2:1). It isn't so much the judging itself that is wrong, because believers are instructed to identify and deal with behaviors that are potentially harmful to themselves or others (Matthew 18:15–17; James 5:19–20; etc.). But, like Jesus, Paul warns of the dangers of hypocrisy in evaluations of other people.

Paul may have the Jewish people in mind here because they tended to look down on Gentiles while overlooking their own shortcomings. In any case, the ones passing judgment (2:3) were doing so with stubbornness and an unrepentant heart (2:5). It is far too common to find those who cherish God's kindness, tolerance, and patience for themselves, yet are reluctant to extend it to others (2:3–4).

Even though people tend to be judgmental when they shouldn't be, God is frequently *not* judgmental when He *could* be. His mercy allows people to repent. Then, rather than being self-seeking and pursuing evil, they are able to seek righteousness instead. Rewards are in store for such people, but God's wrath awaits those who continue to reject truth (2:7–10). God will evaluate people's actions—not their religious affiliations or good intentions. He does not show favoritism (2:11–16).

The reference to "apart from the law" (2:12 NIV) refers to Gentiles. They were never given the Law of Moses, so God will not hold them accountable for it. The Jews, however, were given the Law, so God will rightly judge them by those standards. Yet even the Gentiles have been given enough insight into spiritual things that they cannot plead complete ignorance. God's law is inscribed on their hearts and present through the work of their conscience (2:15). Paul will later clarify that the law is not necessary in order for people to be righteous followers of God.

📖 2:17–29

JEWISH DISTINCTIONS

So far, Paul has demonstrated that a person may be moral, yet still lost and in need of salvation. In essence, he has said no one is moral enough to earn salvation. Then he anticipates the next two questions: What about religious people? Won't God accept them?

His answer (2:17–29) addresses the religious pride of the Jewish people of his time. They felt sure God regarded them with special favor because of their national descent from Abraham and because they bore the mark of the Old Testament covenant: circumcision.

Paul introduces a radical thought: Being Jewish is not a matter of race at all but is, instead, a matter of conduct. He begins by citing five positive distinctions that contributed to religious pride.

First, they were proud to be called Jews (2:17). The term was derived from their ancestor, Judah. Not long after the word *Jew* first appeared in the scriptures, it became the national name the Hebrew people were proud to bear.

Second, Paul acknowledges the Jewish reliance on their scriptures (2:17). They possess God's Word, revealed and recorded. God had entrusted to them the oracles of faith.

Third, the Jews had a special relationship with God (2:17). He had made a covenant with them. He had called them to their land, delivered them from bondage in Egypt, and given them the promised land. He called them His own people. They were special to Him.

Fourth, they were strong moralists with a clearly stated set of values (2:18). They distinguished right from wrong and had a high regard for ethics even though they lived amid a culture that encouraged hedonism and self-indulgence.

And fifth, they were very capable of teaching others (2:19–20). Not only did they discern right from wrong, they could share it with others and instruct them in the ways of God.

Critical Observation

At this point in history, the Jews considered (and called) Gentiles "dogs." The Jewish air of spiritual superiority had created a great animosity and antagonism that had resulted in racial conflict. The Jews had been called by God to be a light to the Gentiles, but rather than witnessing God's love, all the Gentiles were seeing was spiritual snobbery, prejudice, and pride.

It might sound as if Paul is endorsing everything the Jewish people were doing. But all these positive traits are listed in "if" clauses. Paul wants to know *if* they had all these positive things going for them, then why aren't their hearts right before God? He boldly exposes the inconsistency between the Jews' personal claims and their actual conduct. His series of questions (2:21–23) leads to the regrettable consequence that, due to preaching what they didn't practice, the Jews were responsible for God's name being blasphemed among the Gentiles (2:24).

Paul also shows that Jewish emphasis on circumcision was misguided. The Jews had an unwarranted confidence in the rite as a sign that they were special to God. Paul points out that the outer sign was supposed to reflect an inner commitment to God. Circumcision meant nothing to those who chose to neglect God's law (2:25–26). In fact, any uncircumcised individual who kept God's Word was preferable to someone who was circumcised but ignored what God had instructed (2:27).

Demystifying Romans

In essence, Paul redefines what it means to be a Jew in Romans 2:28–29—or at the least, he clarifies the original definition. As God had made clear in the Old Testament, when evaluating the worth of a person, He looks at the heart rather than the outward appearance (1 Samuel 16:7). That is still the case (2:29).

Lest it seems Paul has come down too hard on his Jewish peers, he will continue to expand and clarify his thoughts in the following section. There is still much advantage to being Jewish, which he will soon explain.

Take It Home

The first-century Jewish community certainly isn't the only religious group to get its priorities confused. If Paul had been writing to the twenty-first-century church you're familiar with, what do you think he would have said? Do you think today's church lives up to what it proclaims? If so, in what ways? If not, what are the areas you think could be improved?

ROMANS 3:1–31

BAD NEWS AND GOOD NEWS

Setting Up the Section

Paul continues his evaluation of Jewish religious beliefs and points out that God's righteousness cannot be achieved merely through one's commitment to the law and the practice of circumcision. While knowledge of the scriptures and obedience to their teaching is an excellent start, more is necessary. So first, Paul lays out the bad news of the impossibility of achieving righteousness, but he then follows with the good news of God's plan that overcomes that difficulty.

📖 3:1–8

QUESTIONS AND ANSWERS

In light of everything he had been saying in Romans 2, Paul addresses the advantage in being Jewish. Paul himself was a knowledgeable and well-trained Pharisee. And while it isn't his knowledge or Jewish status that lead to salvation (Philippians 3:3–8), he still sees much advantage in his Jewish heritage (3:1–2).

Critical Observation

As Paul lists the advantages of being Jewish, he begins with the word "first" (3:2). But he seemingly gets so caught up in explaining the importance of being entrusted with the words of God that he doesn't get to the rest of his list until much later (9:4–5).

The questions Paul asks and answers have to do with how his teaching supposedly undermined God's covenant with the Jewish people (3:1), nullified God's promises (3:3), and questioned the fairness of God's judgment (3:5). Whether these objections were literal or only anticipated by Paul, he takes them seriously and responds to them. He is saying things that are hard for his Jewish readership to hear, so he is quick to defend the character of God in each case. He affirms that God's covenant has abiding value, God is indeed faithful to His promises, and God is fair in His judgment.

People tend to take a human, rather than a godly, view of spiritual things. So already some were trying to make a case that their sin only caused God to look more glorious and righteous. And if so, then how could God judge them since they were making Him look better (3:5–8)? Paul categorically denies the validity of the argument and moves on, though he will come back to it later (6:1–14).

📖 3:9–20

THE BAD NEWS

Scripture had already spoken on the subject of whether Jews or Gentiles had a better understanding of God's love and righteousness. Paul quotes a series of Old Testament scriptures (mostly from Psalms, with additions from Ecclesiastes and Isaiah) to show the widespread influence of sin. The grim truth is that no one is righteous. No one understands God's love and mercy. No one seeks God (3:10–11).

The rampant, self-seeking effects of sin have victimized both Jew and Gentile. People can observe the law, but it won't make them righteous (3:20). If anything, the law only makes them more aware of their lack of righteousness (3:20). So what are they to do?

📖 3:21–26

THE GOOD NEWS

The hope for people is not in themselves or in the law, but in God. It is impossible to earn righteousness and salvation, yet God will readily provide it. This should have come as no surprise to anyone who knew the teachings of Old Testament scripture (3:21), but it took the life and death of Jesus for people to have the proper insight and understanding.

From God's perspective, there is no difference between Jew and Gentile. Both are sinful. And neither is there a difference in how they restore a proper relationship with God: He justifies them freely, out of grace, because the death of Jesus paid for their sin (3:22–24). People are still unworthy and unable to do anything to contribute to their own justification, so God does it by His grace. They don't deserve it, but He loves them and initiates action.

Demystifying Romans

Justification is a legal term. When God justifies someone, He declares the person to be righteous. He doesn't make the person righteous. Believers will continue to struggle with sin, yet can continue to be assured of God's declaration of righteousness, thanks to the sacrifice of Jesus on their behalf.

The Greek word for "redemption" (3:24) refers to obtaining something by means of purchase. It can refer to payment of a ransom. Jesus' sacrifice (His blood) was the necessary atonement to pay for the sins of humankind—past, present, and future (3:25–26).

The atoning sacrifice (3:25) is also called *propitiation*. The great importance of such a sacrifice is that it appeases God's wrath so that we don't receive the condemnation that we deserve. God doesn't just choose to overlook our sins; they are fully atoned for from this point forward. Additionally, He had left sins unpunished in the past, knowing that justice would be fulfilled when Jesus eventually paid the price for them (3:25–26).

God is just. He doesn't universally negate the consequence of human sin. Yet He also demonstrates great grace and mercy, and justifies those who have faith in Jesus (3:26).

📄 3:27–31

JUSTIFICATION BY FAITH ALONE

After describing and explaining the concept of justification in regard to his theme of righteousness (3:21–26), Paul emphasizes that people are justified only by faith. He summarizes by returning to a question-and-answer format.

Since Paul has clarified that justification has nothing to do with people's works and is instead an act of God based on the sacrificial death of Jesus Christ on the cross, there is no opportunity for boasting. All have sinned (3:23), so anyone who wants forgiveness must have faith in Jesus. Observing the law is a positive action, yet it has nothing to do with justification (3:27).

The one God has but one way for people to come to Him. Jews and Gentiles alike are redeemed by faith. And lest anyone accuse Paul of suggesting that the law was not important or had become outdated, he boldly declares that placing faith in Jesus is exactly how the law is upheld (3:31).

Paul will continue to explain justification by faith by using an example from the law as he continues his argument in the next section.

Take It Home

Notice Paul's emphasis on faith as he presents his argument in this section. Review Romans 3:22–31, and count the number of times he mentions faith. Then read the section once more and let his words sink in. Do you think most believers today agree that faith is really all that is needed to be justified before God? Or do they tend to add other requirements?

ROMANS 4:1–25

JUSTIFICATION BEFORE THE LAW EXISTED

Setting Up the Section

Paul has been writing about a most significant topic: the fact that salvation is by faith in Jesus alone, and does not require observance of the Mosaic Law or the sign of circumcision. He realizes many of his Jewish readers will find this hard to accept, so in this section he makes an argument using an example out of the greatest hero of their faith: Abraham.

📖 4:1–8

THE PRECEDENT OF FAITH

Earlier in his letter, Paul demonstrated that righteousness (a right relationship with God) comes only through faith. He said that the Law and the Prophets all bore witness to this fact (3:21). He is writing much like a lawyer trying to make his case. And just as an attorney would want to find witnesses who were credible, respected, well known in the community, and possessing first-hand knowledge of the topic, Paul does the same. He refers his readers back to the story of Abraham.

Critical Observation

The Jewish people had a deep reverence for Abraham. His covenant with God had taken him out of Mesopotamia to the land of Canaan. His faith had resulted in the long-awaited birth of Isaac, who gave birth to Jacob (Israel). From Jacob's twelve sons came the Israelites, so the entire nation of Israel was traced back to Abraham. The Jewish people liked to consider Abraham their father (Luke 3:8). And Jesus used the title "son of Abraham" to indicate someone who was not only a descendant of the patriarch, but who also demonstrated the faith of Abraham (Luke 19:9).

Paul's question (4:1) is intriguing: How, exactly, was Abraham justified by God? The Jews had grown so accustomed to thinking that adherence to the law was the way to God's favor that they could hardly conceive of any other way. But by using Abraham—someone they all had the highest respect for—as an example Paul transports them to a time more than four centuries before God had provided the law. If Abraham could find God's favor without the law, so could other people.

Paul quotes scripture to remind his readers that it was Abraham's faith in God that was credited as righteousness (Genesis 15:6; Romans 4:3, 22). To have something credited means the recipient does nothing to earn what is received—just the opposite of working to get a paycheck (4:4–5).

Paul builds his case further by using a second example from the life and writings of David (Psalm 32:1–2; Romans 4:6–8). Since the Jewish people tended to cite the Law and the Prophets, Paul makes his point with an example from both sections of their scriptures.

📄 4:9–17

THE PRINCIPLE OF FAITH

In addition to their intense emphasis on adherence to the Mosaic Law, the Jewish people were just as insistent about the necessity of circumcision. So again, Paul returns to the story of Abraham. Paul's first-century readers would have been more familiar with the facts of the story (4:9–10) than most modern readers, so he didn't need to spell out for them that God had declared Abraham righteous prior to the birth of Ishmael, at which time he was eighty-six (Genesis 16:16). Yet God did not instruct Abraham to receive the mark of circumcision until just prior to the birth of Isaac, when the patriarch was ninety-nine (Genesis 17:1,11; 21:5). So Abraham's circumcision had no direct connection to his righteousness before God.

There was no problem with circumcision being a sign of Jewishness, and the Jews could continue to honor Abraham as their father (4:12). But circumcision was not proof of a person's righteous standing before God, and Abraham was also to be the father of those who came to God by faith and were not circumcised (4:11).

Paul is not disparaging the Jewish devotion to law; he is simply trying to show how futile it is to attempt to use the law to justify oneself before God. The law could define and point out sin because if the law didn't exist, certain actions would still be wrong but would not be identified as such (4:15). And the law could do nothing to permanently free someone from the penalty of sin (4:14–15).

So Paul affirms that the way to God is entirely through faith that trusts Him and depends on His grace. As with Abraham, God first promises to bless people and then invites them to believe and take Him at His word. He does not say to first obey His law, or to receive a mark on their bodies, and *then* receive His blessing. Therefore, the opportunity for salvation is equally available to Jews and Gentiles (4:16–17).

Demystifying Romans

"The God who gives life to the dead and calls things that are not as though they were" (4:17 NIV) is yet another reference to Abraham. "Giving life to the dead" is an appropriate description of Sarah's pregnancy at age ninety. And God had called Abraham the father of many nations, although it didn't seem for many years that the promise would ever come true.

THE PATTERN OF FAITH

Just because justification is by faith alone does not mean it comes easily. Abraham waited a long twenty-five years between the time of God's initial promise to him and its fulfillment in the birth of Isaac. During that time he was hoping against all hope (4:18). His body was "as good as dead" (4:19 NIV), yet God was at work, and Abraham became the father of the Jews physically and the father of many nations spiritually.

Abraham had faith, to be sure, yet he maintained his faith through trust in God and patience. So it is for all who come to God. After making a statement of faith, it is easy to waver (4:20) when God doesn't respond exactly as we might hope or expect. Ongoing faith is necessary in order to remain convinced that God will do as He has said (4:21).

The pattern remains the same. What was true for Abraham was true for the first-century believers in Rome and is true for believers today. Faith is placed in Jesus, and because of His atoning sacrifice on behalf of humankind, God credits faith as righteousness. Believers stand justified in His sight from that point forward. We may never fully understand it, but it's just that simple.

Take It Home

What Paul teaches in this section will be more meaningful if we have a better understanding of the account of Abraham. Spend time during the next week looking over Abraham's story (Genesis 12–22). What can Abraham's life teach you about being a more faithful believer in God today?

ROMANS 5:1–21

THE FRUITS OF SALVATION

Peace with God	5:1–11
One Trespass, One Act of Righteousness	5:12–21

Setting Up the Section

So far in his letter to the Romans, Paul has been explaining the Christian doctrine of justification by faith. He began by describing our need for salvation (1:18–3:20) and followed with the way of salvation (3:21–4:25). In this section, he begins a lengthy examination of the fruits of salvation—the effect salvation has on believers.

PEACE WITH GOD

Paul has just shown that circumcision and adherence to the Mosaic Law are not necessary for salvation. As he begins to detail a number of benefits resulting from being justified by God, peace is first on his list (5:1)—the awareness that we are no longer God's enemies (5:10) and the confidence that comes from realizing we no longer need to struggle to gain His favor.

It is just as impossible to achieve real and lasting peace for oneself as it is to achieve one's own salvation. With the exception of Jesus, no one was ever good enough to uphold the law perfectly. So rather than working harder and harder to do something that is impossible, people can simply put their faith in God, receive His justification as a gift of grace, and experience peace as a result.

It is also due to Jesus that believers have access to God (5:2). The word *access* refers to ushering someone into the presence of royalty, or a ship sailing into the protection of a safe harbor. Paul is saying that Jesus escorts us into the very presence of God; He brings us safely to our resting place.

Critical Observation

In the tabernacle, and later in the temple, a curtain was hung to prevent anyone from entering the Most Holy Place that held the ark of the covenant, which symbolized the presence of God. Even the high priest could enter only one day each year, on the Day of Atonement (Leviticus 16). But as Jesus died on the cross, the dividing curtain was ripped in two, from top to bottom (Matthew 27:50–51). Thanks to the ultimate sacrifice of His Son, believers would no longer be denied access to God the Father.

Believers have good cause to rejoice. First, they rejoice because they have hope (5:2). The Christian's hope is not blind optimism; it is a joyful and confident expectation of blessing, based on the promises of God.

Suffering can also be seen as a source of rejoicing because of the ultimate outcome. From suffering comes perseverance, out of which grows character, out of which comes hope (5:3–4). The Greek word for "sufferings" means pressures. Note that Paul doesn't say we rejoice *because of* sufferings, but rather rejoice *in* them and *through* them. We don't merely endure the pressures of life with stoic fortitude, but rather learn to rejoice throughout *all* the happenings of life—both pleasant and challenging.

We cannot do this in our own power. The power comes from Jesus, who died for us when we were still powerless (5:6). That fact is the final proof of God's love. A parent might gladly die to save a child, or someone might willingly die on behalf of a friend or loved one. But Jesus died for people when they were sinners and still in a state of hostility toward Him (5:7–8).

One more reason for rejoicing is the fact that we have been reconciled to God (5:11). Jesus' death appeased God's wrath and began to remove the enmity that existed because of the presence of sin. The friendship bonds of former enemies are always stronger than those of merely casual acquaintances.

ONE TRESPASS, ONE ACT OF RIGHTEOUSNESS

Paul then goes back to the very first example of enmity with God: Adam. This is the man he refers to in verse 12. Paul had previously stated that all have sinned and fallen short of God's glory (3:23). Here he goes into more detail as to the occurrence and spread of sin.

Demystifying Romans

Adam was the gateway for sin to enter the world. By eating of the fruit specifically forbidden by God, he faced consequences including exclusion from the paradise of Eden, a sentence of both spiritual and physical death, and a curse on humankind and the earth itself (Genesis 3). From that point forward, death and sin were unavoidable aspects of the human condition.

Adam's actions were representative of all human beings. His defiance of God was the way sin entered the world and death came to all people (5:12). His one trespass led to the condemnation of everyone (5:18). No baby born today has the capacity to live a life of perfect righteousness and obedience.

A common initial response after hearing Paul's explanation about Adam's sin is a cry of unfairness. How can God hold people responsible today for something done centuries ago? But Adam had a position of authority and responsibility, representing many others. Just as a king might declare war and the whole country would feel the effects, Adam's actions affected all of humanity. In addition, most people don't *really* think they could have done any better than Adam. They see their human nature much too clearly and realize their powerlessness to overcome their propensity to sin. Even Paul will later admit his helplessness and inability to avoid sinning (7:15–25).

So the judgment that Adam received for his sin is what each person deserves for his or hers. Yet Adam is only the first of the two men Paul writes about. The second is Jesus Christ (5:15). If people think facing condemnation as a result of Adam's sin is unfair, they must realize that receiving the gift (5:15) that became available to all believers after the death of Jesus is even more undeserved. Yet God reaches out in love to offer His grace and righteousness (5:17).

Adam's one trespass condemned humanity to spiritual and physical death; Jesus' one sacrifice conquered death and the grave, providing eternal life for everyone (5:18). It is important not to take Paul's statement out of context, however. When he says that Jesus' act of righteousness brings life for all (5:18), he is saying that everyone will have the *opportunity* for salvation, not inferring that everyone will be saved. He has already clarified the importance of receiving God's offer of salvation (5:17). Not everyone will choose to do so.

Yet for those who seek restoration, forgiveness, and justification, there is no doubt that they can find it. Paul makes it clear that the weight of our combined sin, as abundant as it is, is no match for God's grace (5:20–21). For a period, sin had reigned and death was the result. But from now on, grace and righteousness reign, providing eternal life.

Take It Home

Paul's words on suffering have considerable significance for many believers today. Have you ever experienced a progression similar to what Paul describes: from suffering. . .to perseverance. . .to character. . .to hope? Can you think of any sufferings you are currently undergoing for which you can rejoice, trusting God to eventually teach you something from them?

ROMANS 6:1–23

DEAD TO SIN, ALIVE TO GOD

Setting Up the Section

In Romans 5, Paul wrote about the doctrine of original sin and defined the root problem as the sinful human condition that exists within everyone. The reason Jesus died on the cross was to reverse the problem of sin that Adam brought into the world, providing the possibility of new life and a right relationship with God. Now Paul wants to ensure that his readers don't misapply what he has been saying. If the abundance of sin resulted in an even greater abundance of God's grace (5:20), why not try to sin so God can continue to lavish us with His grace?

6:1–14

CHOOSING TO SIN?

After everything he had presented up to this point, Paul asks the question he imagines some of his readers would raise (6:1). And with no hesitation he immediately answers it with an emphatic *no* (6:2). Genuine followers of Jesus Christ cannot continue to live in sin without sensing their own guilt and conviction before God and seeking repentance.

Critical Observation

The belief that God's grace freed Christians to act however they wished, even if that meant ignoring scriptural (and other) laws, was known as *antinomianism* ("against the law"). It was at the other end of the spectrum from legalism.

Three times in Romans 6:1–10, Paul uses the word "know" (6:3, 6, 9) to remind his readers that they have been joined with Christ. He is speaking of baptism, which involves a personal identification with Jesus and signifies inclusion into the covenant community of faith. Baptism also symbolizes death—burial with Christ, followed by resurrection (6:3–4). Believers die to themselves and bury the sinful nature so they can rise and live for Jesus.

If dead to sin, a person can no longer allow it to control his or her life (6:11–12). Yet it requires a conscious decision to act in harmony with, and on the basis of, one's new relationship with Christ. When tempted to revert to an old way of living, a believer must consider that person—and those behaviors—dead. That doesn't mean pretending the old nature has gone away when he knows perfectly well it hasn't. Rather, he must remember that the former identity died with Christ, so he willingly puts an end to its influence on him.

Rather than offering one's body to sin, it should be offered to God (6:13). Grace should rule a believer's life. Instead of giving in to sin and letting it rule, Paul suggests that Christians pursue a positive alternative. The entirety of one's life should be offered to God—limbs, organs, eyes, ears, hands, feet, thoughts, and dreams. It is inconceivable that Christians should go back to their old way of living by willfully persisting in sin and presuming on God's grace.

📖 6:15–23

THE CHOICE OF MASTERS

In verse 15, Paul reaffirms his opening statement (6:1). He says that everyone is a slave to something. While those in the Western world resist the thought of being a slave and prefer the image of rugged individualism, Paul's Roman readers would be well accustomed to slavery as a way of life.

People begin their lives as slaves to sin—whether or not they realize it (6:16). And sin always leads to death (6:16, 23). But because of Jesus, people have another option. They can choose to become slaves to God, where they discover that obedience leads to righteousness. It's giving up one master for another, but the swap makes all the difference in the world (6:17).

Demystifying Romans

From an American viewpoint, the very word *slavery* brings to mind racism, forced subjection, and harsh treatment. When Rome conquered other nations, their prisoners could face similar treatment. But the Romans also had volunteer slavery. For example, people in extreme poverty could offer themselves as slaves to someone in exchange for food and housing. During the first century, the Roman Empire had as many as six million slaves, so Paul's imagery of being enslaved would have been quite clear to his readers. He admitted later, though, that slavery wasn't the perfect analogy to symbolize one's relationship with God (6:19).

Although many people believe the myth, they are not master of their own fate or captain of their own ship. Everyone is a slave to something, whether to sin or to God. Neither option is static. Both are dynamic. But while one is steadily deteriorating into ever-increasing wickedness, the other steadily progresses toward holiness (6:19).

The decision to follow Jesus breaks the bondage of sin and places the person on the path toward righteousness. But that doesn't mean everything will be easy and auto-matic from that point onward. Slaves—even slaves to righteousness—have to make deci-sions every day about attitudes, actions, and motivations regarding their service. Believers are no longer slaves to the law, yet their new commitment to righteousness and holiness should inspire them to greater acts of love, mercy, and forgiveness.

One of the best ways to keep a proper mind-set is to look back from time to time and remember the quality of life when sin was still master (6:20–22). Everyone recalls things they aren't proud of, which should inspire greater motivation to pursue obedience and godly living.

This passage concludes with one of the great verses in all the New Testament (6:23). In the Greek language, *wages* referred to a soldier's regular pay, something that was due him, while *gift* was something provided out of kindness and grace. Wages were what a person deserved; a gift was an undeserved prize. For those who allow sin to be master, their wages will be death. But for those who are willing to change masters and become slaves to God, the reward is eternal life.

Take It Home

Even among people who choose to live for God, slavery to sin can continue to be a problem. The church has recognized this in recent years and has provided help for those struggling with addictions such as drugs or alcohol. Other people struggle with smoking, pornography, sexual promiscuity, and other things that continue to interfere with their commitment to righteousness and holiness. Do you struggle with any old problems that you would like to eliminate from your life completely, yet haven't been able to overcome? If so, spend some time this week formulat-ing a plan for how you might become less enslaved to the habit in the weeks to come.

ROMANS 7:1–25
THE LINGERING INFLUENCE OF SIN

Setting Up the Section

In anticipation of a personal visit to Rome, Paul is writing to the Roman believers. He has been outlining the message of the gospel, and has just taught that every person has a master. People are either slaves to sin or slaves to righteousness. In this section, he will continue with that theme as he takes up the subject of God's law and its purpose for the Christian.

📖 7:1–13

A LOOK AT THE LAW

Each of the first thirteen verses of Romans 7 makes a reference to "law," "commandment," or "written code." Paul addresses this question: If a person can't find a right relationship with God by keeping the law and doing all God expects, then what is the place of the Old Testament law in the Christian life?

To answer the question, he uses the metaphor of marriage (7:1–6). According to Jewish law, a woman could not divorce her husband. The only way she would be free to marry another man would be if the first husband died. Otherwise, she would be considered an adulteress.

Paul uses this comparison to symbolize the Christian and the law. A believer "dies" to his or her old ways and is reborn without the same obligation to the law. The new believer is dead to both sin (6:2) *and* the law (7:4), and is united with Christ (7:1–6).

It's not that the law was bad (7:7). Just the opposite. The law was holy (7:12) and spiritual (7:14). While it was impossible to follow the law perfectly and achieve one's own salvation, the law served a positive purpose of exposing and identifying sin (7:7–8).

Demystifying Romans

Beginning in verse 7, and continuing through the rest of Romans 7, Paul changes the tense of his writing. He had been writing primarily in third person, switching occasionally to second person or first-person plural. But for this stretch of writing, he shifts to first-person singular, describing his own personal experience—and exposing his own weaknesses and spiritual struggle.

Paul's use of the phrase, "apart from law" (7:9 NIV), was probably his way of saying, "Before I realized what the law meant." Like the Pharisees who lived unaware of what the law really meant, Paul was "alive" for a while. But after coming to see what the law really said, he was confronted with his sin (7:10–13).

📄 7:14–25

GETTING PERSONAL

The struggle that Paul describes in this section is one that each believer wrestles with as well. The more mature the believer, the more aware of sin he or she becomes. The more progress the person makes toward sanctification, the more he or she will abhor sinfulness and see it for what it is.

What Paul expresses is the inner struggle, the personal civil war that all Christians experience. He is refreshingly honest in this passage as he speaks of his thoughts and feelings.

He admits to feeling unspiritual (7:14). Although a believer no longer has the status of a slave to sin (6:6–7), he or she will continue to struggle with the reality of residual sinful thoughts and behaviors. Paul also admits to being confused (7:15). He can't understand why he does some of the things he does. He does things he doesn't want to do, and doesn't get around to doing the good things he intends to do. Inwardly, God's Word gives him great joy, but when it comes to physically doing the right things, he frequently comes up short (7:15–23).

Critical Observation

Not everyone agrees that Paul is speaking of his own experience in this passage. Some believe Paul is describing a nonbeliever because of some of the terms he uses ("slave" [7:14], "wretched" [7:24], etc.). And they say it's a pretty dismal viewpoint if he is describing a Christian experience. Other people argue that the passage refers to an immature believer who has made a Christian commitment, yet continues to live according to fleshly rather than spiritual desires. Still others believe Paul was writing autobiographically about his own internal struggle to live the Christian life.

The word translated "wretched" could also be interpreted "miserable" or "unhappy" (7:24). There are times when all believers grow weary of their daily struggles and just want to give up. Surely, with all of Paul's exceptional trials, he must have felt the same way at times. Related to this is a sense of hopelessness (7:18, 24). It is one of those sinking feelings where he needs help just to get up and get going again. At times he feels like a prisoner (7:23) in bondage with no escape. Confined. Trapped. Yet at the same time, it is like he is engaged in a battle (7:21–23). Good and evil are battling it out within him, creating an inner conflict.

And finally, Paul confesses to feeling condemned (7:24). He realizes he deserves to have God's judgment of death pronounced on his sins. If he were in a court of law, he would plead guilty to the charges.

What a range of thoughts and feelings, and what an honest expression of emotion. Yet few Christians can say they haven't had similar feelings.

Thankfully, that isn't the end of Paul's story. He concludes the passage with an optimistic message of hope (7:25). Who will rescue him from the dire state in which he finds himself (7:24)? Jesus Christ the Lord.

The key to understanding Paul's complete turnaround is to comprehend the already-and-not-yet nature of the kingdom of God. Jesus inaugurated His kingdom at His first coming, but will not consummate it until His second. Believers who live in between will experience the power of His coming in some measure, but not in full. Therefore, it is possible to be assured of victory in Christ, yet still feel defeated from time to time.

Paul's confident conclusion sets up the magnificent and much-quoted chapter that follows. In Romans 8, Paul's outlook improves considerably.

Take It Home

Everyone goes through periods of spiritual struggle similar to those Paul describes. And the sooner such feelings are admitted and dealt with, the sooner the person is likely to get back on track and move forward again. Do you have someone (or a small group of people) with whom you can be honest when your spiritual life seems derailed for a period of time? Rather than just keep going through the motions as if everything is fine, can you open up with someone the way Paul did in this section? If not, perhaps you might consider finding a trustworthy friend to confide in or forming a small group whose members will be willing to share openly among one another.

ROMANS 8:1–39
ASSURANCE AND REASSURANCE

Setting Up the Section

Paul's Epistle to the Romans has been an ongoing defense of justification by faith alone. He has shown that righteousness is the result of one's relationship with God through faith, and not due to adherence to the Mosaic Law, circumcision, or any other external standard. So if believers are not to rely so heavily on such things, what *should* they rely on? Paul's answer in this passage has become one of the most beloved portions of scripture.

📖 8:1–17

THE SPIRIT OF SONSHIP

It may seem that Romans 8 follows naturally after Paul's stark confession of Romans 7:14–25. But the word "therefore" (8:1) actually picks up the thoughts Paul laid out in Romans 3, with chapters 4–7 being somewhat parenthetical. Romans 3:20 described the results of condemnation. Here Paul begins to expound on the results of *no* condemnation.

The Mosaic Law had been powerless to provide a righteous standing before God (8:3). It remains a guide for how believers should live (8:4), yet Paul introduces a new "law"—the law of the Spirit of life (8:2). The Old Testament law could define and prohibit sin, but could never eliminate it. The human nature of the people trying to follow the law could never empower them to live up to its standards (8:3–4).

So Paul begins to contrast the human, sinful nature with that of a person controlled by the Holy Spirit (8:5–17). The difference begins in the person's thoughts and desires. If the sinful nature is in control, the person doesn't want to submit to God—and would be unable to even if the desire was there (8:6–8). But Paul is writing to believers in Rome, so he can assure them that they are under the control of the Holy Spirit. He indicates in this passage that the ministries of Jesus and the Holy Spirit are closely related (8:9–11).

Yet the difference is much more personal than merely determining who is in control. As long as people cling to selfish, natural desires and exclude God, they are unable to experience the relationship that He intends and desires for them. But those who respond to the Spirit of God are led into an intimate relationship—one of Father and child.

Jesus had addressed God as *Abba* ("Father") in His prayers (Mark 14:36). Prior to that, no Jewish person would have addressed God with such a familiar term. Yet here Paul extends the privilege to all believers. The presence of the Holy Spirit is proof that believers are children of God (8:15–16).

Critical Observation

Abba was an Aramaic word for "father." It denoted love and affection, and was the most tender and intimate of the synonyms for father that Paul could have chosen.

"Children" isn't just a title, but a reality. Jesus, as God's Son, is entitled to everything that is the Father's. And as God's *other* children—adopted ones—believers are coheirs with Jesus. They experience similar sufferings, yes, but they also share in the eternal rewards (8:17). This possibility of such a close relationship with God begins to reveal why it's so important not to be misled by legalistic or antinomian doctrines. Paul is advocating the best possible option for followers of God, though he has barely begun.

📖 **8:18–27**

GROANING AND WAITING

Paul was no stranger to suffering, and in this section he explains some of his reasoning. For one thing, it is a matter of return on investment. The sufferings he experienced would be insignificant in light of the glory that would come later (8:18). In addition, creation itself is suffering. Just as Adam, Eve, and the serpent were recipients of the curse after the fall (Genesis 3:14–19), so was the earth. Rather than remaining the perfect paradise that God intended, creation itself is now in bondage, groaning like a woman in labor to produce fruit and be productive (8:19–22).

Believers groan as well, waiting for the time when God will redeem them fully. God's plan is in action. The agreement has been made. The initial stages have begun of God's adoption of believers and their redemption. Yet the full significance won't be realized until resurrection. So the anticipation and assurance of this reality is the believer's hope in the meantime (8:23–25).

Demystifying Romans

Firstfruits was an offering made when the crops started coming in (Exodus 23:19; Leviticus 23:9–14; Deuteronomy 26:1–11). The first of the produce was offered to God in thanksgiving and anticipation of the rest. The same symbolism is applied to the Holy Spirit in Romans 8:23. The appearance of the Holy Spirit in the life of a believer is representative of everything else God will later bring to fruition.

The presence of the Holy Spirit in the life of the believer is first of all the signs that God has begun His work. In addition, the Spirit acts on behalf of the believer, interceding to bring God and the believer closer together (8:26–27).

THE INSEPARABLE LOVE OF GOD

The world can be an evil place at times, yet God works in all things for good (8:28). This is not to suggest that God creates sin or evil; He works in spite of them. When tragedy befalls a believer, the church should not infer that God was responsible for the pain and confusion. Yet He can see His children through such times and teach them valuable lessons about His love and faithfulness.

The meaning of the word "predestined" (8:29) is debated. (Predestination is also called "election," with an emphasis on being specially selected.) Most agree that God did not create a list of people prior to creation that He had chosen for salvation. Rather, *predestination* means that God has predetermined what He will do for those who call on His name (Ephesians 1:4–6). God's foreknowledge is more than simply knowing ahead of time what will happen. It has an added element of regarding with favor.

Justification (being declared righteous) is a matter of how God sees believers now. Throughout the Christian life, God's people should become progressively more Christlike. Similarly, they are also considered glorified (8:30). Ultimately, that means that their human bodies will be transformed into a state like Jesus' glorious body (Philippians 3:20–21). And even though that hasn't happened yet, the promise stands that it will, so believers are already deemed glorified. Therefore, there is good reason for believers to hold fast to their faith (8:31–39).

God's people will suffer, just as Jesus did. That should come as no surprise. Yet God is with them throughout every painful ordeal. The list of potential threats is so detailed that it encompasses all possibilities—trouble, hardship, persecution, famine, nakedness, danger, sword, angels, demons, present, future, powers, height, depth, and anything in all creation (8:39). God will overcome any problem and prove that His love for His people is too strong to be diminished. And since it is God who has justified, sanctified, and glorified believers, there is really very little for them to ever be worried about.

Take It Home

When was the last time you went through a difficult situation and may have questioned God's love? After reading this passage of Romans, do you think God's love for you was ever in jeopardy? When similar hard times arise in the future, what might you do differently?

ROMANS 9:1–33

SOVEREIGNTY, ELECTION, AND LOVE

Setting Up the Section

Paul has been writing about God's sovereignty over death (Romans 5), over sin (Romans 6–7), and over struggles, persecution, and hardship (Romans 8). In this section, he turns his attention to God's sovereignty in regard to salvation. The Jews had always felt they were God's chosen people. Now that the church was growing into an institution, people were asking how God could be faithful to His promises if the majority of His chosen people—the Jews—were failing to respond to the gospel. Paul answers that question here by using familiar stories to remind them of God's sovereign choices throughout their history.

📖 9:1–18

ISRAEL'S REJECTION

The doctrine of predestination (election) is one that many people avoid, whether consciously or not. But it is closely tied to the doctrine of God's sovereignty. Indeed, believers rejoice in God's sovereignty over sin, struggles, and eventual death. Yet many hesitate to accept His sovereignty in the category of salvation.

Paul begins each of the next three chapters of Romans (9, 10, and 11) with a personal statement that identifies himself with the people of Israel and expresses his profound concern for them. He not only acknowledges their unbelief, but he also agonizes over them with sorrow, anguish, and prayer. In fact, he expresses a willingness to sacrifice his own relationship with Christ if that could somehow bring his peers into the fold instead. But the sentiment was moot; Paul had just completed his emphatic proclamation that *nothing* can separate a believer from the love of God (8:38–39).

Still, how could the people of Israel, with their unique privileges and blessings, reject their own Messiah? If God is sovereign, how could the failure of Israel be explained, and why did it seem that God's promises had come up short?

God was true to His promises. He had never forsaken Israel, and Paul mentions eight specific privileges (9:4–5) the people of Israel had been given:

1) They were the children of God, adopted as His own sons and daughters.
2) They had seen the divine glory of God in the wilderness and had beheld the splendor of His presence.
3) The covenants of God had been given to their ancestors and passed down to them.
4) They prized the Old Testament law as the moral code that outlined what God expected of His people.
5) They had the temple, where they could worship and encounter the presence of God.

6) They had seen God's faithfulness with their patriarchs—Abraham, Isaac, and Jacob.

7) They had provided the human bloodline for Jesus, who was providing salvation for the world.

8) They had been given Christ Himself, whose ministry was first to the Jews and then to the Gentiles (1:16; 2:9–10).

Yet the majority of the Jewish people had forsaken God. Their rejection of Jesus was not due to the failure of God's Word and His promise (9:6). It was not because of the absence of benefits and blessing by God. Rather, it was due to their unbelief.

Paul turns to their history to show how God's sovereignty has been demonstrated throughout the centuries. He points out that Abraham's older child was actually Ishmael, yet God had proclaimed that the promise to Abraham would be fulfilled through Isaac (9:7–9), resulting in more of a spiritual relationship than a physical one. Not long afterward, God had chosen to work through Jacob, the younger twin, rather than Esau. And God's decree came even before the birth of the twins (Genesis 25:23), so His decision wasn't based on anything Esau did wrong or that Jacob did right (9:10–13).

Demystifying Romans

The hate of God (9:13) is not hatred as we define it, and it is not directed toward an individual. What Paul has written about the unconditional love of God still holds true. In essence, the statement "Jacob I loved, but Esau I hated" (9:13 NIV) means that God had chosen (loved) the Israelites and had rejected (hated) the Edomites—the descendants of Esau. In this case, human choice had reinforced God's sovereignty—God first chose Jacob over Esau, but Esau had willingly traded away the rights that came with being the older son (Genesis 25:27–34).

The third example Paul uses from Israel's history is that of Pharaoh. It's a sobering reminder that, without God's mercy, no one can escape the penalty of sin and find new life in God. The hardening of Pharaoh's heart that eventually led to Israel's exodus from Egypt was part of God's sovereign plan (9:17–18).

📖 9:19–33

GOD'S SOVEREIGNTY AND PEOPLE'S CHOICES

Paul anticipates a challenge to what he has been saying. It may seem unfair, if God is sovereign, that He still holds us accountable for our choices. Paul isn't putting down honest questions (9:20), because this is a most difficult topic. Rather, he refers to those who want to quarrel with God. That is not our right, any more than a piece of clay has a right to take issue with the potter (9:21). Paul wants his readers to remember who they are and who God is.

Critical Observation

During Israel's exodus from Egypt (Exodus 7–14), Pharaoh's hardness of heart is referred to fifteen times. In some instances it is said that Pharaoh hardened his heart; in other places we read that God hardened Pharaoh's heart. Was God solely responsible for Pharaoh's refusal to cooperate with Moses (9:18)? Pharaoh had numerous opportunities to respond to God and declined each time. The fault was not with God, but with Pharaoh. Yet God used Pharaoh's stubbornness to bless Israel.

The sovereignty of God in regard to whom He would and would not choose had been prophesied (9:22–29). It had been foretold that God would call those who were not His people (9:25). Even when the nation of Israel rejected Him, He would deliver a remnant who would be saved (9:27). It was only God's mercy that kept Israel from being destroyed as completely as Sodom and Gomorrah (9:29).

The obtaining of salvation by the Jews and Gentiles had been much like the race between the tortoise and the hare. The Jews had zealously pursued a legalistic path to God's favor, yet had never accomplished what they hoped. The Gentiles, on the other hand, hadn't been looking for righteousness at all but had found it through faith in Jesus (9:30–33). The Israelites needed to quit depending on their own efforts and put their faith in God instead.

The Bible teaches two truths about election (predestination): (1) God is sovereign, and (2) people are responsible for their choices. Somehow both teachings are true, and God is certain to reward the believer's struggle to integrate and make sense of them.

Take It Home

How does Paul's outlook on the doctrine of election fit with your own spiritual background? How would you define God's sovereignty for a young child who asked you what it meant? How would you explain it to a middle school Sunday school class? What questions would you anticipate in response?

ROMANS 10:1-21

EXPLAINING ISRAEL'S REJECTION

Setting Up the Section

Paul has had much to say about justification by faith so far in Romans. At the end of chapter 9, he had just returned to his running theme of righteousness. As he continues in this passage, he moves from the past to the present and from the aspect of God's sovereignty to individual accountability.

📄 **10:1–13**

ZEAL WITHOUT THE DESIRED RESULTS

Paul is pained to note how hard many of his fellow Jews are working to be righteous and please God when they don't realize that the only source of righteousness is God. Paul knows personally what it is like to be zealous but misdirected (10:1–2). Their hard work had made them self-righteous, and when presented with the righteousness that is attainable only through Jesus, they are too proud to consider it (10:3–4). Jesus put an end to the law (10:4)—the Messiah to whom all the law and Prophets had pointed. And there were other portions of the law that the Jewish people hadn't understood.

Demystifying Romans

In Romans 10:5–21, Paul makes eleven different direct references to the Hebrew scriptures to support what he is saying. He quotes Leviticus 18:5 (10:5), Deuteronomy 30:12–13 (10:6–7), Deuteronomy 30:14 (10:8), Isaiah 28:16 (10:11), Joel 2:32 (10:13), Isaiah 52:7 (10:15), Isaiah 53:1 (10:16), Psalm 19:4 (10:18), Deuteronomy 32:21 (10:19), Isaiah 65:1 (10:20), and Isaiah 65:2 (10:21).

For example, Moses had taught that justification came by faith, and had emphasized obedience out of love rather than legalistic commitment (Deuteronomy 30:6–10). He had also pointed out the nearness of God's law (Deuteronomy 30:11–14). The people don't have to go out of their way to receive insight from God; He has placed it in their mouths and hearts. Similarly, no one has to complete any grand acts or make a special effort to receive Jesus (the perfect fulfillment of the law). It is foolish pride for people to think that they can do anything to help bring the Messiah down from heaven or to raise Him from the dead. Those actions were completely the work of God (10:6–8).

The Word of God is still essential to their righteousness. However, it is not the written law that will justify them, but the Word that became flesh. And God still desires for that Word to be in their mouths and hearts. Salvation comes through believing in their hearts that God has raised Jesus from the dead and confessing with their mouths that He is Lord (10:9–10).

Paul once again quotes Isaiah 28:16 to show that salvation is by faith (9:33; 10:11). And because this was true, salvation is available to anyone and everyone (Joel 2:32; Romans 10:12–13). Much of the zeal in striving to uphold the law was wasted effort. The Jewish people were complicating something that should have been very simple. They were trying to do something God had already done for them.

📖 10:14–21

CONNECTING WITH GOD

Salvation is a matter of hearing the truth of the gospel and responding, so Paul credits those who were involved with spreading the message. The word for "preach" (10:15) means "to proclaim." Paul isn't referring to the position of church pastor, but to *anyone* who has been sent from God to share the good news. According to the words of Jesus, that would include all believers (Matthew 28:19–20; John 20:21).

Critical Observation

"The feet of those who bring good news" (Isaiah 52:7; Romans 10:15 NIV) was a general reference to the messengers who would come running after a battle or other big event to let the general population know the outcome. More specifically, it had come to refer to the announcement that Israel's exile in Babylon had ended, and the people were returning to Jerusalem. Paul adopted the same saying to apply to those who proclaimed the end of the bondage of sin, thanks to the death and resurrection of Jesus Christ.

The news had gone out through faithful messengers and the truth had been proclaimed. Yet that wasn't enough. The Jewish people needed to respond to what they had heard by calling on Jesus (10:14–15).

But what if Israel hadn't heard the message from God? Paul asks that very question (10:18) and then answers it by quoting from Psalm 19. The psalm describes how God reveals Himself both through what He has created (Psalm 19:1–6) and what He has provided in His written Word (Psalm 19:7–11). The Israelites had heard God's message, but they hadn't responded.

Paul anticipates their next excuse: Maybe they didn't understand what God was trying to tell them. He uses two more Old Testament references to show that the Gentiles (a nation without understanding [Romans 10:19]) had figured it out. The Jews believed themselves to be far superior to the Gentiles, and must have felt a bit insulted at Paul's insinuation.

But neither Paul nor God had given up on the Jewish people, even though they still hadn't responded to the message of the love of God. Paul refers back to the Old Testament one more time to remind his readers of God's ongoing patience (Isaiah 65:2; Romans 10:21). Many of the first-century Jewish people were just as disobedient as their Old Testament counterparts. Yet God perpetually held out His hands to them, ready to receive and embrace them whenever they were willing to respond to what they knew.

Take It Home

Based on Paul's (and Isaiah's) statement in Romans 10:15, do you think your feet would be considered beautiful? Think back to your own spiritual journey and recall the people who contributed to your knowledge of Jesus. Then consider if you are contributing to the spiritual growth of anyone today. If so, reflect on what more you might be able to do for that person. If not, how might you get started in opening up about your own spiritual relationship for the benefit of someone else?

ROMANS 11:1–36

GOOD NEWS FOR ISRAEL

Another Jewish Remnant	11:1–10
The Grafted Gentile "Branches"	11:11–24
The Salvation of Israel	11:25–36

Setting Up the Section

In Paul's ongoing treatise on righteousness and justification by faith alone, he has just finished a rather frank commentary explaining that many of the Jewish people had rejected God and missed the significance of Jesus, the Messiah. Even the Gentiles had better spiritual insight. Now Paul asks a different question: Since the Jews had opted to seek self-righteousness rather than God's justification, had God given up on them?

📖 11:1–10

ANOTHER JEWISH REMNANT

Paul's opening question (11:1) is actually a continuation of the writing style he had been using (10:14, 18, 19). It might appear he was saying that because the Jews had rejected Jesus, God was rejecting the Jews. But that isn't Paul's message at all, as he immediately makes clear.

Paul still identifies strongly with the Jewish people, and his own story is proof that God had not deserted the Jews in favor of the Gentiles (11:1–2). In addition, Paul reminds his readers of the story of Elijah, who had served God during a time when many of the Israelites had turned to idols rather than remaining faithful to the Lord. Even then, God had a remnant of faithful people—seven thousand as a matter of fact (11:2–4; see 1 Kings 19:9–18)!

Paul is equally convinced of another remnant of faithful Jewish believers during his time (the elect [11:7]). The existence of such a remnant is evidence of the grace of God (11:5–6).

Paul again returns to Hebrew scripture to cite examples from Jewish history. Both Moses (Deuteronomy 29:4) and David (Psalm 69:22–23) had written about their people being unable to see what God was doing in their midst. Yet the nation had endured because of a remnant of those faithful to God (11:7–10). The same was true for the first-century Jewish nation.

📖 11:11–24

THE GRAFTED GENTILE "BRANCHES"

Paul goes on to say that the rejection of the Jews was partial, was passing, and had a purpose. A remnant continued to believe, the rejection wouldn't last forever, and some good would actually come from it.

Israel's transgression allowed the gospel to be delivered to the Gentiles. And closely related to that fact, a sense of jealousy developed among the people of Israel (11:11–12). When the Jewish people saw God's acceptance of the Gentiles, many would repent and come to God as well. Indeed, Paul's use of the words "fullness" (11:12 NIV) and "acceptance" (11:15 NIV) indicate a positive future for Israel.

In the meantime, the Gentiles have no right to gloat. Their gospel has Jewish roots and a Jewish Savior. Thanks to God's grace, the Gentiles are grafted into God's olive tree (11:17–18), and they are completely supported by the root.

The Jewish nation should not see the inclusion of the Gentiles as a threat. Just the opposite. If God could make a wild branch become productive, it would be no trouble at all for Him to restore some of the natural branches. All the Jews needed to do was show the same degree of repentance and faith as the Gentiles, and they would quickly be reattached to their source of growth and productivity (11:22–24). Ultimately, the restoration of a Jewish person was an easier process than the call of a Gentile to faith, because the knowledgeable Jew understood the need for forgiveness.

Critical Observation

Note that Paul is careful not to say that one day all unbelieving Jews will be saved and grafted back in. What he says is that the grafting can take place *if* they do not persist in unbelief. The way of salvation is open to both Jews and Gentiles in the death and resurrection of Jesus Christ, but it is up to each individual to choose or reject it.

📖 11:25–36

THE SALVATION OF ISRAEL

Paul is going to shift emphasis in Romans 12, so in wrapping up this section he makes a number of important observations. First, he shows that God's sovereignty is undeniable. Even while Israel was rejecting Him, God was opening the doors of salvation to the Gentiles (11:25). And the long-range results of this would be the salvation of Israel (11:26–27).

Demystifying Romans

What did Paul mean that "all Israel" would be saved (11:26)? Some people believe that all Jews are God's chosen people and will be saved regardless of their response to Jesus, but that opinion disregards the death of Christ and the need for repentance in order to receive salvation. Some interpret the phrase to refer to the "elect," including both Jews and Gentiles, but such an outlook doesn't seem to fit the theme of Paul's writing, which focuses on the rejection of Jesus by the Jews. Another interpretation is that at Jesus' return, a large number of Jewish people will believe and come to faith. The word *all* should not be understood in an absolute sense meaning "without exception," but would rather refer to Israel as a whole.

Second, Paul demonstrates that God's mercy is unfathomable (11:30–32). His love and mercy overflowed to the Gentiles, allowing them access to His kingdom. And He used the inclusion of the Gentiles to get the attention of the Jews. God continues to show His mercy, even after His people reject Him and harden their hearts to His love.

Finally, Paul shows that God's mind is unsearchable (11:33–36). At this point it seems Paul stops preaching and starts worshiping. He notes that people, as finite creatures, are incapable of fully comprehending the infinite God. He had previously spoken of a mystery (11:25), and much of what we believe must simply be taken on faith. Yet that which we cannot grasp with our minds, we can entrust to God with all our hearts.

From this point onward, Paul is going to be less theological and a lot more practical. Now that he has explained how God has declared believers righteous, he is going to provide several ways that such a status should affect their lives.

Take It Home

The doxology that ends this part of Paul's letter is a reminder that when we think about God and His incredible love and mercy, our heartfelt response should be one of praise. Theology and worship should go hand in hand. Worship without sound theology is likely to degenerate into sentimentality or idolatry; theology without worship is dead, dull, and boring. Which aspect is most in need of attention in your own life—your theology or your worship? What can you do this week to bring the two into a better balance?

ROMANS 12:1–21

RADICAL TRANSFORMATION

Transformation and Gifts of the Holy Spirit	12:1-8
Love and Other Imperatives	12:9-21

Setting Up the Section

For eleven chapters in Romans Paul has written at length about the mercy of God. When people were lost in their sin and enemies of God, He opened a way of salvation to them through the gift of His Son. Christ died on the cross, taking their place and paying the penalty for the sins of their lives. It is in light of this awesome mercy of God that Paul now urges his readers to live a life worthy of their calling in Christ Jesus.

12:1–8

TRANSFORMATION AND GIFTS OF THE HOLY SPIRIT

Therefore is usually a significant word in scripture to indicate something important is about to be said. It is particularly true in this case (12:1). Everything Paul has written so far in his Epistle is the basis for what comes next. His focus has been on what God has done for humankind; now he explains what believers can and should do in response.

When Paul refers to believers offering themselves as a worship act, he makes a reference to the Jewish sacrificial system. Part of Jewish worship was the sacrificing of an animal, often on an altar. When believers lay their own wills aside and live their lives for the purpose of pleasing and serving God, they become a living sacrifice. Their lives, lived in dedication to the will of God, become acts of worship (12:2).

What God offers His people is not mere improvement, but radical transformation (12:2). It is not simply an offer to make good people a little better, smoothing out the rough edges of their basically pure hearts. It is rather a matter of transforming sinners into saints, of allowing them to exchange their filthy rags of sin for the royal robes of righteousness in Christ. Holy living involves the body, mind, and spirit.

As believers are transformed and begin to comprehend God's will, they see that God designed the church so its members are interdependent on one another. No one has all the available gifts of the Holy Spirit, so it is incumbent that each person identifies his or her gift(s) to use on behalf of the others in the church. Paul uses the metaphor of a human body to describe how individual parts should work together and operate as a unified whole.

Critical Observation

This passage (12:6–8) is just one of Paul's lists of spiritual gifts. Others are found in 1 Corinthians 12:7–11, 28–31 and Ephesians 4:11–13. The lists vary a bit, suggesting that none is intended to be complete. Paul also uses the analogy of the human body in connection with spiritual gifts in other places (1 Corinthians 12:12–26; Ephesians 4:15–16).

Paul identifies seven of the gifts of the Holy Spirit in this passage. When people think of prophecy (12:6), many immediately think of foretelling the future. While that is one aspect of the gift, a wider sense includes the revelation of the Holy Spirit to a believer, concerning the will of God. For example, when an important decision needs to be made, the gift of prophecy might allow someone to know for certain what God wants His church to do.

The gift of service, or helps (12:7), is the ability to assist and support others inside and outside the family of God in practical ways. The believer with this gift is motivated to faithfully demonstrate Christ's love by meeting practical needs and giving assistance. The Greek word for service (*diakonia*) is the root for our word *deacon*.

Teaching (12:7) is the ability to clearly explain what God has revealed. Many people are willing and even eager to teach, yet it is usually evident which have been given the *gift* of teaching.

Encouragement (12:8) is also a spiritual gift. All believers are commanded to encourage one another (1 Thessalonians 5:11), but certain people stand out. (One example in the early church was Barnabas, whose nickname meant "Son of Encouragement" [Acts 4:36].)

The gift of giving (12:8) is the ability to be sensitive and to provide for the needs of others with great joy and generosity. All believers are encouraged to give consistently to the Lord's work, but the person with the gift of giving has an inner, God-given drive to provide for those with needs.

Leadership (12:8) involves being visionary, goal oriented, and decisive.

Mercy (12:8) is yet another characteristic expected of all believers, yet is endowed to certain people in a special way. It involves the capacity to be compassionate and empathize with others' needs, pains, heartaches, disappointments, and sorrows. Mercy can also include being an agent of healing and restoration.

📖 **12:9–21**

LOVE AND OTHER IMPERATIVES

In the rest of this section, Paul compresses a number of instructions for practical Christian living. Nowhere else in his writing is a more comprehensive list of concise commands.

The overriding theme is the importance of love, and how genuine love affects the believer's behavior. Love is the foundation for many traits: humility (12:10), a spiritual zeal for service (12:11), patience (12:12), generosity (12:13), and other desired characteristics.

Certainly, the commitment to express love will be met with certain obstacles, among them persecution (12:14), mourning (12:15), and pride (12:16). Paul repeats Jesus' teaching about persecution and nonretaliation (Matthew 5:44; Romans 12:14). It takes a great commitment to love for one to pray for his or her persecutors (12:14, 17).

Paul stresses the importance of being a peacemaker, yet does not insist on peace at any price. Note his two conditions (12:18) that promote peace, though don't guarantee it.

Demystifying Romans

The reference to heaping burning coals on another's head (12:20) gives rise to various interpretations. Some say the phrase refers to an ancient custom. If a fire went out in someone's home, he or she might go to a neighbor to borrow coals, carried in a pan on the head. Transportation was clumsy and might result in some discomfort for the person, yet the coals were proof of another's love. Similarly, receiving good for evil feels so awkward it may have a lasting effect on the recipient. A more common understanding of the phrase, however, interprets the burning coals as symbols of God's judgment. If one's enemy continues to create trouble, and the persecuted only returns good for evil, he or she can be assured that God will mete out appropriate punishment (coals of fire [2 Samuel 22:9; Psalm 11:6; etc.]) in His own time.

One key to maintaining love, peace, and other godly characteristics is to let God deal with injustices. There is no place for personal retaliation (12:19). Otherwise, it is impossible to overcome evil with good (12:21).

Take It Home

Few people today ever fully appreciate just how damaging sin has been in their lives or how costly the price of forgiveness. But the good news of the gospel is that because of the Father's great love for humankind in Jesus Christ, He has made the means of transformation available to every person. To what extent do you think your own transformation has been completed? Which of Paul's instructions (12:9–21) do you find hardest to comply with?

ROMANS 13:1-14

THE BELIEVER'S PLACE IN THE WORLD

Setting Up the Section

Chapter 12 marked a turning point in Romans, where Paul shifted from a theological presentation to a personal appeal for spiritual transformation and love. He listed a number of spiritual gifts and other admirable behaviors for believers to adopt as they related to one another. In this section, he continues with his treatise on practical living and begins to consider relationships with those outside the church.

📖 13:1–7

THE BELIEVER AND GOVERNING AUTHORITIES

Paul's instructions for his readers to submit to the governing authorities (13:1) take on greater significance in light of the fact that there were few Christians in authority at the time. Those in charge were largely unfriendly and even hostile to the church. Yet Paul viewed the governing authorities as not only having been established by God, but also as the servants of God (13:4). The Greek word translated as "servant" can also mean "minister," and is the same word Paul uses to describe the work of a pastor or elder. So Christians are called to submit to their rulers and pray for them, because rebellion against the leaders is considered rebellion against God (13:2).

Demystifying Romans

A number of Old Testament examples demonstrate the power of a godly person working in conjunction with a secular leader. Joseph had worked with the Egyptian Pharaoh to prepare for and survive a terrible famine (Genesis 41). Daniel had found extreme favor with the kings of Babylon even before impressing Darius the Mede by his faith while in the lions' den (Daniel 2–6). And others demonstrated the benefits of submitting to the authorities rather than attempting to undermine them.

Paul also reminds his readers that the purpose of the state is to restrain evil and promote a just social order. Government originated as an ordinance of God. While it cannot redeem the world, it can nevertheless set boundaries for human behavior. The state is not a remedy for sin, but it is a means to restrain sin. So cooperation with the authorities, in cases where no spiritual beliefs are compromised, goes a long way in removing potential problems (13:3–5).

Believers are not to be anarchists or subversives. Rather, they recognize the state as a divine institution with divine authority. Every believer has a civic duty to show respect for elected and appointed officials, knowing that the offices they hold are ordained of God. The respect for the person and office should be demonstrated in tangible ways as well, such as paying taxes (13:6–7).

Critical Observation

While Paul encourages obedience to and prayers for those in civil authority, he is not calling for unequivocal and blind submission to the state. Submission must not require the believer to violate his or her conviction as a Christian or demand a loyalty that is superior to one's allegiance to God. In situations where the state requires something contrary to God's commands, the believer may be called to disobey (Exodus 1:15–21; Daniel 6:6–10; Acts 4:18–20).

The basic principle of scripture is clear: Civil authorities are to be obeyed except for cases where they set themselves in opposition to God's divine law.

📖 **13:8–14**

THE DEBT OF LOVE

Giving what is due has been a running theme in Paul's letter so far. He has written of the obligation he felt to spread the gospel (1:14–15), the believer's debt to the Holy Spirit to live a holy life (8:12–14), and one's debt to the state to pay taxes (13:6–7). Now he writes that the one outstanding obligation every believer should have is continuing love for one another (13:8). No one ever comes to the point in his or her Christian life where it can be said, "I have loved enough."

Paul ties together love for one another with fulfillment of the law. Some argue that love and law are mutually exclusive—that love has its own moral compass and anything that feels good can't be wrong. But Paul teaches that love cannot operate on its own without an objective moral standard.

For example, a person who truly loves will not commit adultery (13:9), because real love shows respect and restraint. If someone allows physical passion to sweep him or her into an affair, then that person loves too little rather than too much. A person who truly loves will not murder, because love never seeks to destroy. A person who truly loves will never steal, for love inspires giving more than getting.

Why does love sum up all the other commandments (13:9)? Paul says it's because love does not harm its neighbor (13:10). The final five of the Ten Commandments address sins that hurt other people: murder, adultery, stealing, giving false testimony, and coveting (Exodus 20:13–17). The essence of love is to serve one's neighbor and his or her highest good. So the demonstration of love does away with the need to spell out all the individual "You shall nots" of the law. Yet human love is never as complete as it should be, which is why we carry a debt of love at all times.

The importance of love should take on greater meaning in light of the present time (13:11). The Bible divides history into two periods of time—this present age and the age to come. The New Testament writers show that the kingdom of God (the age to come) was inaugurated by Christ at His first coming, but will not be consummated until His second coming. So believers from the first century onward are living between the two comings of Christ.

With each passing day, Jesus' return nears. So as believers anticipate that event when night gives way to day and darkness to light, Paul reminds them to wake up (13:11) and be aware of their behavior (13:12–13). He provides the image of taking off nightclothes and putting on the armor of light, suitable daytime equipment for soldiers of Christ (13:12, 14). As the time grows shorter, the need for love takes on greater urgency.

Take It Home

Sometimes believers are taught to see obedience only as a spiritual discipline, which it is. Yet Paul demonstrates one very practical benefit of obedience: the dispersal of fear. In a practical, civil sense, if people pay their taxes and obey the laws, they have no fear of the authorities (13:3). Likewise, if they submit to God and obey His instructions, they have no fear of being embarrassed when Jesus returns (13:11–14). Can you identify any areas in your own life—civil or spiritual—where increased obedience or submission might result in a lessening of fear?

ROMANS 14:1–15:13

WEAK AND STRONG BELIEVERS

Setting Up the Section

As Paul continues the practical application section of his letter to the Romans, he deals with conflicts that can arise between people who have different levels of spiritual maturity. What may seem completely appropriate to those in one group can appear wrong (if not outright sinful) to those in another. His exhortation to love one another (13:8) still applies as fellow believers learn to respect one another's opinions.

📄 14:1–12

DEALING WITH DISPUTABLE MATTERS

Scripture is clear as to whether many things are right or wrong. But in this section, Paul addresses those "gray" issues. It's not surprising that these matters were becoming potential problems in the early church. The Jews had a long-established pattern of worship that they naturally planned to continue. The church/worship experience was new to the Gentiles, who had no religious traditions.

Two frequent points of contention were food-related regulations (14:2–3) and the observance of special days (14:5–6). Paul implored his readers not to be so quick to judge one another on these matters. Just because one person found one particular method to be more satisfactory didn't mean that everyone would. Before getting into the specific problems, Paul asked for acceptance of one another and the avoidance of passing judgment (14:1).

Critical Observation

We tend to think that those who follow the most stringent religious disciplines are the most mature. Yet it is interesting to note that the Roman Christians who tended to adhere to the strictest rules and probably felt more superior were those labeled weak by Paul (14:2). Others, generally those who weren't bound to all the Old Testament laws, had experienced the freedom of the gospel to a much greater degree.

No matter the religious practices, a believer had no justification for feeling superior to others. All believers were accountable only to God. Whether or not someone observed all the feasting and fasting days or included meat in a daily diet was inconsequential in terms of his or her salvation and overall relationship with God. After God had accepted someone (14:4), what right did that person have to stand in judgment of a fellow believer?

Believers suffer when they compete with one another. No one is self-sufficient, so all need to acknowledge the right of other believers to worship in a different way. Rather than being critical of one another, people should attend to their own spiritual condition and devote themselves to God (14:6–8).

Paul reminds his readers that there will indeed be a day of judgment (14:10–11). Everyone will stand before God and give an account (14:12). So in the meantime, judgment of one another is a useless exercise.

📄 14:13–23

REMOVING STUMBLING BLOCKS

In addition to judging, another problem between "strong" and "weak" Christians is the exercise of one's religious freedom with a callous disregard for how it might affect others. In the first century, when one group was sensitive to dietary restrictions and whether or not meat had been sacrificed to idols and another group had no concern about such things, sharing a meal together could be awkward.

One might think that the mature believers would be expected to set an example for the others. They were to an extent, but not by blatantly ignoring how their actions would be perceived by less mature members. They weren't to flaunt their spiritual freedom before those who hadn't yet reached that point in their spiritual journeys. Paul explains that the unity of the church is the primary issue; food and other matters are secondary. So even if mature believers (rightly) feel no unease with eating foods others believed were unclean, Paul asks them to forego doing so within group settings. It didn't bother them and it didn't bother God, yet it was a distraction for less mature believers.

Demystifying Romans

The Old Testament prohibition against eating certain foods had been removed by Jesus (Mark 7:14–15) and reinforced to Peter through a vision that symbolized the inclusion of the Gentiles into the early church (Acts 10:9–23). Yet many believers still clung to those teachings, as do certain groups today.

The word translated "stumbling block" (14:13 NIV) is a literal reference to an object in a path over which someone would trip and fall. The more traditional believers were becoming distressed (14:15), finding fellowship with other Christians (and perhaps even with God) to be difficult. What the "strong" believers saw as good was being perceived as evil (14:16). So Paul encourages the more mature in the church to be sensitive to the feelings and beliefs of the others and, out of love, not to practice those things in a mixed group.

Christian freedom is not license. If one's Christian freedoms are impairing the growth of others, it's better to voluntarily do without those things (14:20–21). Paul himself recognized that believers develop at their individual paces, and left it to those who were more mature to not create more difficulty for them. People are not required to reach total agreement in all matters of church function, and should learn to respect one another's differences of opinion (14:22–23).

ACCEPTING ONE ANOTHER

In some of Paul's other writings, he warns against becoming intent on pleasing other people (Galatians 1:10; 1 Thessalonians 2:4; etc.). Those who are too concerned with pleasing others are in danger of falling away from God. That's not what Paul means when he writes of sacrificing one's rights and pleasing his neighbor (15:2). The other instances refer to pleasing people instead of pleasing God. In this case, the desire to find favor with other believers is so that God will be pleased as they continue to grow spiritually.

It is not easy or natural to bear with the failings of the weak (15:1), but it is achievable through knowledge of scripture (15:4), prayer, and praise (15:6). Jesus has already accepted both the stronger and weaker believers, so now they need to learn to accept one another (15:7). He has already set the example to follow, and because of His willingness to set aside His own rights and privileges, He brought salvation not only to the Jews but to the Gentiles as well (15:8–12).

As Paul concludes his writing on the righteousness of God and prepares to make a few closing statements, he prays for joy and peace for all his readers (15:13). Rather than letting their differences of opinion lead to arguments and divisions, they could grow stronger by working through them, with hope and the help of the Holy Spirit.

Take It Home

Deciding where your freedom needs to take a backseat to your responsibility to influence is something that all Christians must navigate in their spiritual journeys. If Paul were writing to the church of the twenty-first century, what issues do you think he would address in regard to mature and immature believers?

ROMANS 15:14-33
PERSONAL COMMENTS

Paul's Ministry to the Gentiles   15:14–22
Paul's Plans   15:23–33

Setting Up the Section

Paul has just finished with the "business" of his letter to the Romans after calling on all the believers to accept one another and not let their differences get in the way of spiritual growth. He has completed his thorough explanation of justification by faith and other doctrinal matters. As he begins to close his letter, he turns his attention to some personal matters, including another affirmation of his genuine concern for the believers in Rome.

📖 15:14–22

PAUL'S MINISTRY TO THE GENTILES

Keep in mind that Paul has not yet set foot in Rome. He knows some of the believers there but has never personally visited. Yet he has just written a very bold letter and wants to ensure it is received well and not misinterpreted. So in this section, he elaborates on the nature of his ministry.

First, he describes his work as a priestly ministry (15:15–16). A priest was responsible for offering the sacrifices of the people, and Paul had been able to offer to God a great number of Gentiles who had converted to Christianity under his ministry. Although the Gentiles were excluded from participating in the temple at Jerusalem and from sharing in the temple sacrifices, they were living sacrifices (12:1).

Paul then speaks of his work as a powerful ministry (15:18–19). Yet he never takes credit for anything that was accomplished. He gives credit to the Holy Spirit and gives glory to Jesus. As Paul had earlier explained, he had chosen to be a servant to Christ (1:1–2; 6:22; 15:17). It is Christ living in Paul whom he credits with the results of his ministry.

Paul also writes that his was a pioneer ministry (15:19–20). Paul had spent ten years in ministry and had gone on three missionary journeys to places where no evangelist had gone before, preaching to people who had never heard the gospel of Jesus. Yet his description is a rather modest summary. His work has prevented him from traveling to Rome, but he is hoping that is about to change.

📖 15:23–33

PAUL'S PLANS

Having clarified his ministry for his readers, Paul outlines his future travel plans. He specifies three destinations: Jerusalem (15:25), Rome (15:24), and Spain (15:24). Assuming he would travel by sea, going to these locations would require a journey of three thousand miles—an ambitious undertaking given the difficulties of first-century transportation.

Paul and others had collected a special offering from a number of Gentile churches in Greece. Before doing anything else, Paul wanted to deliver the gift to the Jewish believers in Jerusalem who were suffering from a severe famine.

Demystifying Romans

Though Paul doesn't say much in his letter to the Romans about the financial gift for the Jerusalem church, he provides a number of details in 2 Corinthians 8–9.

The gift of the Macedonian churches was significant for a number of reasons: It fulfilled the request of the apostles to remember the poor (Galatians 2:10), it demonstrated the solidarity of God's people across various geographic regions and economic levels, and it broke down racial and social barriers. Paul recognized the gift from the Gentile churches to the Jewish believers as a humble, material, and symbolic demonstration of the oneness of the body of Christ.

Paul has wanted to visit Rome for a while (1:15), but has been unable to. Now the time seems right. Paul senses that his missionary service in the eastern Mediterranean area is sufficient. Rome was the center of the empire, and the church there had great opportunities for ministry. Paul wants to visit as well as establish a base of operation prior to going on to Spain. He is also counting on them to help support his ministry as he moves on (15:24).

As far as Paul's hopes to see Spain, we don't know if he ever made it. The entire Iberian Peninsula was under control of Rome and had many flourishing Roman colonies. But if Paul took that trip between his first imprisonment in Rome and the later one that led to his death in AD 64, it isn't on record anywhere.

Critical Observation

Paul was by no means tentative about his traveling. However, his bold statement in 15:29 is not an expression of self-confidence, but rather his faith in Jesus. He knew that when he arrived in Rome both he and the believers there would be blessed.

Paul concludes this section with a heartfelt request for prayer (15:30–33). He had begun his letter with the assurance that he was praying for the believers in Rome (1:8–10), so it is not unusual that he would ask for their support in return. He is quite specific in his prayer requests. He asks for prayers for safety in his travels, for deliverance from his enemies, and above all, for the opportunity to visit with the church in Rome. He does not pray in order to bend God's will to his, but rather to align his plans with God's will.

Paul's request is a reminder that all people need prayer. It is easy to assume that mature spiritual leaders don't really need prayer, encouragement, or affirmation. But the fact that the apostle Paul coveted the prayers of fellow Christians demonstrates the responsibility for believers to pray for all their leaders.

The three concerns of Paul in this section—his apostolic service, his plans for travel, and his need for prayer—all reflect the providence of God in his ministry. As believers are reminded of God's sovereignty, they can take great comfort to realize they are never alone in any of their endeavors.

Take It Home

This personal section at the end of Paul's letter is a good reminder that sometimes we address spiritual matters with a businesslike attitude. Paul had certainly written a deep and insightful letter that dealt with many of the doctrines of the faith. Yet he didn't stop there; he also made it personal. Can you think of ways either you or your church might need to include more of a personal element in your spiritual dealings?

ROMANS 16:1–27

PAUL'S FELLOW MINISTERS

A Series of Greetings 16:1–16
Final Exhortations 16:17–27

Setting Up the Section

As Paul concludes his lengthy letter to the Romans, he personally acknowledges dozens of people who were working for God. It is a personal and intimate conclusion to his Epistle, and was surely an encouragement to those who might have felt unnoticed.

🕮 16:1–16

A SERIES OF GREETINGS

When it comes to lists of names in the Bible, whether they comprise tribes, genealogies, the great gallery of faith in Hebrews 11, or other groupings, many people have a natural tendency to skip over them. Yet, in most cases, there are valuable lessons to be discovered by those who slow down and take a look.

In this passage, twenty-six people are mentioned by name, and there are twenty-one titles attached to the various names (sister, servant, helper, etc.). Some names are familiar; many are not. Yet a quick look at the people and Paul's comments may provide some surprising insight.

For one thing, Paul's list reflects the importance of hospitality in the body of Christ. He begins his closing with a personal request that the church in Rome would welcome

Phoebe (16:1-2). Perhaps she was the one entrusted with carrying Paul's letter to the believers in Rome. Paul explains that she had been a big help to him and asks the Roman Christians to do whatever they could to help her.

Hospitality is also evident from the mention of the church in the home of Aquila and Priscilla (16:3-5). Paul had met this couple on his second missionary journey while traveling through Corinth, and had formed a strong bond with this husband-and-wife team (Acts 18:1-3, 18-19). But they were originally from Rome, and had apparently returned home to minister there. They were at the top of Paul's list of greeting.

A second significant point about Paul's list is that it is comprised of people of different rank and race. There are Jews and Gentiles, men and women, slaves and free people. Aristobulus (16:10) was a grandson of Herod the Great and friend of Emperor Claudius. Narcissus (16:11) was a rich and powerful freed slave who served as the secretary to Claudius. Ampliatus, on the other hand (16:8), was one of several common slave names on the list. Rufus (16:13) may have been the son of Simon of Cyrene, the bystander who had been unexpectedly forced into Roman service to carry the cross of Jesus to Calvary (Mark 15:21).

Critical Observation

In the cemetery of Domatilla, one of the oldest Christian catacombs, is a decorated tomb with the single name AMPLIATUS carved in bold and decorative lettering. A Roman male would usually have his three names carved on his tomb, which suggests that Ampliatus was a slave. And if this is the same person mentioned in Romans 16:8, it suggests that this slave held a position of leadership in the church in Rome.

And yet, in spite of the fact that this assortment of people came from different backgrounds, social standings, races, and encounters with Christ, there was great unity within the diversity. Four times in this chapter Paul describes the believers at Rome as being "in Christ." Twice he uses family language of "sister" and "brother." He also refers to "fellow workers" and fellow sufferers, two expressions that strengthen Christian unity.

Paul's list of names also includes the extensive involvement of women. Nine of the named people on the list (one-third) are women. Tryphena and Tryphosa (16:12) may have been twin sisters (based on the similarities in their names). Their names mean "dainty" and "delicate" respectively, yet Paul praises them for working hard for the Lord—a phrase that indicates working to the point of exhaustion. In addition, the list contains the names of Priscilla, Mary, Junia, Persis, Rufus's mother, Julia, and Nereus's sister.

Some people point to other passages of Paul, taken apart from the rest of his writing, and suggest that he taught against women serving in leadership positions in the church. Yet here we see his commendation of Phoebe (16:1), who was most likely a deaconess. (The word for "servant" can also mean "minister.") He referred to Priscilla as a fellow worker. He honors Junia as outstanding among the apostles. He acknowledges the good work of many women in the church and does nothing to criticize their leadership.

Clearly, Paul was not the male chauvinist some have made him out to be. He appreciated the gifts and ministries of women, and he commended them for their service to him and to Christ.

📄 16:17–27

FINAL EXHORTATIONS

Even though this is the longest of Paul's greetings in any of his letters, he still isn't finished with his list of acknowledgments. After greeting many of the individuals who were in Rome, Paul credits a number of people who were with him (16:21–24).

Demystifying Romans

Timothy (16:21) was a young pastor and Paul's protégé, whom Paul mentions frequently in his letters. Jason (16:21) may have been the man who had taken some heat for Paul in Thessalonica (Acts 17:5–9). Sosipater (Romans 16:21) may have been the Sopater who traveled with Paul in Greece (Acts 20:4). Tertius (Romans 16:22) was Paul's secretary who had written the letter to the Romans as Paul dictated. Gaius (16:23) was Paul's host in Corinth; Paul had led him to Christ (1 Corinthians 1:14). The others were evidently believers in Corinth.

Between the list of people Paul greets and the list of Paul's companions, he provides a word of warning. False doctrines were beginning to circulate, promoted by smooth-talking people (16:17–18). Paul challenges his readers to be both wise and innocent (16:19). Naïve people are easily fooled, so wisdom is needed. Yet the more the believers could keep themselves removed from evil things (innocent), the better off they would be.

Paul's doxology (16:25–27) is a final reminder that the mystery of God had been revealed through Jesus Christ. What had been written in the law and proclaimed by the prophets could at last be fully understood. And for that, God was due praise and glory forever.

Take It Home

Paul's lists in this section remind us of how interconnected we are in the body of Christ. Whether it's an appreciation for people we haven't even met or the acknowledgement of those who regularly support and inspire us, it is good to let others know we are thinking about them. Make a list of the people you are thankful for. Then, as soon as you get the opportunity, contact each one to express your gratefulness for his or her influence in your life.

1 CORINTHIANS

INTRODUCTION TO
1 CORINTHIANS

Corinth was a Roman colony and capital of the province of Achaia. Its population probably reached as many as two hundred thousand free citizens, with close to half a million slaves. The city had been in existence since the Bronze Age. It was located in a most strategic position, midway along a five-mile stretch of land between the Saronic Gulf and the Corinthian Gulf. The city would therefore get all the travelers going to the isthmus at the south of Greece, or north to the continent. Additionally, the hazards of sea travel made it advisable for ships to dock, unload, and transfer their cargo to another ship across the isthmus, east to west or vice versa. Small ships would be dragged across the land bridge while still fully loaded.

With all the people and money going through Corinth, it was naturally an influential city. And along with the crowds and wealth came immorality. The city had a reputation for both idolatry and prostitution. The city's less-than- stellar reputation is mentioned in numerous ancient writings. Paul had started a church there during his second missionary journey (Acts 18:1–18). This Epistle to the Corinthian believers alludes to many of the aspects of social life in the city.

AUTHOR

The Epistle of 1 Corinthians both begins and ends with an identification of Paul as the author (1:1; 16:21). The early church was quick to affirm his authorship, and few modern scholars dispute it.

OCCASION AND PURPOSE

During his second missionary journey, Paul remained in Corinth for about eighteen months (about AD 51–52), teaching and establishing the church there. He then returned to his home base at Antioch, and subsequently set off on his third missionary journey. He traveled to Ephesus, the key city in the Roman province of Asia, where he remained for three years, establishing churches there and in the surrounding regions.

While in Ephesus, Paul began to hear of troubles in the young church at Corinth. One of these problems was related to sexual sin, and Paul seems to have written a short letter (now lost) to correct it (5:9). The church was also suffering from division (1:12). In response to the problems in this immature church, Paul wrote this letter, known to us as 1 Corinthians (about AD 55).

Shortly before writing the letter, a delegation from Corinth (Stephanas, Fortunatus, and Achaicus [16:17]) came to Paul with a financial gift from the church. They probably also brought a list of questions from the church, since Paul answers these questions in his letter (7:1). The report of these three men, along with a report from members of the household of a woman named Chloe (1:11), and perhaps a report from his fellow missionary Apollos (1:12; 16:12), prompted Paul to write the letter.

Paul was planning another trip to Corinth. His letter was an attempt to correct some of the problems in the church before he arrived (4:18–21). He also was collecting gifts for the church in Jerusalem because its members were facing tough times, and he wanted the Corinthians to be ready to give (16:1–4).

Paul considered himself the spiritual father of the Corinthian church (4:14–15). It was his love for the believers that motivated him to confront them so directly concerning spiritual and moral issues. Personally, he had experienced weakness, fear, and trembling in his previous association with the church (2:3), but Paul knew it was the power of God that would sustain both him as the messenger and the Corinthian believers as a body.

THEMES

Because of the many ongoing disputes in the church, one of the continuing themes of 1 Corinthians is unity. Paul repeatedly challenges the believers to resolve their conflicts, dissolve their factions, and let God's love rule in the church to bring them together as one body.

Related to unity is the work of the Holy Spirit, especially in regard to spiritual gifts. It is the Holy Spirit who provides the needed wisdom and equips the believers in various ways to minister to one another and the world outside the church.

The sanctification of believers, therefore, is also stressed throughout Paul's letter. Whether supporting their church leaders, addressing sexual sin, foregoing lawsuits against one another, feeling gratitude for their spiritual gifts, or living in anticipation of the resurrection, believers need wisdom from God and the maturity of personal discipline. God has sanctified His people, and in response they are to live accordingly.

CONTRIBUTION TO THE BIBLE

The first letter to the Corinthians is a good example of the importance of integrity within the local church. Much of the focus of scripture is frequently applied to the worldwide church, but here we find a call for each individual body of believers to attend to its own spiritual life and growth.

Paul writes about spiritual gifts in various places, yet his comprehensive explanation in 1 Corinthians 12, using his analogy of the human body, is perhaps his best. The "one body" concept is a universally understood image of the church.

In addition, 1 Corinthians 13 is one of the best-known passages of scripture. Paul's description of love has become a classic piece of literature throughout the centuries since the church at Corinth first read it.

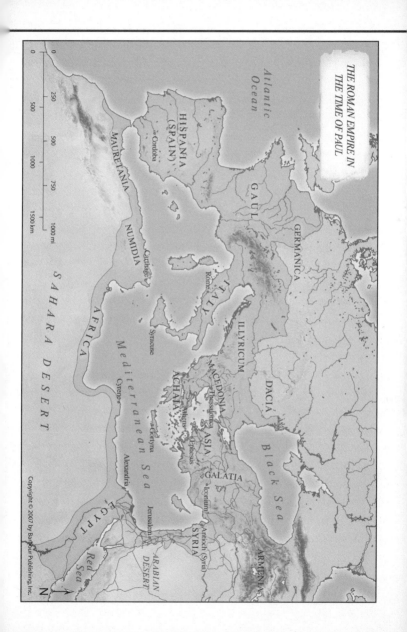

THE ROMAN EMPIRE IN
THE TIME OF PAUL

Atlantic
Ocean

HISPANIA
(SPAIN)

Córdoba

GAUL

GERMANICA

MAURETANIA

NUMIDIA

Carthage

Rome

ITALY

ILLYRICUM

DACIA

AFRICA

Syracuse

Mediterranean Sea

MACEDONIA

Thessalonica

Black Sea

SAHARA DESERT

Cyrene

ACHAIA

Corinth

Athens

ASIA

Ephesus

GALATIA

Iconium

Alexandria

EGYPT

Jerusalem

Antioch (Syria)

SYRIA

ARMENIA

Red
Sea

ARABIAN
DESERT

N

0   250   500   1000   1500 km

0   250   500   750   1000 mi

Copyright © 2007 by Barbour Publishing, Inc.

1 CORINTHIANS 1:1–2:5

A CHURCH DIVIDED

Setting Up the Section

The church at Corinth was undergoing a number of problems. Paul begins by addressing the main source of trouble: division among church members. This issue was evident in a number of specific ways, which Paul will get to in subsequent chapters. But here he deals with the matter from a broader perspective.

📖 1:1–9

GREETING AND GRATITUDE

As was customary for first-century letters, Paul begins by identifying himself and his recipients, and then provides a brief greeting. He refers to his apostleship as well as his calling (1:1), both credentials that attest to his being sent out by God. Later in the letter, he will reveal that his authority is questioned, so from the beginning he makes his intentions clear.

Paul's recipients were Christians in the city of Corinth (1:2). He referred to them as a collective whole, although they may have been members of assorted house churches. Even in the salutation, Paul reminded his readers of their purpose in the Christian life—to be sanctified and holy.

Demystifying 1 Corinthians

Paul adds no details about his companion, Sosthenes (1:1). However, a man by this name appeared in Acts. A synagogue ruler named Crispus had become a believer in response to Paul's preaching (Acts 18:8), and Sosthenes appears to have been his replacement. Perhaps after the unfortunate events described in Acts 18:17, Sosthenes also became a Christian. If Paul's companion isn't this same Sosthenes, we know nothing about him.

The usual Greco-Roman greeting was "rejoice" or "be well" (*chairein*). Paul turned this into a Christian greeting by making it "grace" (*charis*), a Greek word that sounds similar. "Peace" (*shalom* in Hebrew; *eirēnē* in Greek) was the typical Jewish salutation. So Paul combines Greek and Jewish greetings (1:3), and acknowledges their significant theological overtones by citing the origin of grace and peace—the one, true, living God revealed in Jesus Christ.

In his greeting, Paul expresses thankfulness for the believers in Corinth (1:4–6), even though he will soon confront them with a number of problems and shortcomings. Paul trusts God's character and faithfulness to see the Corinthians through their human frailties and flaws (1:7–9).

📄 **1:10–17**

DIVISIONS AMONG THE BELIEVERS

Before going into detail, Paul appeals to his readers for greater unity (1:10). The Bible urges believers to maintain unity and work toward that goal. The unity of the Spirit can be achieved despite differences and even disagreements.

Yet the Corinthians were divided for various reasons. Foremost among them was the tendency to align themselves with different Christian leaders, as if it were a contest. Paul names four different leaders (1:12), and it's not surprising that they would have appealed to different personalities.

Some believers aligned themselves with Paul. They were probably of Greek ancestry and wanted to be loyal to the one who had founded the church. Others aligned themselves with Apollos. He would have appealed to the intellectuals, because he was well-educated in the city of Alexandria and was known for his oratorical abilities and vast knowledge of the Old Testament (Acts 18:24–28). The third group supported Peter (Cephas), and was probably of Jewish background. Perhaps they were attracted to the forcefulness of Peter's personality or the fact that he had spent three years interacting with Jesus personally. Finally, one group professed devotion only to Christ. While all believers should be aligned with Jesus, perhaps this faction thought they were superior because they acknowledged no human teacher and felt overly spiritual in their walk with the Lord. They were actually using the name of Jesus to separate themselves from others in the church!

Critical Observation

Although the Bible contains 1 Corinthians and 2 Corinthians, apparently these weren't the first two letters Paul had sent to the church in Corinth. He makes references to at least one previous letter he had written (5:9) and one he had already *received* from the church (7:1), yet those correspondences have never been found.

Paul minimizes his own leadership role (1:13–17), and in doing so also downplays the other human leaders of the church. This was to assure his readers that Christ was indeed the leader of the church. Paul was one of the spokespeople, but his preaching was not based on his own wisdom. The power of his message came through the death and resurrection of Jesus.

📄 1:18–31

GOD'S WISDOM VS. HUMAN WISDOM

After contrasting human wisdom with the power of the cross of Christ (1:17), Paul continues the comparison in the next section of his writing. The cross was far from becoming an accepted religious sign. At the time, it was still a horrific symbol of cruelty and death. So for believers to make the cross a major issue seemed foolish to those who didn't understand the necessity and benefits of Jesus' death (1:18–19).

At the time, wisdom was perceived less a matter of genuine intellect and intuition than an ability to articulate a clever-sounding worldview that spoke to the grand themes of life. Two philosophers could expound on their opinions and reach quite different conclusions, yet both were considered wise. God's wisdom had little to do with such showiness. The simple message of the gospel was God's wisdom, yet some people continued to look for wondrous signs and others for bold declarations and hidden truths (1:22–24).

However, there was no comparison. God's "foolishness" is wiser than all of humankind's wisdom (1:25). And God intentionally chooses "foolish" and "weak" things to accomplish His will, which undermines all the arguments of the "wise" and "strong" (1:26–31). As a result, all the credit for a believer's wisdom and strength goes to God rather than oneself.

📄 2:1–5

PAUL'S MODEL OF WISDOM

Paul gives God credit for everything in his ministry. Though well educated and quite knowledgeable about everything he wrote, he refuses to package his message in pretentious speech or high-sounding eloquence. The content of his message is powerful enough without attempting to bolster it in manipulative ways. Paul is able to maintain great humility and vulnerability among those he ministers to (2:2–5). He could have made a dazzling presentation of the gospel, using various secular techniques. But by choosing not to do so, his readers are able to see the supernatural nature of what he is preaching. Paul doesn't want the attention to be on him, but on God (2:4–5).

Take It Home

Paul's emphasis remained on the content of the gospel rather than the presentation of it. Do you think most churches have a similar commitment, or do they try too hard to use human wisdom to attract attention? To what extent do you think it is appropriate for Christian leaders to concern themselves with the presentation of God's Word?

1 CORINTHIANS 2:6-16

THE HOLY SPIRIT'S ROLE IN WISDOM

The Value of God's Wisdom	2:6–10
The Illumination of the Holy Spirit	2:11–16

Setting Up the Section

Paul begins this letter to the Corinthian church by contrasting human wisdom with the wisdom of God. Those who value their own wisdom too highly tend to think that the truth of the gospel is foolishness. Paul continues his clarification in this section, where he explains how the Holy Spirit contributes to a believer's genuine wisdom.

📖 2:6–10

THE VALUE OF GOD'S WISDOM

As Paul continues to differentiate between various definitions of wisdom, he explains that the wisdom of believers is mature, and not at all like what was being presented as wisdom in the secular culture (2:6). The difference is due to the work of the Holy Spirit.

God's wisdom, Paul writes, had been hidden (2:7). But what was once secret has been revealed and is now accessible (2:10). Until the Spirit enlightens someone, however, the person is incapable of realizing the truth about God, Jesus, and the gospel. All the so-called wisdom of the rulers of that time would come to nothing (2:6). Some people think Paul may have been writing of spiritual rulers here rather than (or in addition to) human ones.

Demystifying 1 Corinthians

Paul was not endorsing the new teaching beginning to circulate through the church (later to be labeled Gnosticism) that said the way to God required much deep thought and secret knowledge. Rather, Paul was speaking of a matter of timing. After the coming of the Holy Spirit, access to God's truth required only simple faith rather than intellect or religious zeal.

In Paul's day, the secular culture attempted to approach God through reasoning and argument. The result was a deity created in the people's own image that in no way resembled the real and personal God. In their minds, God was what they called *apatheia*— He had a total inability to feel. They saw God as detached and remote, and the preaching of Christ (with its emphasis on suffering and reconciling the world to Himself through death on a cross) as incomprehensible and foolish.

If the first-century crowds had been able to discern the true wisdom of God, they never would have crucified Jesus (2:8). Indeed, for those who believe, the wisdom of God is profound. But human wisdom alone is not enough. Jesus said He chose His disciples, not the other way around (John 15:16). And the author of Hebrews confirms that Jesus is the author and perfecter of faith (Hebrews 12:2). If people begin to think they are smart enough to comprehend the truths of Christianity on their own, they don't fully understand the ministry of the Holy Spirit in their lives.

📄 2:11–16

THE ILLUMINATION OF THE HOLY SPIRIT

Human observation and careful study can never fully penetrate the deep truths of God. But where human imagination fails, spiritual illumination prevails. Through the power of the Holy Spirit, God reveals the light of the gospel to believers and convicts them of the truths of their faith.

To illustrate his point, Paul asks his readers to consider the human spirit. It is impossible, simply by looking at someone else, to determine that person's deepest thoughts, inner dreams, and strongest desires. But the spirit within the person is aware of such things. Similarly, people had spent centuries trying to understand and relate to God. But it wasn't until the Spirit of God revealed God's truth that people could really comprehend (2:11–12).

Similarly, people without the help of the Spirit can't understand spiritual things (2:14). Those with the Spirit not only are given insight to understand, but also to communicate what they have discerned. Believers learn to translate their spiritual thoughts into spiritual words (2:13). Just as the Holy Spirit provides the enlightenment needed to comprehend the mystery of God's truth, He also enables believers to speak with a type of wisdom far superior to the rhetoric of any orator.

In conclusion, Paul refers to a question from Isaiah: "Who has known the mind of the Lord?" (Isaiah 40:13 NIV). And the answer, from a New Testament perspective, is that with the help of the Holy Spirit, *all believers* can know the mind of Christ. Paul doesn't go into detail here, but his definition of the attitude of Christ (Philippians 2:6–11) is not a bit mystical or mysterious. The mind of Christ is an attitude of humility and sacrifice. And anyone who understands this spiritual truth is accountable only to God—not to those who lack the same spiritual insight (2:15).

Sadly, many in the church at Corinth were still far from understanding the mind of Christ. They had a long way to go in their process of spiritual maturity, as Paul will explain in the next section.

Take It Home

Consider your own opinion about what it means to be "wise." Do you think most people are impressed by a simple demonstration of spiritual maturity and reliance on the truths of God? Or are they looking more for eloquent answers to hard questions? Would you say you tend to display more human wisdom, or do you display godly wisdom that is expressed by spiritual truths (2:13)?

1 CORINTHIANS 3:1–23

A PLEA FOR COOPERATION RATHER THAN COMPETITION

Setting Up the Section

In this section, Paul continues his appeal to the Corinthians to quit dividing into factions based on their personal preference of church leadership. As long as jealousy and arguments continued, the church would never unite. And in addition to the church as a whole, Paul speaks to the importance of individual commitment and work for God.

📖 3:1–4

INFANTS IN CHRIST

Paul had just gone into considerable detail (2:6–16) describing the difference between people who attempt to get by with only human wisdom (nonbelievers) and those who have responded to the Holy Spirit and are able to discern the mind of Christ (believers). Here he begins to differentiate between mature and immature believers.

Overall, the church in Corinth was immature. Although the members had been Christians for several years, they were still babes in the faith. They should have possessed a mature hunger for real Christian teaching, but they were still acting immature (3:1–2). They wanted milk (probably a reference to justification and all the other benefits of a Christian relationship), but hadn't moved on to the solid truths of Christianity: choosing righteousness, making sacrifices, submitting to others, and so forth.

Infants can be cute, but not when they are uncompromisingly self-centered, so Paul calls them on their behavior. It must have been particularly disheartening to realize that he was part of the reason the Corinthian believers were jealous and quarreling among one another (3:1–3).

Demystifying 1 Corinthians

Paul considered himself the spiritual father of the Corinthian believers (4:15), and wanted his "children" to mature as they should. Every parent wants to see his or her child grow out of the self-centered stage after a reasonable amount of time.

📖 3:5–9

GOD'S FIELD

To make his point, Paul uses a couple of analogies for the church. The first is that of a field (3:9). Jesus had used the image of a seed and soil as a symbol of the human heart and its response to God's Word (Matthew 13:3–23). Paul makes a similar comparison, but with an application to the entire church instead of a single person. For some of the Corinthian believers to align behind Paul while others supported Apollos—and to argue about which leader was more important—made about as much sense as cheering for one farmer over another in regard to crop growth.

Paul had sown the seed of God's Word in Corinth, and a church had sprung up. Apollos had come along later to "water" the young church. But Paul makes it clear that only God is responsible for any growth (3:6–7). The Corinthians needed to see that Paul and Apollos had played different—but equally important—roles in the ministry of the church. Both would be rewarded by God (3:8), and should be respected by the believers.

📖 3:10–17

GOD'S TEMPLE

Next, Paul uses the illustration of a building to further clarify his point. Jesus is the foundation of anything a believer hopes to construct. Paul had laid that foundation in the sense that he had first preached the gospel in Corinth (3:10–11). And again, Apollos had played a part in the growth by building on the foundation—strengthening the belief of the Corinthian Christians.

But not every builder has the same results. Those who work with valuable materials—the truths of God—would have a lasting ministry. Others who settled for less wouldn't see the same results. The references to wood, hay, and straw probably represent work based on the limited human wisdom Paul described in 1 Corinthians 2. Believers should be capable of better, more productive ministry, yet some settle for less.

Critical Observation

Although God will judge and reward individuals for the work they do (3:12–15), believers are not to operate independently of one another. When Paul wrote, "you yourselves are God's temple" (3:16 NIV), the word *you* was plural. Believers are not individual *temples* of God, but are collectively the *temple* of God.

📖 3:18–23

WISE FOOLS

Up to this point, Paul has been contrasting foolishness and wisdom. He concludes this passage by urging his readers to risk being perceived as "foolish" in order to adopt the true wisdom of God that is found in unity with others in Christ (3:18–20). Christianity is at odds with the worldview of nonbelievers, so believers should not be surprised to find themselves out of step with the secular world as they faithfully follow the Savior.

The Corinthians seemed worried that they might miss out on something if they backed the wrong leader, so they tended to boast about their minister of choice. Paul concludes this section by assuring them that God has provided everything for them (3:21–23)—people, the world, life, death, the present, and the future. Each leader belongs to the entire church. No subgroup can lay claim to a servant of Christ at the exclusion of the other church members. Everything belongs to the church, the church belongs to Christ, and Christ belongs to God. And *that* is something to boast about (1:31)!

Take It Home

Think about your current level of involvement in the church of Christ. Would you say you are contributing to the growth of the church with gold, silver, and costly stones, or with wood, hay, and straw? Do you foresee lasting effects of the work you are doing? (If not, do other people?) What might you do to improve the quality (not the quantity) of your work in the future?

1 CORINTHIANS 4:1–21

PROPER REGARD FOR CHURCH LEADERS

Setting Up the Section

In the previous section, Paul had explained to the Corinthian believers some of the wrong ways to respond to their church leaders. He challenged them to quit boasting about human leaders (3:21) and to quit allowing their leadership to create jealousy and quarreling among the church members (3:3–4). In this section, he continues to explain how the church should properly respond to and support its leaders.

📖 4:1–7

FAITHFULNESS IN SERVING

Paul begins his letter to the Corinthians by explaining the wrong way to treat apostles of God. The Corinthians were prone to overly exalt them, and Paul corrects their way of thinking. Next, he brings the discussion full circle and suggests that the Corinthians see their spiritual leaders as servants—servants entrusted with secret things of God (4:1).

Church leaders are stewards. The steward was the highest-ranking servant of a wealthy landowner—the one in charge of the entire estate in his master's absence. The primary responsibility of the steward was faithfulness to his master, so he had to resist kowtowing to the demands of those who served under him.

The church leaders were servants, yet they were servants with authority. It was improper for others to exalt them, yet they were due respect as God's designated stewards. Ultimately, both the leaders and the other church members would have to give an account to the Lord. It meant little to Paul how the Corinthians regarded his ministry, because all that really mattered was God's divine assessment (4:2–5).

Paul further challenges his readers not to impose standards on their leaders that scripture didn't require (4:6). He identifies the Corinthians' problem as one of pride, and then immediately challenges them by asking how they had acquired the things that made them proud (4:7). His point was that they had no right to be proud and boastful, since God had provided them with everything they had.

📖 4:8–13

SACRIFICE IN SERVING

Paul wasn't beyond using a little sarcasm to make his point. He derisively portrays the Corinthian believers as rich and wise kings, filled with strength and receiving honor. In contrast, he describes the apostles as a spectacle, fools, weak, homeless, and scum of the earth. Paul's words are harsh, indeed, yet his illustration isn't far from reality. The Corinthian believers were bickering about minor things while Paul, Apollos, Peter, and other leaders were suffering, going hungry, working hard, and facing persecution.

Demystifying 1 Corinthians

When a Roman general won a great victory, he would parade his triumphant army through the streets of the city, displaying all the spoils of their conquest. Following at the end of the parade was a group of people who had been taken captive. Soon this group would be taken to the arena to fight against wild animals or armed gladiators, where most would die. This is the image Paul uses, describing the proud Corinthians as victorious kings and the church leaders as the doomed prisoners.

📖 4:14–21

A MODEL OF SERVICE

There was an antidote to pride, but it wasn't popular in first-century culture. Paul doesn't use the word *humility* here as he does in other places (Philippians 2:3), but that is his intent. According to Greek philosophy, humility was a trait associated with slaves, a sign of weakness, and not to be associated with men of character. Paul (in imitation of Jesus) had a completely different philosophy that prized humility. It was his humility that allowed him to return cursing with blessing, persecution with tolerance, and slander with kindness (4:12–13).

In fact, Paul pleads with the Corinthians to follow the example he had set in his ministry (4:16). And since Paul couldn't be in Corinth right away, he was sending Timothy to set the same example for them, and to remind them of what Paul believed and practiced (4:17).

Paul isn't afraid to chastise the Corinthian church a bit. Even though there were thousands of people who might weigh in with opinions of how they were doing and what they might need to do, Paul is their spiritual father, in that he had originally gotten the church up and running (4:15).

In the final section of this passage, Paul alerts his readers to a problem that he will revisit later in his letter (9:1–3). When he makes reference to *some* of them (4:18), he is acknowledging his awareness of personal animosity toward him by several in the Corinthian church. This dissentious group had been trying to convince others that Paul was not as sincere or as competent as he purported to be (2 Corinthians 10:10; 11:13). He will deal with them more directly later.

Paul acknowledges that it's easy for the Corinthians to be arrogant when he isn't there to rebut or to defend himself, but he assures them of his intent to visit very soon (4:18–19). If his critics demand a showdown, he will be ready. He hopes it won't come to that, but he will leave it up to them (4:20–21). Do they prefer a whip (a rod wielded by someone in a position of authority)? Or will they rather come to agreement through love with a gentle spirit?

Paul's preference would be the latter. But he isn't afraid to confront the Corinthians on issues he feels are completely out of order, as he will demonstrate in the next section.

Take It Home

When Paul taught others how God intended for them to behave in the world, he was able to urge them to imitate himself (4:16). Can you do the same? Do the people closest to you see the love and humility of Christ evident in your own words and actions? Identify someone you would like to have a stronger influence on, and then consider what you might do to change yourself in order to make a positive impression on that person.

1 CORINTHIANS 5:1–13

DEALING WITH SIN IN THE CHURCH

Setting Up the Section

To this point, Paul has addressed the problems in the Corinthian church in general terms. But here he gets quite specific. He cites a particular—and particularly offensive—problem, and then provides instructions for how to deal with it. This is the first in a series of specific issues Paul will deal with throughout his letter to the Corinthian believers.

📖 5:1–5

UNADDRESSED SEXUAL SIN

The church frequently came into conflict with the secular culture during the first century. For example, the Greek attitude toward prostitution was rather lax. To most Gentiles, it was a small matter whether someone frequented brothels or participated in an ongoing affair, even if he were married. The Greek word for "sexual immorality" (5:1 NIV), when used by the church, refers to numerous sexual sins they found immoral and inappropriate: fornication, adultery, homosexuality, and more. One of the few specific requests the early church leaders made of Gentile converts was to abstain from sexual immorality (Acts 15:20, 29).

Yet the church in Corinth had reversed the sides of the conflict over sexual propriety. One of its members was living with his father's wife (5:1). Most likely the woman was his step-mother. It is possible that his father had already died and that he and the woman were approximately the same age. But the relationship was still considered incestuous. Pagan society would have looked down on such a bond, and it was prohibited by Roman law. Yet members of the Corinthian church took pride in the tolerance they showed in allowing the relationship (5:2).

The problem in the church went unresolved, largely because the issue of leadership had not been settled. But Paul writes with authority, prescribing specific and immediate action. He doesn't have to be present, he says, because he is acting under the authority of Jesus (5:4).

Paul's concern is not simply for the offending church member. Rather, he views the problem as church-wide. He doesn't address the man, but rather scolds the church as a whole for allowing the problem. And since it hadn't taken action, he dictates what it should do: excommunicate the man for his own good and the good of the church (5:2, 5). It was a severe punishment. Yet Paul later makes a reference to a similar event (2 Corinthians 2:5–11). If he is referring to the same man, it is good news indeed that the man did repent and return to good standing in the church.

Demystifying 1 Corinthians

Paul's instructions to hand the offending church member over to Satan (5:5) can be interpreted in various ways. Most agree that this was primarily a command to expel him from church fellowship into the secular world (the realm of Satan). But the reasons vary. Some believe that by being cut off from worship, the painful isolation would create the strong desire to repent and correct his sinful behavior. Some believe that the expelled man's physical body would suffer as a result of divine chastisement, perhaps even leading to premature death like Ananias and Sapphira (Acts 5:1–11). Some believe the destruction of his sinful nature (or flesh) meant the cessation of his desires. Some propose that the man himself was the sinful nature, and that the spirit of the church would be saved as a result.

📄 5:6–13

THE LESSON OF LEAVEN

Paul had recently warned against judging other people (4:5), but his intent there was in regard to the person's relationship with God. When the issue is obvious immorality in the church, the church leaders have not only the right but also the responsibility to speak up and take appropriate action.

He compares this responsibility to the old Jewish tradition of removing all the yeast from the household during Passover. Just as a tiny amount of yeast in dough has a surprising effect, so does the toleration of just a little sin in the church. It is definitely not something to be proud about! The lingering presence of such "yeast" results in malice and wickedness, while the church without yeast is marked by sincerity and truth (5:6–8).

Critical Observation

The Israelites removed all leaven (yeast) as they prepared the annual Passover dinner. It wasn't enough to put it away; they literally threw it out so it would be far removed from the unleavened bread they were baking (Exodus 12:15; 13:6–7).

In Paul's previous letter (the one that has never been found), he had apparently dealt with a similar problem, but the church members had misinterpreted his instructions. So here, he reiterates his point and makes himself very clear. It is not right to judge those *outside* the church. The church had a ministry to those people. If outsiders choose to ignore the truth of the gospel, then God will be their judge (5:12–13).

Paul's point is to disassociate with immoral people *within* the church (5:11). Perhaps the person is a Christian in name only or a believer who reverted to the ways of his sinful past. Paul prescribes complete removal from such people to the point of not even sharing a meal (5:11). Otherwise, nonbelievers might witness the intimacy between the two and assume that the church approves of such sinful behavior.

Later, Paul will be even more specific concerning the sharing of the meal that was served in connection with the Lord's Supper (10:21; 11:17–34). But first he will return to the topic of sexual immorality as well as lawsuits among believers (chapter 6).

Take It Home

One of the most offensive insults today is to be called judgmental, and few people want that reputation. Conversely, most people like to be considered tolerant of the rights and opinions of others. Yet the refusal to pass judgment in the church at Corinth created a lot of problems both within and outside of the church. Where do you think people should draw the line between tolerance and confrontation? Do you think Christians should be more tolerant or less tolerant of other Christians in comparison to their attitudes toward nonbelievers?

1 CORINTHIANS 6:1–20

LITIGATION AND LICENTIOUSNESS

Lawsuits between Believers	6:1–8
Sexual Impropriety	6:9–20

Setting Up the Section

Paul had begun to respond to specific problems in the Corinthian church he had learned about through correspondence with the believers there. He continues to address their issues in this section, writing about two issues that continue to be problems in many churches today: lawsuits and sexual immorality.

📖 6:1–8

LAWSUITS BETWEEN BELIEVERS

The ancient Greeks loved courtroom drama. In Athens (which was not far from Corinth), the courts of law were a primary source of entertainment. The culture was so litigious that essentially every male citizen was involved with the legal system to some degree, and in the process, tended to cultivate oratorical skill as well. But then, as the citizens became believers and started attending church, they carried their tendencies for lawsuits and rhetoric with them.

Critical Observation

When there was a dispute in ancient Athens, the first attempt to settle the matter was through private arbitration. One arbitrator was chosen by each party, and the two agreed on a third arbitrator to serve as an impartial judge. If that failed to settle the problem, it went to a court known as The Forty. This court referred the matter to public arbitration by Athenian citizens. And if this group couldn't reach agreement, the case went to a jury court that consisted of 201 citizens for small matters and 401 citizens for major issues. Jurors had to be at least thirty years old. Records exist of some cases where the juries numbered in the thousands.

The Jews, on the other hand, had always avoided the public courts. They tended to settle disputes before the leaders of the community or elders in the synagogue. Justice was a matter best left to the spiritual community. So Paul is especially distressed to hear of the Corinthian believers' willingness to allow secular courts to settle their disagreements (6:1–6).

Christians have access to the wisdom of God through the Holy Spirit. They will one day rule with Christ and supposedly be qualified to judge the world (Matthew 19:28) and even angels (Jude 6). Yet the Corinthians couldn't even settle their own minor disputes.

Instead of feeling proud of their legal victories in secular courts, the Corinthian Christians should have been ashamed of extending the problems of the church into the public arena. Paul writes that the result of Christians taking other Christians to court is shame, defeat, and ineffective witness for Christ.

If Christians cannot resolve their disagreements short of secular litigation, there is something fundamentally amiss in the church of Jesus Christ. Even if the Corinthian believers couldn't settle a matter to their satisfaction within the church, for the good of the gospel they should have been willing to be wronged (6:7–8). What offense would be severe enough to sacrifice one's Christian witness to nonbelievers?

Demystifying 1 Corinthians

Paul's instructions in this section apply specifically to Christians involved in lawsuits with other Christians. In such cases, much harm can be done in the resulting misperception of Christian fellowship. But Paul's admonition does not address potential instances of due legal process a Christian might pursue with people outside the church or even with the state. Paul made extensive use of Roman courts and asserted his rights as a Roman citizen. Yet he had the same goal in mind: the spread of the gospel.

SEXUAL IMPROPRIETY

Corinth was a city with a reputation for sexual promiscuity. Prostitution was rampant, much of it connected with the large temple of Aphrodite, the Greek goddess of love. Many of the Corinthian men no doubt visited prostitutes before they became believers, and it appears that some continued to do so even afterwards. (If so, it was no wonder that they had little to say about the man living with his step-mother [5:1–5].)

Paul first lists a number of sexual sins, along with other sins including greed, drunkenness, slandering, and swindling (6:9–11). He acknowledges that numerous believers had once participated in such things, but had since been washed and sanctified. They should have been experiencing the joy and freedom of their salvation rather than desiring to revert to their previous sinful ways.

Paul appears to be responding to specific arguments, suggesting that the Corinthians had given three reasons why they thought they should be included in the anything-goes sexual attitudes of their culture. First was the social argument that everyone else was doing it. They didn't want to be left out of the citywide parties occasionally held at Aphrodite's temple and be considered antisocial. Second was the philosophical argument that sex didn't really matter, because things such as food and sex were physical matters, not spiritual ones (a philosophy known as dualism). The physical body would eventually pass away, leaving only the spirit, so what people did with their bodies was of no lasting concern. And third was a spiritual argument that God's grace was so all-encompassing that the greater a person's sin, the more abundant His grace would be.

Paul counters these arguments one by one and refutes the false thinking of the Corinthians. Everyone else may be doing the wrong things, but believers are not their own. They have been bought with a price and therefore should glorify God with their bodies (6:20). Food may be for the stomach and the stomach for food, but God will destroy them both. The body is not meant for sexual immorality, but for God. And even of all the things that are permissible, not everything is beneficial. Christians should not be mastered by anything (6:12–14).

The Spirit of God dwells in the bodies of believers (6:15–20), so even their physical (bodily) lives should honor God. Clearly, this is not done through sexual promiscuity. And the principle holds true for numerous other behaviors in addition to sex. Freedom in the Christian life is never an excuse to live however one wants. Rather, it is a holy calling to find the power to exhibit self-control in every aspect of life.

Finally, sexual purity is one of God's most precious gifts. Sexual intercourse goes beyond mere biology or physiology and encompasses the totality of one's humanity. So Paul is not being prudish in his instructions. Rather, he is attempting to lift this wonderful gift of God above the cultural standards that tend to debase and demean it.

Many people settle for a cheap imitation of what God intends for sex. In pursuit of selfish gratification, they sacrifice true freedom and miss the ultimate fulfillment of sexual fidelity within the covenant of marriage.

Paul will have much more to say about marriage (as well as singleness) in the next section.

Take It Home

Paul asks the question "Do you not know. . . ?" six times in this section of 1 Corinthians (6:2, 3, 9, 15, 16, 19). In each case, he is chiding the church in Corinth because its members were not following the clear teachings of scripture. They either weren't aware of what its members should do, or were ignoring what they knew. Can you think of anything you are doing that you either suspect or know for sure is not in line with scriptural teaching? What potential harm could come of such behavior?

1 CORINTHIANS 7:1–40

GUIDELINES FOR MARRIED AND SINGLE BELIEVERS

The Issue of Marriage	7:1–16
The Issue of Singleness	7:17–40

Setting Up the Section

Paul had just answered questions concerning sexual behavior. So it was only natural that he would follow by discussing the believers' questions on marriage. He rebuked their improper attitudes, but spent considerably more time prescribing positive behavior.

▤ 7:1–16

THE ISSUE OF MARRIAGE

Having just told his readers to flee from sexual sins (6:18), Paul turns to the option of marriage. In previous correspondence, he had received questions about the topic, which isn't surprising because Greek philosophy and cultural values were quite different from the standards God had established for His people.

In fact, the Greek culture distorted scriptural teachings on marriage at both ends of the scale. Those who practiced dualism believed that body and spirit were completely separate entities within a person. In their way of thinking, nothing done to the body had a lasting spiritual effect, so why not engage in hedonism and sexual pleasure-seeking? Another philosophy was asceticism, where the practitioner sought to purify his spirit by depriving his body of any pleasure—sexual or otherwise.

Paul had already addressed the hedonistic group (chapters 5–6), and here he turns his attention to the ascetics. Both extremes were prevalent in the church, so he tries to establish a balance. Rather than attempt to sway everyone to his personal preference of celibacy, or to go the other way and declare the proponents of celibacy to be too legalistic, Paul acknowledges the strengths and weaknesses of both alternatives.

When Paul opens with the statement that it is good for a man not to marry (7:1), he may have been quoting a popular ascetic saying because he follows immediately with the argument *for* marriage. Not only is marriage preferable to rampant immorality, it is a gift from God for some people (7:7). In explaining, Paul's words stood in stark contrast to the highly patriarchal societies of antiquity. When he suggests that neither husband nor wife should deny the other sexual intimacy, this principle of mutual submission is revolutionary. A Christian's body belongs to God (6:19–20), and also to his or her spouse. It is inappropriate to deprive one another of sexual intimacy unless it is a mutually prearranged and temporary agreement to devote themselves to spiritual disciplines (7:2–5).

Critical Observation

One might wonder how Paul knew so much about marriage. He was clearly unmarried at the time of this writing (7:8), although some people speculate he could have had a wife who died young. They base the opinion on the fact that he might have been a member of the Sanhedrin (Acts 26:10), which only accepted married men. Also, he wrote with great understanding and sensitivity for what it meant to be married, suggesting personal experience.

Paul was unmarried and found singleness both satisfying and beneficial in his ministry, yet realized that God had different plans for different people (7:7). Being single and miserable was not a desirable state (7:9).

Yet a commitment to marriage is to be lifelong. God's plan for marriage is for one man and one woman to leave their parents and be joined together in a permanent and exclusive union throughout the course of their earthly lives. Divorce, though allowed by the Mosaic Law in limited circumstances (Matthew 19:8), was never designed nor desired by God.

With the rapid growth of the church, it is not surprising that the question of divorce came up. Paul provides guidelines for when one spouse becomes a believer and the other doesn't. He says if the unbelieving spouse leaves, the believer is no longer bound to the marriage. Yet if the unbeliever is willing to continue in the marriage, the Christian is not to leave his or her spouse. The godly influence of one spouse on the other may result in the other's salvation (7:12–16).

7:17–40

THE ISSUE OF SINGLENESS

Paul provides an underlying principle for marriage and other aspects of life in 1 Corinthians 7:17. Becoming a Christian certainly changes a person's spiritual life and outlook, yet it doesn't mean the person will necessarily change in other ways. Gentiles remain Gentile. Slaves may remain slaves (but are under no obligation to do so if they can obtain their freedom). So happily single people need not rush out looking for a mate, and married believers need not pursue singleness. Instead, everyone should attempt to do whatever God directs (7:17–24).

Demystifying 1 Corinthians

The word translated "virgins" (7:25) allows numerous interpretations. Various opinions of who Paul is addressing include: (1) fathers who were responsible for their unmarried daughters; (2) unmarried couples involved in the ascetic practice of living together before marriage in a purely platonic and spiritual relationship, sharing the same bed but having no physical relations; (3) couples who went through the marriage ceremony but then decided to live as a celibate couple and devote themselves entirely to a spiritual life; and (4) young engaged women who, along with their fiancés, were being pressured by the ascetic group and wondering if they should go through with their weddings as planned.

Paul clearly preferred the single life, yet insists it is not the only option for people to be faithful to God (7:25-28). However, ministry was always foremost on Paul's mind. His reminder that there is little time (7:29) may be a reference to Jesus' return, because Corinth was prosperous at the time, and not yet facing the Christian persecution that would eventually become a problem.

It is logical that a single person is freer to serve God. Marriage is a commitment to another person, and such a commitment requires time and attention or, as Paul wrote, divided interests (7:34). People can serve God, married or single, but God is not honored by the neglect of a spouse.

So while Paul tends to lobby for people remaining single, he still extols the role of marriage (7:36-40). As long as people choose wisely and act appropriately, one choice is as good as the other.

Take It Home

There seemed to be a bias in the early church toward remaining single and serving God more intently rather than getting married. Today the bias might be the other way: Perhaps Christian couples and families are taken more seriously than singles. Have you detected a bias in either direction? Does your church provide equal opportunities for service, whether single or married?

1 CORINTHIANS 8:1-13

QUESTIONS OF CHRISTIAN FREEDOM

Setting Up the Section

Paul has been answering questions from a previous letter from Corinth. He has just responded to questions about marriage (7:1) and singleness (7:25). Now he turns to a topic that was a major problem in Corinth, yet not a concern in most modern Western cultures. Still, Paul's approach to the issue provides insight for how to deal with a number of contemporary spiritual problems.

📄 8:1-3

THE PROBLEM OF FOOD SACRIFICED TO IDOLS

Paul had been asked (via mail) to provide some guidelines for how believers should feel about and react to meat that had been sacrificed to idols (8:1). At this time in the city of Corinth, most of the meat available in the community was somehow associated with idol worship. Most of the meat in the marketplace came from sacrificial animals that had been slaughtered at pagan temple ceremonies.

The Corinthian believers no doubt had a number of questions. Did the pagan rituals somehow taint the meat? Could a Christian buy meat that had been sacrificed to an idol? Should a believer eat sacrificed meat if it was served at a friend's home? What about a believer's involvement at various social events, such as weddings and parties, that served the meat and often utilized a temple dining hall for the festivities?

Demystifying 1 Corinthians

For pagan worshipers in Corinth to incur the favor of a god or goddess, an animal would be sacrificed and divided into three portions. One small portion was burned on the altar as an act of worship. The priest received the second portion as payment for his services. The worshiper kept the rest of the meat and could do one of two things with his portion: He could either give a banquet for a number of guests in his home or at the temple, or he could sell the meat in the marketplace.

This issue had become another dividing factor within the church. The members of one group strongly felt that meat sacrificed to idols was indeed tainted and would have nothing to do with it. Nor would they attend any secular social function because they felt they would compromise their witness for Christ and their pursuit of holy living. Others felt that wherever their food came from, it was ultimately from God. They didn't consider eating meat sacrificed to idols a problem. The conflict between the two groups had become so great that Paul addresses the issue at length, from 1 Corinthians 8–10.

Before he even starts to answer, Paul warns that he isn't attempting to prove one group right and the other wrong (8:2–3). Knowledge without love is prideful. Love is the ultimate goal.

📖 8:4–6

WHEN TO EAT

Paul says that idols have no objective spiritual existence, so essentially the meat had been dedicated to nothing. The one God that Christians serve is the provider of all things (8:4–6). Although other people recognized various gods and goddesses, none of those so-called deities had anything to do with the creation, sustenance, or redemption of the world. Therefore, a Christian was free to eat meat that had been sacrificed to an idol because the idol had no spiritual power or authority.

His comments seem to validate the opinions of the okay-to-eat group. But Paul isn't finished.

📖 8:7–13

WHEN NOT TO EAT

Paul had declared that there was no ontological or theological basis for refusing to eat meat that had been sacrificed to an idol. But the fact remained that some of the Christians in Corinth could not in good conscience eat sacrificed meat in the privacy of their own homes, much less in the pagan temples of the city. Many of them had no doubt been involved with idol worship and ceremonial sacrifices, and wanted nothing to do with that past (8:7). They would have felt compelled to abstain from anything associated with such ceremonies.

Therefore, in consideration of the brothers and sisters in Christ who continued to struggle with the issue, Paul asks other believers to willingly abstain from the practice as well. Even though they had freedom in Christ, the highest calling for the believer is love. And love should constrain them to limit the exercise of their Christian freedom. Concern for one's fellow Christian takes precedence over personal freedom in Christ.

Critical Observation

It is faulty thinking to believe that freedom in Christ entitles a person to do anything he or she wants to. Any fool can do that. True freedom in Christ is having the courage and will to do what *ought* to be done. One of the most important exercises of Christian freedom is willfully abstaining from certain things in order not to cause someone else to stumble in his or her walk with the Lord.

Where does a believer draw the line and set boundaries? Paul indicates that the gray areas of the Christian life will depend on the circumstances and the people affected by one's choices (8:10–12). Personally, Paul is willing to give up eating meat altogether if that's what it takes to bring others closer to Christ (8:13).

It would have required much less thought and care to either create blanket prohibitions of certain practices or to authorize them indiscriminately. But Paul's approach is much truer to reality and to biblical revelation. Christian freedom can certainly be exercised, though believers first need to exercise prayerful thought and godly concern for fellow Christians. They might also seek out wise counsel from other mature believers in order to do God's bidding and bring glory to Him in all areas of their lives.

Take It Home

Eating meat offered to idols isn't much of an issue for most Christians today—at least in the Western world of America and Europe. But what other practices can you think of that tend to create tensions between groups of Christians? How would Paul's advice to the Corinthians apply to such contemporary issues?

1 CORINTHIANS 9:1–27

AN APOSTLE'S RIGHTS

Setting Up the Section

Paul has just encouraged the Corinthians to willingly forego their Christian rights if by doing so they could prevent more immature believers from stumbling. In this section, Paul gives a personal example of how he had sacrificed his rights for the good of others. By doing so, he also addresses some underlying resentment from a portion of the Corinthian church.

📄 9:1–14

WHAT AN APOSTLE IS DUE

Because of the way chapter divisions have been added to the original scriptures, it appears that Paul is beginning a new thought in 1 Corinthians 9. But chapters 8 through 10 are a continuation of the same theme. Paul had just expressed a willingness to never eat meat again if his choice would keep a weaker believer from stumbling (8:13). As he continues, he will list other things he has given up to minimize problems and dissension in the church.

If anyone was skeptical about Paul's right to be an apostle, it shouldn't have been the Corinthians. Paul's credentials were not only that he had seen the living Jesus on the road to Damascus, but also that he had begun the church in Corinth—sure verification of his calling (9:1–2).

Paul was a proven apostle, and apostles had rights. Although the church should have been supporting him, he never demanded it even though other churches were taking care of the expenses of their leaders—and the leaders' wives as well (9:3–6).

Demystifying 1 Corinthians

In the custom of the time, philosophers and wandering speakers had various means of support. Some charged fees, some enlisted financial backers, some would beg as they went, and others would work. Paul had been taught a trade, as had all educated young Jewish men, and had been willing to work when necessary (Acts 18:1–3). However, the Greek mentality looked down on physical labor, and many Gentiles preferred to leave manual work to their slaves while they pursued art, philosophy, sport, and leisure. This may have been true of some in the Corinthian church.

It was common sense that someone who did so much work should be recompensed in some way. Soldiers were paid for their service to the nation. Gardeners ate the fruit they planted. Shepherds drank their animals' milk. People were sure to feed the oxen that turned the mill wheels (9:7–12). A priest got a share of what was offered at the temple (9:13–14). So how much more should a church take care of its spiritual leader?

Paul's argument is strong that he should be entitled to certain rights and privileges in return for the work and service he is doing for others. Yet he refuses to demand anything because of his high regard for the gospel of Christ (9:12).

📄 9:15–27

WHAT AN APOSTLE IS WILLING TO DO WITHOUT

It might be natural to think that Paul is complaining about what he doesn't have in order to goad his readers into providing him with more support. But that is not his intent. The very point he is trying to make is that the purpose of Christian freedom is to allow believers to choose to do without personal entitlements for the sake of others. It is a matter of love, not privilege.

Paul doesn't require financial support because he is more than satisfied with the reward he has received—the privilege of preaching the gospel without charge (9:18). If he were performing his ministry only because he was getting paid, he wouldn't have found it nearly as fulfilling.

Because of Paul's willingness to minister without remuneration, it not only benefited those he preached to, but also gave him great freedom. He didn't have to justify an expense form or give regular reports to a patron. He used his Christian freedom to live for Christ as fully as possible. When around fellow Jews, he would adhere to all Jewish customs and dietary restrictions, even though he felt no spiritual obligation to do so.

When among Gentiles, he adapted to their less traditional practices and menus. When around immature believers, he would practice no spiritual freedom that might alarm them and cause them to stumble in their progress. In devotion to Jesus, Paul attempted to be "all things to all men" (9:22 NIV).

Critical Observation

The concept of becoming all things to all people in order to win them over to the kingdom of God is frequently misunderstood and misapplied. Paul never neglected or compromised his firm Christian convictions. He wasn't willing to water down his theology in an attempt to appease others. But he was always willing to set aside his Christian freedoms if by doing so he would benefit others.

Many of Paul's readers would have been aware of, if not involved in, the Olympics in Greece, as well as the nearby Isthmian Games that took place every two to three years. So if they missed the point of sacrificing to get ahead on a spiritual level, they would have understood the athletic metaphors (9:24–27). A runner intent on winning would deny himself certain things while in training. Similarly, a boxer would toughen himself up to receive the blows he was sure to receive. But if such efforts resulted in a victory, then the outcome would be worth all the training and sacrifice (9:24–27).

Paul's reference to being disqualified (9:27) is not a suggestion that salvation could be lost. He is emphatic that nothing can separate a believer from the love of God (Romans 8:29–39). But a Christian "runner" who didn't abide by the rules could lose rewards that might be his or hers.

So just as Paul had previously expressed willingness to become a vegetarian in order not to offend a group of weak Christians (8:13), he also proclaims his willingness to set aside other Christian freedoms for the glory of God. He is more than willing to deny himself certain things if the result is the ongoing progress of other believers in their spiritual journeys. He is in the race and striving to win the prize at the end. And he is doing everything in his power to encourage others to do the same.

Take It Home

Paul's willingness to become "all things to all people" (9:22 ESV) allowed him to expand his ministry effectiveness beyond his natural Jewish comfort zone into Gentile territory, and beyond that into the realm of immature believers. He was able to adapt his behaviors without sacrificing his foundational beliefs. Have you had a similar experience where you were able to minister across cultures or across other potential barriers? If so, what were your biggest challenges? What were the results?

Setting Up the Section

In this section, Paul continues to follow up on the issue of eating food sacrificed to idols. He had previously stated that since idols were nothing of substance, it didn't matter if believers ate meat that had been sacrificed to them (8:4). But he had added warnings to avoid anything that would create spiritual difficulties for immature and growing Christians, and had provided an extensive argument for voluntarily suspending the exercise of Christian freedom for the good of others. As he now continues his train of thought, he warns of the danger of temptation for those who take too much pride in their freedom.

📖 10:1–13

LESSONS FROM THE PAST

Paul had just asked his readers to forego their personal rights in cases where they could promote the gospel and win others to Jesus Christ. In this passage, he continues his argument by including examples from Israel's history.

When believers fail to exercise self-control, they expose themselves to danger. Paul points to several examples as the Israelites wandered in the wilderness of the Exodus. Paul begins by listing four privileges the people of Israel had received that could have led to subsequent blessings, yet didn't (10:1–5): They were guided by God's presence in the form of a cloud (Exodus 13:21–22); they safely escaped the Egyptians by crossing the parted Red Sea (Exodus 14:21–29); they feasted on manna and quail in the desert (Exodus 16); and they were provided with water supernaturally (Exodus 17:1–7).

With God providing such amazing feats for such a crowd of people, one might think the Israelites would have responded with gratitude and praise. But they didn't, and Paul lists four specific ways the people had proved faithless and suffered as a result (10:7–10): They repeatedly complained to Moses and God about their conditions in the desert (Exodus 17:2–3); they committed idolatry by worshiping the golden calf (Exodus 32:1–6); their grumbling turned into rebellion, which resulted in a widespread plague (Numbers 16:41–50); and they engaged in sexual immorality with women of Moab in connection with Baal worship (Numbers 25:1–9).

Paul connects the experience of the Israelites with that of the Corinthian church (10:6, 11). He is illustrating that even those who enjoy the greatest privileges of God are not immune to temptation. The experience of the Israelites should serve as a warning to the Corinthians believers, who were beginning to behave in a similar way. Like the offenses of the Israelites in the wilderness, the pagan temple feasts in Corinth involved idolatry and sexual sin, and tested God's patience.

Demystifying 1 Corinthians

The meaning of testing God (10:9) is to do something wrong to see what He will do in response. Like children who test parents with defiant behavior, believers sometimes flirt with danger or see how far they can go with rebellion before God steps in and does something about it.

It is a mistake to think that the Lord is indifferent or will look the other way when believers do wrong. It is precisely because they are His children that He will be stirred to action. He disciplines those He loves (Hebrews 12:5–6) to guide them back to the path of righteousness.

It is best to heed the mistakes of others to avoid similar failures and consequences (10:11). Everyone faces occasional temptations. No one is exempt. Believers will confront many of the same temptations that others have endured throughout human history, yet they can experience God's faithfulness during such times. Paul assures them that God will not give them more than they can handle, provided they rely on His strength and yield to the power of His indwelling Spirit (10:12–13).

📄 10:14–22

LESSONS FROM WORSHIP

This brief history lesson serves to support what Paul has been saying about eating meat sacrificed to idols. Here he clarifies that while the food itself is morally neutral, the corresponding idolatry is not to be tolerated. To illustrate, Paul uses two more analogies. He begins with the Lord's Supper—something his Gentile readers would be familiar with. The sacrament connected the participant with the risen Lord through the appropriation of the symbols of His broken body and shed blood. And Jewish believers would have understood that after Old Testament sacrifices, those who ate the sacrificial meat in the temple communed with the Lord and appropriated the temporary forgiveness that was associated with those animal sacrifices.

Similarly, pagan sacrifices were not only offered to idols, but part of the meat was given back to the worshiper to hold a feast, with the belief that the god himself would be a guest. So while a believer need not be overly concerned about the meat itself, he or she should not participate in the pagan festivals (10:18–20). The idols may have been only wood and stone, but they had real spiritual forces behind them that believers were to avoid.

So whether Jewish, Christian, or pagan, a meal in connection with a sacrifice was intended to connect the worshiper with the deity. The common loaf of Communion represents a unity in Christ, which necessitates a separation from all false religions. Someone who sits at the table of the Lord in Communion could not then participate in a table that was an instrument of demons and pagan idols (10:21–22).

SPECIFIC GUIDELINES

Paul concludes what he had been saying for the past three chapters. The overall rule is that love for others should dictate a believer's choices and behaviors (10:23–24).

Critical Observation

What may be only a matter of dietary choice for a mature believer might be a major spiritual issue for another person. So those who are mature (and supposedly living their lives for God) are asked to sacrifice for the good and salvation of other Christians.

More specifically in the area of meat sacrificed to idols, what a believer did in his or her own home was of no concern. To a Christian, it was just a piece of meat (10:25–26). If believers were invited out to dinner where the meat was served, they could eat it in good conscience (10:27). But if a fellow believer was at the dinner and was troubled by what was served, the more mature believers should refuse to eat, lest he conform and feel that he was sinning.

All areas of life—including eating and drinking—should glorify God (10:31–33). It is easy enough to make an occasional sacrifice that would keep someone else from stumbling. By doing so, who knows when someone might find salvation or spiritual growth as a result?

Take It Home

Many people go through a stage in life where they tend to test God. Did you ever go through such a period? If so, what did you learn from it? Do you think everyone needs to go through the same process, or is it possible to learn from the mistakes of others?

1 CORINTHIANS 11:2–34

GUIDELINES FOR WORSHIP

Women and Worship   11:2–16

Bad Table Manners at the Lord's Supper   11:17–34

Setting Up the Section

After a comprehensive response to the Corinthians' question about eating meat sacrificed to idols (chapters 8–10), Paul moves on to another topic in this section. For the next several chapters he will address various issues of church propriety. In this passage, he addresses gender issues and provides clear instructions for the observance of the Lord's Supper.

11:2–16

WOMEN AND WORSHIP

During Paul's day, it was customary for a woman to wear a veil, similar to a scarf, which covered the head and hung down over her neck. No respectable woman would think of appearing in public without it. Recent immigrations of Arabic people have exposed more Westerners to such dress, and many tend to identify the dress as a religious requirement. However, Paul was writing seven hundred years before Islam came into being. Wearing a veil was widespread among women throughout the ancient Near East as a sign of honor, dignity, security, and respect.

The first-century attitude toward women was that they were inferior and subordinate to men. Jewish women could attend synagogue worship, but they were segregated from the men, in a separate part of the building. Greek women were not allowed to attend school and get an education.

So as women became believers and joined the church, they were viewed with a degree of discrimination and narrow-mindedness. While the question of whether or not a woman should have her head covered or have a particular hairstyle may not seem important to most today, it was a very sensitive matter for the early church. Would the church also impose discrimination and second-class status onto its female members? Would women have all the same rights as men—including dress and hairstyles? Or would some middle ground need to be reached?

Demystifying 1 Corinthians

Bible scholars disagree about the exact problem Paul is addressing. A number of the words in the passage can be translated a variety of ways, and some of the language is metaphorical and symbolic in nature. The apparent meaning of the text has to do with the wearing of a veil, or head covering. Some think Paul is describing the practice of certain women to wear their hair cropped very short in contrast with the custom of the day. Others feel his reference is to women who wore their hair long and flowing in public, which was typical of prostitutes.

Paul first praises the Christians in Corinth for their faithfulness in responding to his teaching about freedom in Christ, but then explains that some of them had carried things too far (11:2). Although God may see males and females as equals and joint heirs of His kingdom, that doesn't mean that all the differences between the sexes have disappeared.

Freedom in Christ is no reason for either gender to abandon appropriate behavior and clothing to send the wrong signals about sexuality. Paul says believers should be careful how they present themselves to a watching world (11:3-6). They should err on the side of modesty.

Among the teachings of Gnosticism, a problematic philosophy that was beginning to influence the first-century churches, was the belief that spiritual purity would transcend one's gender. The Gnostics viewed an androgynous human as a pristine ideal. But Christianity has always recognized that God created men and women as sexual beings with sexual differences. Paul writes that it is unwise to attempt to blur the distinctions. He encourages the Corinthians instead to celebrate the differences between male and female (11:7-10). Modern studies verify specific differences between the genders, physiological and otherwise, so why not find great satisfaction in one's God-created design?

Paul is not, as some accuse him, trying to "put women in their place." Just the opposite. He had already acknowledged the right of women to pray and prophesy in the church (11:5), and he continues by clarifying that men and women cannot operate independently of one another (11:11-12). For a male writing in the first century, Paul's teachings were progressive and radical. He was one of the first advocates for the legitimate role of women in church leadership, but he also wanted to ensure that both women and men were submissive to God and acted appropriately (11:13-16).

📄 11:17-34

BAD TABLE MANNERS AT THE LORD'S SUPPER

Paul usually tries to acknowledge what a church is doing right before correcting its members or challenging them to do better. But when it came to the Corinthians' behavior during celebrations of the Lord's Supper, Paul could find nothing good to say (11:17).

The early church met weekly at a potluck-supper-type meal called the Agape Feast that would culminate with the celebration of Communion. But at Corinth, the wealthy people (who didn't have to work until sunset as did the poorer manual laborers) would go early and eat their fill, leaving little, if anything, for those who needed the food most. Some would drink their fill to the point of drunkenness (11:18-22). The very meal that was supposed to bring people closer to one another and to God had become an embarrassment and yet another source of division within the Corinthian church. And the people's self-centered behavior had not gone unnoticed; God was passing judgment (11:30).

Critical Observation

Since Paul's letter to the Corinthians was written before the Gospels, this passage contains the first recorded words of Jesus. Paul's instructions to the Corinthians about the appropriate procedure for celebrating the Lord's Supper (11:23–26) have become known as the Words of Institution and are used in some form in most Christian churches around the world.

Paul reminds the Corinthians of the proper procedure and purpose of the Lord's Supper (11:23–26). He also instructs the believers to examine themselves before participating (11:28). They should not see the meal without seeing the body and blood of Jesus. And he tells them to consider the others involved (11:27–34).

Jesus died to bring people closer to God. A believer's spiritual rebirth places him or her in the spiritual family of the church with an ongoing calling to be mindful of other believers. And there is no time a Christian should be more aware of this fact than during the solemn reminder of the Lord's Supper.

Take It Home

Paul's instructions for the Corinthians to examine themselves (11:28) apply to the modern church as well. It is easy to get into habits or traditions that require little thought about the things that should be most important in one's life. Think about your own attention to the celebration of the Lord's Supper, and your attitude toward gender differences in the church as well. Can you think of anything you might do to renew your spiritual commitment or heighten your experience in either of these areas?

1 CORINTHIANS 12:1–31

UNDERSTANDING SPIRITUAL GIFTS

Setting Up the Section

In this section of Paul's Epistle, he continues to respond to a number of problems that have been creating divisions in the church at Corinth. In the previous section, he addressed some women who were disrupting worship services with the way they prayed and prophesied. He also dealt with the terrible things the Corinthian church members were doing to demean the Lord's Supper. Now he turns his attention to the topic of spiritual gifts—yet another part of church life meant to bring people closer together, but was having the opposite result.

📖 12:1–11

AN EXPLANATION OF THE GIFTS OF THE SPIRIT

Continuing his critique of the worship problems in the Corinthian church, Paul moves on to the practice of spiritual gifts. The Greek word translated "gifts" is *charismata*, the source of our word *charismatic*. The word could also be interpreted as "gifts of grace." Paul says that the church was to be a charismatic, Spirit-gifted community.

Many of the Corinthians had come from pagan backgrounds and had worshiped idols. But the idols were mute, and provided them with no help or direction. The Holy Spirit of God, in contrast, would provide them with knowledge and spiritual substance (12:1–3).

This group of spiritual gifts that Paul lists (12:8–11, 28–30) is not exhaustive. He provides lists in other places as well (Romans 12:6–8; Ephesians 4:11–13).

Critical Observation

Spiritual gifts are not the same as natural abilities. Spiritual gifts are special abilities given by God after a person has become a Christian. The Spirit of God infuses natural skill with a new spiritual dynamic to empower the person to be productive in the work of Christ. As each believer identifies and begins to use his or her spiritual gifts, the church grows stronger.

Scholars have identified ninety-six different New Testament images to describe the church, including the household of God, the people of God, the bride of Christ, and the fellowship of the Holy Spirit. But the symbol that dominates the New Testament is the perception of the church as the body of Christ.

📄 12:12–20

UNITY AND DIVERSITY IN THE CHURCH

Paul emphasizes the importance of unity in the body of Christ. The church, though comprised of many members, is intended to be a single unit (12:12–13), an organic whole regardless of racial or religious backgrounds (Jews or Greeks) or social standing (slave or free).

Unity, however, is not the same as uniformity. Paul is not writing about an institutional unity. Various groups within Christianity, and even within denominations, will have different opinions and emphases that should be respected as long as all agree on the great orthodox spiritual truths that all Christians share.

Then Paul moves on to the obvious fact that there exists diversity in the body of Christ—as there *should* be. Yes, the human body is a single unit, but is comprised of a great many diverse parts. Paul's logic is compelling. No physical body can function as all seeing, all hearing, or all smelling (12:14–20). So why should the church expect to function with a focus on only one spiritual gift?

Still, many believers (whether first century or twenty-first century) tend to separate themselves from others whose gifts appear too different. They understand their own gifts and trust those with similar gifts, which is a natural response. But the work of the Holy Spirit is supernatural. People are not all the same, their gifts will differ according to God's will, and believers should learn to accept one another. They are called to celebrate their diversity within the unity of the church, which provides a place of belonging for a wide range of followers of Jesus Christ.

📄 12:21–31

INTERDEPENDENCY IN THE CHURCH

The various members of the body of Christ are not just to learn to tolerate one another. Like the parts of the human body, there is a principle of mutual interdependence that is critical to proper operation. While some parts of the body function differently from others, there is nevertheless mutuality to common life together. The effectiveness, health, and vitality of the church are dependent on how well its various members function together as a whole (12:21–26).

No individual has the right to say to another, "I don't need you." And whether or not church members realize it, each person is indispensable for collective effectiveness in the world. Indeed, unity and interdependence create a richness and texture for the collective witness of the church.

Demystifying 1 Corinthians

Paul points out a concern that is still a problem for many churches today: The Corinthians' perception of spiritual gifts wasn't accurate. Some of the gifts that *seemed* less important were actually indispensable. Others that appeared quite special were not any more special than the others (12:22–23). Therefore, it is important to trust God in the dispersal of gifts and to put one's gift(s) to use without questioning or comparing.

Not everyone can preach. Not everyone can sing. Not everyone can teach. But everyone is gifted to do *something* (12:29–30). Apparently, the problem in Corinth was a rivalry between spiritual gifts and a jealousy that caused some people to covet the gifts of others. There was no unity, no positive diversity, and certainly no interdependence.

Paul will get to the root of the problem in his next section. But he provides a clue about where he is headed as he concludes this section by telling believers to "eagerly desire the greater gifts" (12:31 NIV).

Take It Home

Rather than focus on your own spiritual gift(s) as you contemplate this section of Paul's writing, think of other believers you know and try to identify *their* gifts. Be sure to differentiate between natural abilities and spiritual gifts. Then, when you get the opportunity, contact those people and thank them for the specific contributions they make to the body of Christ.

1 CORINTHIANS 13:1–13

THE DIFFERENCE LOVE MAKES

Setting Up the Section

Paul has just finished a rather harsh scolding of the Corinthians—first for their self-centered and unacceptable behavior during the Lord's Supper (11:17–22) and then for the arguments they were having over spiritual gifts (chapter 12). Throughout his Epistle, Paul has tried to emphasize the importance of love in dealing with the various problems of the church. In this passage, he offers a definition of love, and his words have become a cherished portion of scripture as well as a classic piece of literature.

📖 13:1–3

THE NECESSITY OF LOVE

The widespread popularity of 1 Corinthians 13 is understandable, considering the magnificent depiction of love that Paul provides. Yet Paul never intended it to be a stand-alone chapter. In the context of what he had been writing, the importance of love was provided as a solution for the various problems that had been dividing the church. He intended this passage to help the Corinthian believers understand the destructive ways in which they had been using their spiritual gifts, especially in regard to worship.

It seems that many people were prideful of their gifts and thought they were better than others because of what God had enabled them to do in the church. Paul counters this notion and points them to a more desirable way (12:31).

The first point Paul makes is that love is absolutely necessary if the church is to function as God intends. People can use their Spirit-given gifts and generate some big actions in the church. They can speak in angelic tongues, understand deep mysteries, give all their possessions to the poor, and sacrifice their very bodies. But actions performed without love don't count for anything (13:1–3).

Love is to be the centerpiece of a Christian's life. Evidently, the Corinthians had been arguing about who was performing the greatest works. Instead, they should have been considering who was showing the greatest love.

📖 13:4–7

THE CHARACTER OF LOVE

The word *love* is tossed around in literature, music, advertising, and visual arts. Surely it was much the same in ancient Corinth, especially with the rampant sexual promiscuity in the culture. Even believers are frequently misled into thinking that love is primarily an emotion—something a person falls into and out of. So Paul provides a description that has nothing to do with hearts and flowers.

True Christian love is not a warm and sentimental feeling. It has little to do with emotion at all. By Paul's definition, it is action in response to the conviction of one's heart and mind. With a series of fifteen succinct descriptive phrases, he explains why this degree of love is necessary for a believer in Jesus Christ (13:4–8). The terms he uses are not romantic sentiments, but rather commitments requiring active choices. This kind of love should be the goal of anyone who desires to live out the majestic and holy calling believers have in Christ.

📖 13:8–13

THE PERMANENCE OF LOVE

Most likely, the arguments about spiritual gifts and divisions in the Corinthian church were centered on those that were most apparent: speaking in tongues, prophecy, healing, and so forth. It would have been quite clear who had those gifts in contrast to the gifts of faith, helping others, administration, etc.

So Paul concludes by clarifying that just because a spiritual gift is clearly from God and being used for the good of the church doesn't mean it is permanent. The time will come when those gifts are no longer needed. Prophecies will cease. Tongues will be stilled. Knowledge will pass away. Only three will always remain: faith, hope, and love. And love is the greatest of the three (13:13).

Many of the gifts of the Spirit are a temporal provision by God in order to equip people for the works of service to which He calls them. Yet those provisions for an imperfect world will one day be rendered unnecessary when the perfection of heaven comes (13:10).

No matter how hard believers try to relate to God, they cannot do so perfectly. Paul compares the process to childhood, when thoughts and reason are far from mature. But one day Christians will leave behind their childish ways and achieve full spiritual maturity.

Paul also compares a believer's image of God to what he or she might see in a mirror of the time. The reflection is helpful, but far from satisfying. It only makes the person wish for a clearer view.

Demystifying 1 Corinthians

The city of Corinth was known for its production of mirrors. But the modern mirror that we are familiar with didn't emerge until the thirteenth century. Mirrors in Corinth were made by polishing bronze until it was completely smooth and reflective. Even so, the bronze mirrors provided an imperfect reflection.

Paul's final promise is that someday believers will see God face-to-face. They will have answers for the things they don't understand. Imperfections will be left behind as they experience God's perfect light.

But in the meantime, they can try to comprehend God's love and apply it to those around them. Now is the time for them to develop faith, hope, and love, because those three gifts will always be around.

Take It Home

Two thousand years after Paul's writing, the church continues to struggle with the human limitations of love. In an attempt to come closer to true self-sacrificial love, review Paul's description in 1 Corinthians 13:4–7. Does that sound like a description of you or anyone you know? If not, identify one specific aspect of love where you could use some improvement. Then focus on that one aspect for a while, asking God for help in becoming a more loving and effective believer.

1 CORINTHIANS 14:1–40

THE PROPER USE OF SPIRITUAL GIFTS

Setting Up the Section

In 1 Corinthians 12, Paul listed a number of spiritual gifts and challenged the believers to use them for the benefit of the church as a whole. He followed in 1 Corinthians 13 with the importance of love in connection with the exercise of gifts. In this section, he returns to a discussion of spiritual gifts and provides some specific guidelines for how they should be properly exercised in a church context.

📄 14:1–12

DIFFERENT GIFTS, DIFFERENT PURPOSES

Paul is about to make some direct and perhaps confrontational comments, so he begins by making himself clear that people should be eager to receive the gifts of the Holy Spirit. And he reiterates what he had just written about the importance of love in connection with spiritual gifts (14:1).

Apparently the believers at Corinth had become enamored with the gift of speaking in tongues. Paul assures them that the gift has its place, yet needs to be used with love and discretion. He contrasts the gift of tongues with the gift of prophecy (14:2–5). The role of the New Testament prophet was to discern God's message to the church through the Holy Spirit. Unlike the modern church, the early believers had no Bibles for reference; even Old Testament scrolls were costly and difficult to secure. So the role of the prophet was very important.

Critical Observation

Believers are divided as to what "tongues" really means. Some believe the gift to the church in Corinth was no different than that to the church in Jerusalem on the Day of Pentecost (Acts 2:1–13): existing languages that could be understood if someone knowledgeable of that language were present. Throughout Corinthians, Paul uses the words *tongues* and *languages* interchangeably. Others believe the tongues in the Corinthian church were divine ecstatic utterances with no earthly equivalent. But either way, Paul's advice was valid. Without an interpreter, the church as a whole benefited little from proclamations that could not be understood.

Although the Corinthians were extolling speaking in tongues, Paul tells them to especially desire the gift of prophecy (14:1). Even though both tongues and prophecy require special revelation from God, there are significant differences. Foremost among them was the fact that everyone in attendance could understand what God was saying through the prophet. But the person speaking in tongues didn't know what he or she was saying, nor did the church. An interpreter was needed, but none was present. The person speaking in tongues would feel edified, but only in a mysterious spiritual way. No one else was benefiting.

Paul provides some practical examples to make his point (14:6–12). First, he asks the Corinthians to suppose he had come to them speaking only in tongues they could not understand. Clearly, they had needed clear knowledge and instruction, as did the newer believers currently in their midst. He uses music as a second example. The cacophony of an orchestra warming up doesn't warrant anyone's attention. But when the notes are arranged to provide a symphony, it means something to the listeners. Third, Paul refers to a military trumpet giving signals to the soldiers. If it is unclear whether the signal is to advance or retreat, how could the army function?

The church needs clear signals. Those with the gift of prophecy, who provide vital information, should not be disparaged. Using the gift of speaking in tongues without having an interpreter is not much different than having a foreign-speaking visitor give the sermon with no translator (14:10–11).

📄 14:13–25

SPEAKING IN TONGUES APPROPRIATELY

Paul never tells the Corinthians *not* to speak in tongues. In fact, he expresses thanks that he had the gift himself (14:18). But he is firm in clarifying the right way to use the gift. He insists that gifts that benefit the church should always be given preference over those that only edify the individual. The people who took undue pride in the gift of tongues thought they were the mature segment of the church, but Paul says they are thinking like children (14:20).

Demystifying 1 Corinthians

In verse 22, Paul comments that tongues are significant for unbelievers. This is in reference to his previous quotation from Isaiah (1 Corinthians 14:21). When God's people stopped believing in Him, they were taken into captivity where they heard strange tongues that symbolized God's rejection. Paul goes on to explain that church attendees who heard people speaking in tongues without explanation would have no idea what was going on (14:23).

People who spoke God's Word in an understandable language would benefit both the believers and unbelievers in the assembly. People would hear and respond, and the church would grow. *That* was the mature outlook.

ORDER IN THE CHURCH

As he starts to conclude this section, Paul writes that all spiritual gifts should be used in an orderly, helpful, productive manner. If speaking in tongues, the public expression should be limited to two or three people, with interpretations for each one. Otherwise, the person(s) should worship silently and privately (14:2–28).

If prophesying, again, the number should be limited to two or three. And the speakers shouldn't compete. They were to take turns so those assembled could hear each one to receive instruction and encouragement. Otherwise, it would appear that believers serve a God of disorder (14:29–33).

Paul's shift to address women at this point (14:34–35) is the cause of much debate, but he doesn't seem to indicate that *all* women should be silent at *all* church functions. He had previously validated their participation in prayer and prophesying (11:5, 13). Most likely his comments were intended to reduce potential confusion in the worship services. It might be that some of the women were asking questions or initiating debates over what was said.

One opinion is that Paul is speaking primarily to women married to believers, asking them to allow their husbands to speak for both of them. Others think he is simply asking the women to keep quiet just as (by limiting the number to three) he was asking some of those who would otherwise speak in tongues or prophesy to keep quiet. His mention of the law (14:34) might have been a reference to Genesis 3:16.

Paul reiterates the right and the privilege of putting all of the gifts of the Spirit into practice (14:39–40)—as long as they are carried out properly. He isn't just expressing his opinion, but using *his* gift to let the Corinthians know how God felt about their worship (14:36–38). And with that, he concludes his writing on spiritual gifts. He had other essential matters to cover before ending his letter.

Take It Home

Do other people do things during worship that make it difficult for you to keep your focus on God? Can you think of anything you do that might inhibit another's worship? How would you feel if those in authority asked you to submit and keep quiet for the good of the church as a whole?

1 CORINTHIANS 15:1–58
RESURRECTION AND EXPECTATION

Setting Up the Section

In the previous section, Paul concluded a rather extensive passage examining spiritual gifts and their proper place in worship. He had addressed the Corinthians' past behavior and provided instructions for the current state of the church. In this passage, he turns their attention to the future as he writes of what they can expect at resurrection and beyond.

On the basis of a "dualistic" worldview that viewed the physical world as evil and only the spirit world as good, some of the Corinthian believers were evidently claiming that there would be no resurrection of the body. Paul responds by affirming both the certainty of Christ's bodily resurrection and the centrality of the resurrection for the Christian faith. He also discusses the nature of our glorified bodies.

📖 15:1–11

A MATTER OF FIRST IMPORTANCE

Paul had been dealing with problems and issues that had recently come up in the church at Corinth. So he uses the opportunity to remind the believers of a few things he had already taught them—things that should have been having an effect on their behavior.

He assures them that they had indeed received the gospel (15:1). Salvation is a gift from God. No one ever discovers it on one's own or accomplishes it by clever insight, imaginative thinking, or hard work. In addition, the gospel is the foundation on which they stood. They based the weight of their lives, hopes, and dreams of heaven on what Paul had originally preached to them. By his own estimation, the most important message is that Jesus had died for the sins of humankind, was buried, raised from the dead, and had made numerous undeniable appearances (15:3–8).

Critical Observation

Although the word *gospel* (generally translated as "good news") has come to be closely associated with Christianity, its roots go further back into pagan and Jewish culture. The Romans used the word to mean "joyful tidings." But Paul and other early Christian writers adopted *gospel* to refer to the coming of Christ for the salvation of the world. The "good news" is that Jesus had been resurrected after His death on the cross, providing eternal life for those who believe in Him.

After His resurrection, Jesus had appeared to Peter, the eleven remaining apostles (still referred to as the Twelve), James, a group of more than five hundred, and others. Peter had denied Jesus. James had doubted Him. And Paul was the worst of them all (15:9).

Still, Paul spoke with authority about the effect of the gospel on a person. Although Jesus had already ascended, He showed Himself to Paul on the road to Damascus, and Paul received the grace of God to turn his life completely around and discover his calling (15:9–11). Paul considered himself the least among the apostles, so he could attest to the Corinthians that holding firmly to faith in Christ and His resurrection was their only hope in this life and the life to come.

📄 **15:12–34**

THE POWER OF RESURRECTION

The debate about whether or not the dead would be resurrected had been going on for a long time. It was a major point of contention between the Pharisees (who said yes) and the Sadducees (who said no). The issue of Jesus' resurrection made the topic that much more relevant (15:12).

Paul says there are only two options: Either Jesus was resurrected, or He wasn't. If Christ had *not* been resurrected, then nobody else would be either. And that would also mean that Christianity was a lie and all preaching was in vain. Sin would still reign. People would have no hope. And to attempt to live a victorious life on earth with no anticipation of eternal life was simply pitiable (15:13–19).

But Paul makes it clear that the other option is the truth. Jesus has indeed been raised from the dead. Adam's sin has separated all humankind from God, but Jesus' sacrifice has redeemed them all and restored an intimate relationship. Jesus has been resurrected, and all believers will follow Him into eternal life after their deaths (15:22–23). The resurrection of Jesus is God's ultimate victory over sin and death (15:24–28).

No one could question Paul's commitment to his belief in Jesus' resurrection. He proved it by facing danger every day (15:31). The beasts he fought in Ephesus (15:32) were probably the people in an angry mob out to find him (Acts 19:28–31). His point is that it would be foolhardy to keep putting his life on the line for a faith that ended at his death. If that were the case, the live-for-today philosophies would make more sense. But the reality of resurrection makes a difference in how believers should live. The Corinthians had no excuse to be indifferent to God (15:32–34).

Demystifying 1 Corinthians

Paul doesn't clarify what he means by his reference to those "baptized for the dead" (15:29), and there have been around two hundred various theories to explain what he was referring to. Just north of Corinth in Eleusis, members of a pagan religion practiced baptism in the sea that was connected with expectations of afterlife bliss. Perhaps Paul was making mention of this mysterious practice. Maybe he meant that the baptism of new believers filled the spots left by the deaths of older believers. Or possibly living believers wanted to be baptized as surrogates for believers who never had the privilege before they died.

PERFECT, IMPERISHABLE BODIES

The attempt to comprehend biblical truths like the resurrection can be overwhelming, and people can begin to pose all sorts of questions (15:35). But just as amazing, Paul points out, is how plants grow from seeds. A shriveled, dead-looking seed can be placed in the ground to produce not the same plant it once was, but the same *kind* of plant with far more fruit than was buried (15:36–38).

In addition, there are all kinds of "bodies"—human, animal, heavenly, etc. The resurrection body will differ from the earthly body in that it will be glorious, imperishable, and spiritual (15:39–44).

Human beings first bear the likeness of Adam in a natural body that eventually returns to the dust of the earth. But after death, believers can look forward to receiving an eternal body with form and structure that bears the likeness of Christ (15:45–49).

Finally, Paul tells his readers why they shouldn't fear death. For believers, it is only a passageway to immortality and eternal life with God. Jesus has removed the sting of sin and the power of death. Victory over death is assured (15:57). Whether dead or alive when Jesus returns, believers' bodies will be changed.

So rather than sit around and speculate about matters that God has already taken care of, Christians should stand firm and get to work (15:58). The assurances of God should not lull them into self-satisfaction, but motivate them to greater love and service.

Take It Home

Today's believers have had two thousand years of history and theology to help them deal with the concept of death and resurrection, and still we have questions. But put yourself in the place of a believer in the first century, when the topic was still very new. What questions would you have had? How would you have felt after hearing Paul's words in this passage?

1 CORINTHIANS 16:1–24

GIVING AND GREETING

Setting Up the Section

Paul is wrapping up his lengthy letter to the Corinthians. Before ending, he has one more matter of business to address, and he wants to convey a number of personal greetings and make a few final requests.

📄 **16:1–4**

THE GIFT FOR FELLOW BELIEVERS

Before signing off his letter to the Corinthians, Paul wants to answer one final question. Someone had asked about the collection he was taking for the church in Jerusalem. There is no additional information to be found about what he had told the Galatian churches (16:1).

The first day of the week was not yet called the Lord's day, even though Christians had already begun to assemble on that day in memory of the resurrection of Jesus. And it was never called the Sabbath, which was Saturday, the day the Jews met for group worship. Paul tells the Corinthians to regularly bring their financial gifts on the first day of the week. He doesn't want to have to take up a special collection when he gets there; he prefers that the believers make giving to others an ongoing commitment and have their gift ready when he arrives.

Demystifying 1 Corinthians

Tithing is never mentioned in the New Testament. It had been a method of giving prescribed for the Israelites under the Mosaic Law as well as a method of taxation in certain circumstances. Some feel Christians should still tithe because Abraham's tithe to Melchizedek (Genesis 14:18–20) predated the law. Others feel New Testament giving should be less dictated and more heartfelt, based on this passage and 2 Corinthians 8–9.

The church in Jerusalem had been suffering from both persecution and famine. The churches in Greece and Galatia owed their existence to the people God had called out of Jerusalem to go out and minister. So it should have been a natural response for them to help out their sister church financially.

When Paul wrote, he wasn't sure if he would personally take the collection back to Jerusalem (16:4). As it turned out, he did (Acts 21:17; 24:17).

🔖 16:5–24

SOME FINAL PERSONAL MATTERS

Paul closes by sharing some of his plans with the Corinthian believers. His phrasing shows that although he was making plans, his ultimate itinerary depended on God. He demonstrates that a believer can use God-given wisdom to keep moving ahead rather than waiting for detailed knowledge of God's will before even getting started.

Paul also acknowledges his fellow ministers, as he usually does in his letters. He is thankful for Timothy (16:10); Apollos (16:12); Stephanas, Fortunatus, and Achaicus (16:15–18); and Aquila and Priscilla (16:19). Divided loyalties between church leaders was one of the problems at Corinth (1:11–12), but Paul always gave credit to *everyone* whom he saw at work for God—whether they were ministering alongside him or elsewhere.

Critical Observation

Although Paul had written a lot of things to correct unwarranted behavior among the Corinthians, he closes with an emphasis on unity and love.

Paul wants to spend a considerable amount of time in Corinth (16:6–7), which is not surprising considering the number and the severity of the issues that demanded his attention. This letter must have been helpful to the Corinthian church, yet its problems would continue. Paul's next Epistle (2 Corinthians) will provide further details of the issues that threatened the unity of the believers in Corinth. Among them would be the resistance to Paul's authority by several of those in the church. Paul will ably defend himself, yet his love and concern for those in Corinth will never waver.

Take It Home

The money Paul was collecting was from primarily Gentile churches to benefit a church with mostly Jewish believers. It was more than a financial gift; it was a symbol of interconnection between two groups who were quite different. Does your church (or your personal) giving ever accomplish a similar goal of reaching out to those beyond your immediate community, based solely on your unity in Jesus?

2 CORINTHIANS

INTRODUCTION TO
2 CORINTHIANS

This epistle from Paul to the Corinthian church is a follow-up letter to 1 Corinthians. The topics he discusses are similar, particularly the concern with the false teachers who continued to plague them. Though Paul addresses both general principles and issues specific to the Corinthian community, there is much here for the church today.

AUTHOR

Paul not only identifies himself as the author of 2 Corinthians (1:1; 10:1) but also provides more autobiographical information than in any of his other letters.

OCCASION

After establishing a church at Corinth (Acts 18:1–11), Paul continued to correspond with the believers there. Some of the correspondence between them has never been discovered (1 Corinthians 5:9; 7:1; 2 Corinthians 2:4; 7:8). In 1 Corinthians, Paul had addressed specific issues that had been raised in previous communications. He firmly advised the church how to handle its problems.

Some time later, while Paul was ministering in Ephesus, he took a trip to Corinth to correct some of the problems that his first letter had not resolved. This was an unsuccessful mission, and Paul was hurt and embarrassed by his reception at Corinth (2:1; 12:14, 21; 13:1–2). In response, he returned to Ephesus and wrote a severe and sorrowful letter (now lost, but referred to in 2:4; 7:8) to the Corinthians, calling them to repent of their disobedience. He sent this letter to Corinth with Titus (7:8–13).

Paul then traveled north from Ephesus to Troas (in modern northwest Turkey), expecting to meet up with Titus and to learn about the response of the Corinthian church. But Titus was not there, so Paul moved on to Macedonia in northern Greece (Acts 20:1; 2 Corinthians 7:5). There he finally met up with Titus who brought the good news that many in the Corinthian church had repented and were greatly appreciative of his ministry. Paul sat down and wrote 2 Corinthians to express his great joy and to encourage the believers further in their faith.

PURPOSE

Although many Corinthian believers had acknowledged and respected the apostolic authority of Paul, there were others who hadn't. A number of self-designated church leaders had appeared in Corinth and set out to undermine Paul. They accused him of being bold in his letters but weak in person. They said that since he didn't charge the

Corinthian church for his service to them, his ministry must essentially be worthless. And as they continued attempts to erode Paul's integrity, they began to attract followers from among the Corinthian Christians. Therefore, throughout this Epistle, Paul tends to defend his ministry more than usual. He remains highly supportive and encouraging toward the Corinthian believers, yet targets the troublemakers and rebuts their accusations.

In addition to responding to these criticisms about his apostolic credentials, he needed to ask them to forgive someone who was seeking to restore fellowship with them (2:5–11), and to prompt them to prepare their offering for the church in Jerusalem (chapters 8–9).

THEMES

Paul's appeal to the Corinthians reveals his vulnerability. Even during times of dire distress and deep disappointment, Paul demonstrates the value of trust in "the Father of mercies" and "the God of all comfort" (1:3 NASB).

His writing also reflects ongoing encouragement. Throughout this letter, when Paul had every reason to be offended, he instead focuses on the encouragement and comfort he received not only from God, but from the Corinthians as well.

And as Paul provides a reluctant, but necessary, defense of his ministry, he writes of authenticity. His work for God is based on genuine love for others and commitment to his calling, as contrasted to the self-serving and manipulative tactics of the false apostles in Corinth.

HISTORICAL CONTEXT

Corinth was a much-traveled city and heavily influenced by Greek culture, including its idolatry and sexual promiscuity. Not surprisingly, the church had to deal with members affected by such temptations. Additionally, enough time had passed since the death of Jesus and introduction of the gospel for false teachers to begin to infiltrate the churches. This problem was particularly evident in the Corinthian church.

CONTRIBUTION TO THE BIBLE

Second Corinthians is a valuable book because it reveals not only the trials and tribulations, but also the joy and fulfillment that come from Christian ministry. Paul's directness, his "tough love," his encouragement, and his compassion, had initiated the repentance of many of the believers at Corinth.

In defending his ministry, we see Paul at his most human. In many of his writings, Paul's tremendous zeal and devotion seem almost unreal and unattainable for most people. Yet all believers can identify with the personal sufferings and frustrations Paul expresses in this letter.

Paul's Corinthian Contacts and Correspondence	
First Visit	ca. AD 51; Paul establishes the church; stays 18 months
First Letter	A short letter to respond to immorality in the church (1 Corinthians 5:9)
Second Letter	**1 Corinthians** written from Ephesus: *Dealing with problems and questions in the church*
Second Visit	ca. AD 56–57; Journey from Ephesus; painful visit.
Third Letter	A severe and sorrowful letter (2 Corinthians 2:4; 7:8)
Fourth Letter	**2 Corinthians** written from Macedonia: *Restoration for some; rebuke for others*
Third Visit	ca. AD 57–58; Paul comes and stays 3 months in Corinth; writes **Romans**.

2 CORINTHIANS 1:1–2:11

SETTING THE RECORD STRAIGHT

Setting Up the Section

Paul writes this letter with mixed emotions. Although he knows of some problems in the church at Corinth, he also feels a sense of great relief. He had been hoping to receive word from the Corinthians in response to his previous letter (2:4; 7:8), but was unable to locate the messenger, Titus, for a while (2:13). Later, in Macedonia, Titus catches up to Paul and tells him of the Corinthians' repentance and love for Paul (7:5–7). So even though Paul writes of trials and suffering, he does so out of a heart filled with joy.

📖 1:1–11

GREETINGS AND COMFORT

The fact that Paul opens this letter by identifying himself as Christ's apostle by the will of God (1:1) is significant. In later sections he will address the fact that a segment of those in Corinth were challenging his integrity and his call to be an apostle.

Paul may have been away from the Corinthians and uncertain about their response to his previous letter(s), but at least he had Timothy with him (1:1). Timothy was a regular comfort to Paul in his travels. Even though Timothy was quite young when Paul recruited him, Paul considered the young minister a brother.

Paul could experience great comfort because of his understanding of God. All three titles he uses for God (1:3) are not only assurances for Paul, but for all believers as well. Paul will have much to say about suffering in this letter, but he begins with the outcome of his sufferings: comfort. He makes it clear that believers will sometimes share in the sufferings of Jesus, but they will also share in the comfort that only God can provide (1:3–7).

Paul's sufferings are no small matter. He had encountered situations that were literally life-threatening (1:9). As a result, the grace and subsequent comfort of God were very real and dear to him. And because of his personal experience, he could make a very persuasive argument to the Corinthians (1:5–7).

Critical Observation

One example of Paul's sufferings is found in Acts 14:8–20, where Paul is stoned by an angry crowd and left for dead. During the experience, he likely didn't expect God to spare him. He was prepared to face death, which eventually became an ongoing attitude for him (Philippians 1:21–24).

The peril of which Paul refers to (1:10) is unclear. He had previously written of fighting wild beasts in Ephesus (1 Corinthians 15:32), which is usually considered to be a reference to the events of Acts 19:23–41. But nothing had actually happened to Paul during that fracas, so this may be reference to a different experience.

Paul notes that his own weaknesses and limitations only cause God's power to be more apparent (1:10–11). This is a point he will emphasize throughout this letter.

📖 1:12–2:4

A CHANGE OF PLANS

Paul's boasting (1:12–14) had a present dimension; he could declare a clear conscience regarding his conduct among believers and nonbelievers. But it also had a future dimension that looked ahead to the day of the Lord Jesus—the Day of Judgment when Christ would return to establish His kingdom. When that time came, Paul could take pride in his association with the Corinthian church, and the believers could be proud of him. Conversely, Paul's opponents might be proud and boastful now, but would be silenced in the day of the Lord.

Demystifying 2 Corinthians

To *boast* usually has negative connotations, and rightly so. Yet this is the word Paul uses in his defenses throughout 2 Corinthians. Modern readers might not realize, though the first-century believers would have, that Paul had been verbally attacked by a group at Corinth. They wanted to discredit him and had accused him of a number of things. His boasting is simply a statement of his service to Jesus.

Paul never tries to infer that spiritual maturity requires special status or hidden knowledge. His writing style is simple and easy to understand (1:13–14).

While in Ephesus, Paul had made plans to visit Corinth twice, once on the way to Macedonia and once returning from Macedonia (1:15–16). His first visit, however, ended in disaster and disappointment when he was publicly harassed and embarrassed (2:1; 12:14, 21; 13:1–2). False apostles had attacked his authority, and the Corinthian congregation apparently sided with them against Paul. Paul therefore altered his plans and did not visit Corinth a second time, instead returning to Ephesus (2:1). This change of plans only gave his opponents more ammunition. They accused him of waffling on his promises, saying one thing and doing another (1:15–17). Their underlying charge was that since his plans seemed to waver, how could they trust his message?

Paul goes to great lengths to justify his change in plans and to explain that it in no way affected the truth of what he taught (1:15–20). He makes it clear that God's promises are sure. God keeps His word. Likewise, those who serve Him must also keep their word. It would be wrong if Paul had made a foolish promise he had no intention of keeping; but it was quite different to make plans that were subject to the will of God and leading of the Holy Spirit.

Besides, Paul wanted to spare the Corinthians any undue discomfort. His previous visit had been difficult (2:1). Perhaps he felt it was too soon to revisit. It was in this sense that he was sparing them (1:23)—by not wishing to confront them again until he had provided them with enough time to address their problems. Paul seems to realize that being there for someone is not always the best course of action. There are times when love may be better demonstrated by keeping one's distance rather than being present. It is Paul's intent to demonstrate love for the Corinthians rather than cause them further grief (2:4).

So Paul's plans had changed. Yet he was not at all casual in making this choice. Throughout his explanation, he emphasizes God's role in the decision (1:20–23) and what is best for his friends in Corinth (2:1–4). His critics were by no means justified in their accusations.

📖 **2:5–11**

PUNISHMENT AND FORGIVENESS

Paul refers to a specific individual in this section. Some assume it is the man who was excommunicated for having an improper relationship with his father's wife (1 Corinthians 5:1–5). But it is just as likely that it was someone whom Paul had confronted on his most recent visit to Corinth.

If the latter case is true, it appears that one individual had reacted in an unseemly manner toward Paul. The church members had apparently rushed to Paul's defense to censure the man by excluding him from their fellowship. It also seems that the man had repented, yet the church had not reinstated him (perhaps thinking Paul would want it that way).

But Paul was not one to hold grudges. As long as the church failed to reinstate the offender, the believers would not have unity and would be vulnerable to Satan's attacks. So Paul entreats the Corinthians to forgive and comfort the man, assuring them that his forgiveness would be added to theirs. While Paul had rebuked the previous inaction of the church (1 Corinthians 5:1–5), the Corinthians more recent overzealous attempt to invoke discipline in the church was also a problem.

Paul shows concern for both the individual involved and the church as a whole (2:7–11). Excluding someone from fellowship is a drastic action—necessary at times, but not to become a regular solution for all problems in the church.

Take It Home

It can be a fine line between imposing discipline for the good of an offender and forgiving the offense. As most parents will attest, hasty forgiveness before the offender has repented may not be appreciated or even acknowledged. Where do you tend to draw the line when someone has seriously offended you? What do you think should be the guidelines to apply to a church setting?

2 CORINTHIANS 2:12–4:18
PAUL'S CONFIDENCE

Setting Up the Section

Paul here starts to describe what happened when he finally met up with Titus after sending his severe letter to the Corinthians (2:4). He had come to Troas, where he had successful ministry. But he could not find Titus and so was still distraught, wondering how the Corinthians had responded to his stern message (2:12–13). Yet as Paul remembers his anguish, he also recalls the joy he experienced when he finally met up with Titus in Macedonia and learned that the Corinthians had repented. At this thought he breaks into joyful praise to God: "But thanks be to God. . ." (2:14). Paul seems to lose himself in this joy now, launching into an extended discussion of the joys and victory of the Christian ministry (2:14–7:1). He won't resume his discussion of the circumstances of the letter for five more chapters! In chapter 7 he will pick up with, "For when we came into Macedonia, this body of ours had no rest. . ." (7:5 NIV)—exactly where he left off at 2:13! Second Corinthians 2:14–7:1 is therefore an extended parentheses in Paul's letter, a masterful celebration of the trials and joys of the Christian ministry.

📖 2:12–17

SWEET FRAGRANCE OR FOUL SMELL?

In this section and following, Paul addresses two matters of concern for church leaders throughout the centuries. One is a tendency to "burn out" over time due to the continual demands of the position. The other is the temptation to "spice up" the gospel to make it more palatable to a wider cross-section of society.

Even Paul was subject to the pressure of seemingly endless responsibility and account-ability. He was always quick to share news of his associates and how much they meant to him. In this case, he had failed to connect with Titus in Troas, which left him without any peace of mind (2:13). Even though he felt that God had opened a door to that city, Paul didn't linger long. Things would be little better for him in Macedonia, although he does catch up with Titus there (7:5–7). And he raises an obvious question: Who is equal to the task he had taken on (2:16)?

Critical Observation

Paul's mention of a triumphal procession (2:14) would have caused his readers to think of Roman generals returning from battle. If victorious, the officer led the way with his armies fol-lowing, trailed by the people they had defeated and taken captive. Meanwhile, those in the crowd would burn incense. Paul envisioned Christ, having overcome sin and death, leading His followers in a triumphal parade.

The response to the gospel is polarized. For those who believe and respond in faith, the good news is like a sweet aroma. But for the ones who reject the truth that Paul and others proclaim, the message is like the smell of death (2:14–16).

Yet Paul refuses to cater to the whims of his listeners. Unlike others, he didn't minister for the money (2:17). He could therefore speak simply and sincerely.

📄 3:1–6

PROVEN COMPETENCE

In Paul's day, as Christianity was just beginning to spread, it was easy for unscrupu-lous characters to pose as apostles and proclaim false information, teaching it as truth. So as a safeguard, it was common for a church to vouch for someone traveling to another congregation by means of a letter of recommendation. For example, Paul includes a personal recommendation on behalf of Phoebe within his letter to the Romans (Romans 16:1).

But even as Paul's reputation is being besmirched, he doesn't provide the Corinthian believers with such a letter. Rather, he reminds them that they are his "letter" to prove his authority as an apostle. They are the proof that the Spirit of God had worked to authenticate Paul's ministry (3:2–3).

Paul wasn't out to prove himself. Instead, he wanted to prove the adequacy of God. His confidence was not in himself, but in his Lord. Paul's adequacy, therefore, was as a minister (servant) to God. Those who held to the old covenant focused only on the letter of the law. The new covenant initiated by Jesus, however, provides access to the Spirit of God and to life (3:4–6). And it is the Holy Spirit that provides Paul's competence.

COMPARING THE COVENANTS

Paul continues to contrast the old covenant with the new covenant. The old covenant—as spelled out in the Law of Moses—produced condemnation. It set a standard of righteousness that no one could meet (3:6–7). And while the glory of God was occasionally evident under the old covenant, it was a fading glory. Even the glory that lit Moses' face after his time with God did not last. And Paul notes that the old covenant itself was fading away, to be replaced by something much brighter and better (3:11).

The new covenant makes available righteousness and life rather than condemnation and death. The old covenant was like a dim flashlight in a completely dark room—helpful, but only to a certain extent. The surpassing glory of the new covenant is like someone coming in and hitting the switch, flooding the room with light. The old covenant had no glory when contrasted with the new covenant.

Paul uses the veil that Moses had worn over his face (Exodus 34:29–35) to symbolize the spiritual "veil" over the hearts of many of the Jewish people (3:15). In their devotion to the old covenant, they were unable to see the glory that was available to them. The Spirit of God is the One who lifts the veil and enables believers to behold the glory of God in the face of Christ. And it is the hope of glory (3:12) that emboldens believers to proclaim the gospel. With the veil removed, all believers should reflect the glory of the Lord (3:18).

TREASURE IN A CLAY JAR

The power of the Holy Spirit is especially relevant to Paul. He had previously mentioned personal experiences that were impossible to endure (1:8). Yet his reliance on God enabled him not to lose heart or give up in his ministry (4:1). Similarly, the Spirit of God allowed him to continue to proclaim the gospel without distorting it or attempting to deceive his listeners. (Again, Paul had a specific group of people in mind who were guilty of both of those offenses.)

Paul returns to his image of the veiled light of God. His previous application had been made toward the Jewish people (3:14–15). Here he applies the concept to the Gentiles (4:3–4). In all his teachings, he never tries to make himself the object of attention, but faithfully keeps his focus on Jesus Christ as Lord (4:5–6).

Yet the wonder of the gospel is that human believers carry the glory of God within them. Paul describes it as having treasure in jars of clay (4:6–7). The treasure is the glory of God in the person of Jesus Christ. It is quite clear that the glory is God's and not the believer's, although Paul's critics in Corinth were trying to build themselves up with little regard for the truth of the gospel. The image of oneself as a clay pot may not be consoling at first, but when considering the treasure within, it takes on a whole new perspective.

Clay jars are weak, fragile, and subject to being broken. But like the pots used by Gideon's army (Judges 7:15–25), they may be broken for a purpose. If, and when, the jar is broken, the light within shines brightly and does not go unnoticed. Indeed, it may have a powerful effect. Numerous people throughout Christian history have been "broken," only to reveal the great power of the Spirit of God—beginning with the martyrdom of Stephen (Acts 7:54–60) and continuing to the present day.

So the believer is not as fragile as he or she may appear. Paul again writes from personal experience. He knew it was possible to be: (1) hard-pressed without being crushed; (2) perplexed, but not in despair; (3) persecuted, but not abandoned; and (4) struck down, but not destroyed (4:8–9). A believer's afflictions do not result in complete failure or destruction.

People are not made righteous by trying to live for Christ, but by dying to self and to sin so that Christ's life is lived out in them. Paul emphasizes this truth by repeatedly emphasizing death to self in three consecutive sentences (4:10–12). As clay pots, believers must be broken in order for the light of the glory of Christ to shine.

📄 **4:13–18**

THE BENEFIT OF SUFFERING

In verse 13, Paul references Psalm 116:10. He echoes the psalmist's faith and confidence that he could call on God when in great danger, believing that God would rescue him. Strengthened and encouraged by his faith, he could face and endure persecution, adversity, danger, and even death. In the meantime, he need not be silent about his suffering, for his faith acknowledges the reality of resurrection beyond his suffering and death (4:14).

Demystifying 2 Corinthians

Throughout this passage, Paul uses the first-person plural much of the time (*we*, *our*, etc.). In some cases, he appears to be speaking of all believers (4:7). In other instances, however, his intent seems more focused on those who are conducting the ministry of an apostle (4:1, 5, etc.).

Paul's suffering was for the benefit of the Corinthians (4:15). As they and others were coming to believe in Christ and being strengthened in the faith, God was receiving praise and thanksgiving.

Paul found comfort in knowing that while his physical body was deteriorating, his inner spirit was being renewed daily. In fact, his body was being destroyed at a more rapid pace than most due to the abuses he received as an apostle determined to spread the gospel. Still, he could endure and remain encouraged as he boldly proclaimed Christ, and he was able to perceive bodily suffering as light and momentary. He could see the unseen glory ahead of him, and encourages his readers to do the same.

Take It Home

Paul's response to the troublesome events of life is quite impressive. His dependence on God is exemplary (4:7–9). If you were asked to comment on the same situations, what would you say? Complete the following statements:

1) When I am hard-pressed by the stresses of life, I. . .

2) When I am perplexed by a spiritual crisis, I feel. . .

3) When I am persecuted by others, I want to. . .

4) When I am struck down after trying my hardest, I feel. . .

2 CORINTHIANS 5:1–7:1

NEW DWELLINGS, NEW CREATIONS, AND NEW ATTITUDES

From a Tent to a House	5:1–10
Reconciled to God	5:11–19
Ambassadors for Christ	5:20–6:10
Choosing Sides	6:11–7:1

Setting Up the Section

Paul is writing to the Corinthians, fully aware that some of them are actively opposing his authority. He is defending himself and his ministry, to some extent, even while addressing his concerns for the genuine believers. In this section, he continues to emphasize the impermanence of human life as he turns his readers' attention to eternal things yet to come.

5:1–10

FROM A TENT TO A HOUSE

Paul had just compared a person's earthly body to a jar of clay (4:7). When the clay pots are shattered by opposition and persecution, the glory of the Lord is made visible to the world. The "shattering" should come as no surprise to believers, since a degree of suffering is typical for all who consider themselves dead to self and alive for Christ.

Here Paul uses the image of a tent to build on what he is saying. The earthly body is temporary and far from perfect. At death, believers leave behind their physical bodies and are provided vastly superior heavenly bodies. The frailty of the human frame is replaced by the permanence of an eternal dwelling place (5:1). It is only natural that people would groan because of their imperfections and the desire for a more perfect body. For now, however, the Holy Spirit is God's pledge to the believer of a future in heaven and a glorious body as well (5:4–5).

Knowing that their earthly bodies are only temporary and that death is only a gateway to something much better, believers have great confidence to live and to proclaim the gospel boldly. If they hasten the day of their deaths by living courageously for Christ, they are only closer to the day they receive their glorious heavenly bodies and go to be with their Lord. They should not fear death (being away from their bodies), but should look upon it as the arrival of what they have long been hoping for (5:6–8).

However, the assurance that they will leave their temporary bodies is no excuse for being careless about the way they live now. The physical body will perish, but the deeds a believer has done in them (whether good or bad) are the basis for future judgment. The resurrection of Jesus should remind people of their own future resurrection, as well as Jesus' promise to return to earth to subdue His enemies. He will then judge everyone according to their deeds, so believers should desire to please God as they live in their earthly bodies (5:9–10).

📖 5:11–19

RECONCILED TO GOD

When faced with the choice of pleasing other people or pleasing God, believers should always choose pleasing God. Some, however, try so hard to win human approval and favor that they corrupt and pervert the truth of the gospel. For such people, the coming Day of Judgment is something to be dreaded.

Knowing that his references to the Day of Judgment would likely evoke fear and dread among those who resisted the truths of God, Paul sought to persuade his readers to turn to Christ and be reconciled to God. The false apostles in Corinth had been telling people what they wanted to hear in order to entice listeners to follow them. Paul, on the other hand, appealed to the conscience of the Corinthians, hoping they would acknowledge his apostleship.

Critical Observation

Paul, as an apostle, was certainly not opposed to attempting to persuade others to put their faith in Jesus. Yet he always did so with a respect for the Lord (5:11). He vocally opposed other methods of persuasion that were unacceptable to God. Salvation was not the result of appealing to fleshly lusts or distorting the truths of the gospel. Paul and his colleagues were fully aware that not only their message, but also their accompanying methods and motives, were evident to God.

If Paul's readers thought he was out of his mind, he wanted them to know it was because he was determined to please God. If they believed him and considered him sane, he let them know it was for their sake that he spoke as he did. Paul and other true apostles were motivated by the love of Christ (5:12–13).

As a result of grace, every Christian has been reconciled to God by identification with Christ in His death, burial, and resurrection. All who are saved have the same general calling (5:14–15). As far as one's standing before God, believers are all the same, in Christ.

Just as believers come to see Jesus through a different lens—as Savior and Lord rather than simply a notable rabbi who had lived and died—so Paul encourages them to see one another differently. According to Paul, believers are new and should be acknowledged as such (5:16–17). Christians dare not view others merely by outward appearances.

Apart from Christ, all people are dead in their sin, enemies of God, and alienated from Him. They do not seek God, but He seeks them through His Son, Jesus Christ. As sinners acknowledge their sin and trust in Jesus for forgiveness and the gift of eternal life, they are reconciled to God. Those who know and trust God are given the privilege and responsibility of proclaiming the gospel, which includes an appeal to others to be reconciled to God through faith in Jesus Christ. In this regard, believers are Christ's ambassadors (5:18–19).

Demystifying 2 Corinthians

In the original language of 2 Corinthians 5:20, the word *ambassador* is used not as a noun, but as a verb. (Believers *ambassador* for Christ.) This responsibility entails: (1) Entreating unbelievers to be reconciled to God (5:20–21); (2) urging believers to properly value the grace of God (6:1–2); and (3) commending oneself as a servant of God without creating stumbling blocks for others (6:3–10).

🔖 5:20–6:10

AMBASSADORS FOR CHRIST

Paul describes the importance of ministering to believers as well as unbelievers. Those who are lost need to be reconciled to God and experience the righteous life that He intends for them (5:20–21). In addition, some of those who are already believers need to be reminded of the incomparable gift of grace they have been given.

Paul knew the Corinthian church had been divided into competitive cliques. Some were looking to their leaders or their spiritual gifts as a basis for boasting over others. They needed to experience genuine salvation and then grow up in unity to maturity. Otherwise, they received the gift of God's grace in vain (6:1–2). Because Christ has come, the day of salvation is now.

Paul provides four aspects of the life of an ambassador of Christ (6:3–10). First, he states that true apostles do not create stumbling blocks for others. Note that Paul does not say he avoids offending unbelievers altogether. He knew the truth and power of his message was a problem for many people (1 Corinthians 1:22–23). Yet he is scrupulous to avoid offending anyone unnecessarily or in a way that adversely affects the gospel.

Second, Paul says that ambassadors of Christ suffer for the sake of the gospel. False prophets had minimized sin and its consequences throughout biblical history, as had the false apostles in the church at Corinth. Such people were motivated by greed and self-indulgence, and were quite unwilling to wholeheartedly follow Jesus. But true apostles endure hardships.

Third, Paul writes that ambassadors manifest the character of Christ by the way they suffer. People can suffer for a lot of reasons (1 Peter 4:14–16), but an authentic believer will suffer for the right reason. Throughout their sufferings, ambassadors of Christ are guided by the Word of God, enabled by the power of God, indwelt by the Spirit of God, and characterized by the fruits of godliness (purity, knowledge, patience, kindness, love, etc.). God's authentic apostles manifest Christlikeness in the midst of their adversities.

And fourth, ambassadors of Christ employ godly means and methods. The false apostles in Corinth were religious hucksters who modified the gospel to sell it like a product and satisfy their own desires to feel important. They loved glory and boasted in it. In contrast, authentic apostles know that the crucifixion of Jesus for the salvation of humankind is not a popular message, yet they rely upon the power of the Holy Spirit to convince and convert unbelievers. Ambassadors of Christ do not always seem to succeed or garner the approval of others, yet they are faithful to the God who uses them in their honor and dishonor, for the sake of Christ.

📖 6:11–7:1

CHOOSING SIDES

Throughout both of his letters to the Corinthians, Paul has been hinting at divisions and problems within the body of believers. In this passage, he gets right to the point. The Corinthians had a serious problem regarding their relationships. They had distanced themselves from Paul and other genuine apostles, while at the same time drawing close to those who sounded good but twisted the truth of the gospel. Paul urges those in the church to do as he had done to them: to open their hearts and stop withholding affection (6:11–13).

As Paul continues, his language becomes stronger. His instruction to not be yoked with unbelievers (6:14) is not just a warning, but also an intimation that such an illicit intimacy and partnership with unbelievers already exists. Their association was not just with some misguided church leaders, but with Belial (a term for Satan) and idols. They were much farther from God than they realized (6:15–18).

Christians cannot be yoked together with unbelievers in God's work because of moral incompatibility. Christians are to pursue righteousness; unbelievers are accustomed to lawlessness. Christians have been exposed to the light of God's truth; non-Christians remain in darkness. The distance between the two is so significant that they find no basis for a partnership in spiritual ministry.

The first verse of 2 Corinthians 7 is actually Paul's conclusion to his argument. Paul refers to the Old Testament prophecies as promises because they are yet to be fully realized. They are the basis for his appeal to the Corinthians to put off all defilement—both physical and spiritual. The knowledge that a holy God dwelled in their midst (and would do so even more in His coming kingdom) should have resulted in prompt repentance and pursuit of holiness.

Believers must look to the holy scriptures for guidance so that they can follow the Lord (and His called leaders) in obedience. They are not to avoid association with unbelievers because they are to model Christian living and point others to Christ. Yet Paul's warning is to identify and shun those who claim to be followers of God, but are not. The Holy Spirit works in the lives of believers to provide discernment in such situations.

Take It Home

Religious hucksters wouldn't get by with as much as they do if people weren't so gullible. Even many of today's professing Christians tend to judge leaders on their methods, their personalities, their success rates, or some other trivial standard. Paul has repeatedly attempted to convince the Corinthians not to succumb to such a temptation, but rather to support those who remain faithful and true to God. Can you think of a consistently conscientious and hardworking Christian leader (or lay person) who may not be as flashy or popular as others? If so, try to take some time to call or write that person to offer your appreciation and support.

2 CORINTHIANS 7:2–9:15

GRIEVING AND GIVING

Godly Sorrow, Godly Joy	7:2–16
Exemplary Giving	8:1–15
A Delegation to Precede Paul	8:16–9:15

Setting Up the Section

Earlier in this letter to the Corinthians, Paul had written about the circumstances he was facing (2:12–13). In the midst of that discussion, however, he suddenly launched into an extended discussion of the joys and challenges of Christian ministry (2:14–7:1). In this section he returns to where he left off, writing about his joy at the church's repentance and his reconciliation with them.

📖 7:2–16

GODLY SORROW, GODLY JOY

Paul describes some of the serious problems he faced in Macedonia (7:5), and throughout the letter he describes some significant problems within the Corinthian church. Certain false teachers had managed to gain a following as they proclaimed another gospel and undermined Paul's authority. Some of the Corinthians had even become embarrassed by Paul and his colleagues, and drew back from them.

Yet Paul is surprisingly upbeat in this passage (7:2–4). What enabled him to write with such confidence after so many wrongs had been committed against God and against him?

Paul had just pointed out that he and his colleagues had not closed themselves off to the Corinthians; it was the Corinthians who had withdrawn from the apostles (6:11–13). Yet instead of writing them off and moving to the next ministry opportunity, Paul communicates his desire to restore the relationship he previously had with the Corinthians. It was a state of the heart that needed adjustment. He had already asked them to open their hearts (6:13); here his request is that they make room in their hearts (7:2).

Paul also enumerates evidences of the love the authentic church leaders had for the Corinthians. It would be understandable if the Corinthians had grown suspicious of Paul and others if they knew the apostles had wronged them in some way. But Paul makes it clear that he had not done so. More than that, Paul felt great pride because of his association with the believers in Corinth. Paul could attest to the list of statements he made in 2 Corinthians 7:2–4; the false apostles in Corinth could not.

Paul had crossed over from Troas to Macedonia, looking for his companion Titus and wondering how the Corinthians had responded to his strong letter of rebuke and correction. During this time of great distress (7:5), he finally met up with Titus, who reported that the Corinthians had repented and wanted to be reconciled with Paul. God encouraged Paul not only through the presence of Titus, but especially through the positive report about the Corinthians' repentance. The letter had been hard for Paul to write, knowing that his candor would cause them sorrow. But he had sent it for their own good, so it was with great relief that Paul discovers they had taken his words to heart and repented (7:8–9, 12).

Critical Observation

Paul seems to infer that if he had known about the problems in Corinth and ignored them, he would have actually harmed the people there (7:9). When one believer knows of another who is caught up in some sin, the failure to speak up makes the observer a partner in the other's sin. Writing the letter caused Paul sorrow, but he would have been sorrowful for the Corinthians even if he hadn't written. So by taking the difficult step of writing, he and the Corinthians experienced godly sorrow that led to repentance, restoration, and a renewed bond between them.

Sometimes sorrow is according to the will of God because it produces repentance that leads to salvation and life. Consequently, there are no lasting regrets. In contrast, worldly sorrow leads to death (7:10–12). After denying Jesus, Peter's great sorrow eventually resulted in his repentance and his bold leadership in the early church. Judas, on the other hand, had only regrets and committed suicide.

One other great source of joy for Paul was seeing how excited Titus was after he had delivered Paul's difficult message. Paul had boasted about what kind of believers the Corinthians were. The fact that they responded so well had been a tremendous relief for Titus, and seeing Titus's enthusiasm was pure delight for Paul (7:13–16).

EXEMPLARY GIVING

Paul now turns to the second major reason for writing this letter (chapters 8–9). He is gathering a collection of money for the poor and persecuted believers in Jerusalem, and wants to encourage the Corinthians to give generously. By way of incentive, he points to the generosity of the churches in Macedonia.

Paul's collection was no surprise to the Corinthians. He had told them about it in his previous letter (1 Corinthians 16:1–4). Perhaps the Corinthians had begun to lose heart in the prospect of helping the Jerusalem believers due to the problems in their own church. But since Paul had just heard of their renewed excitement, he broaches the topic again. On his next visit to Corinth, Paul would collect their gift, and he wanted them to be prepared.

The churches in Macedonia (including Philippi, Berea, and Thessalonica) had been models of sacrificial giving. However, the actual amount of their contribution is not mentioned. The size of their donation did not impress Paul as much as the willingness of their giving.

The believers in Macedonia were poor to the point of extreme poverty. In addition, they were facing a severe trial (8:2). Under such circumstances, most would not expect much in terms of a contribution for *others*. Yet, clearly, Paul's expectations were considerably exceeded.

The Macedonians *first* gave themselves to the Lord, and then to the apostles. They realized the great significance of their salvation, and gave back to God what they had. They gave generously, voluntarily, gratefully, and joyfully. They set a high standard for other churches to imitate (8:3–7). The Corinthian church had many strong points (1 Corinthians 1:4–7), and Paul challenges its members to add this level of generosity to the list (2 Corinthians 8:7). Yet he makes it clear that he is not commanding them, but rather encouraging them, to give as proof of their love.

Then Paul provides an even higher standard to strive for: The ultimate example of selfless giving is the Lord Jesus Christ, demonstrated by His atoning work on the cross of Calvary. He was infinitely rich in the presence of His Father, yet gave it all up during His incarnation (Philippians 2:5–8). Because of His sacrificial life and death, He made all who trust in Him exceedingly rich (8:8–9).

Paul was convinced that generous giving was a desirable thing that worked to the donor's advantage. The Corinthians had been the first to begin to give, and if they were not yet ready with their contribution, it was certainly time to finish the matter. The desire to give should continue throughout the process of giving (8:10–12). Paul refuses to use guilt to prompt the Corinthians to give more than they are able, but he doesn't hesitate to urge them to finish what they had started.

Paul concludes his exhortation to give by setting forth two governing principles. The first is the principle of equality (8:13). The secular world is familiar with a structure where the rich get richer and the poor get poorer. But the biblical model is one where political and economic power should be used not to oppress the helpless, but for the good of those who are weak and powerless. Paul never suggests that people give up their rights to own private property or be expected to live on exactly the same standard. But when one believer has more than enough and sees another believer in need, he or she should seek to narrow the disparity rather than widen it.

Paul also promotes the principle of reciprocity (8:14–15). He suggests that although one group of believers may *now* have an abundance and the ability to help another group in need, there may come a day when the tables are turned and they will find themselves in need. Generosity shown toward a brother in need may result in generosity from that same brother at a later time. When people are blessed with prosperity, it is not so they can go overboard in self-indulgence, but rather so they can share with those who have less than they need.

Demystifying 2 Corinthians

In explaining his principle of reciprocity, Paul uses an example from when the Israelites were in the wilderness after leaving the slavery of Egypt (8:15). In an area with essentially no food, God provided for the Israelites by sending manna for them to eat. Each person was allowed a certain allotment per day. Some gathered much. Some gathered little. Yet when the portions were measured, everyone had just the allotted amount (Exodus 16:16–18). Paul seems to believe that those who collected more than enough gave to those who came up short, and he uses the same principle to demonstrate how believers should use their money and possessions.

8:16–9:15

A DELEGATION TO PRECEDE PAUL

Paul had assured the Corinthians that he would soon visit them, but he isn't going right away. He wants to see that they keep their commitment to give not only for the good of others, but for their own reputation and, of course, for the glory of God. So Paul sends this letter to them along with a small group of trusted associates who will help them out. One is Titus, who had recently been to Corinth and has a personal interest in their lives. Although Paul is asking Titus to go, he makes it clear that Titus is eager to make the trip (8:16–17). He will be accompanied by at least two other "brothers" (8:18, 22), who are not named. Some speculate the group might have included Luke, Barnabas, or Apollos. Even though their names aren't provided, these men had outstanding credentials.

Why would Paul send such an esteemed group ahead of him? First, they were to facilitate the financial follow-through Paul had detailed in 2 Corinthians 8 and 9. Their gifts of teaching and exhortation would not only inspire giving, but also help the Corinthians rebut the erroneous teachings they had been hearing from the false apostles. Second, a group (rather than a single person) would ensure the integrity of the financial matters. Paul and his colleagues were scrupulous about money matters. They were consistently trustworthy, but wanted no opportunity for questions to be raised about their integrity.

Just as Paul had told the Corinthians about the selfless giving of the Macedonian churches (8:1–5), he had also told the Macedonians about the commitment the

Corinthians had made (9:1–2). So the delegation would help ensure that things were in proper order in case Paul shows up in Corinth later, accompanied by Macedonian believers (9:3–5). Paul wants the Corinthians' gift to be generous and heartfelt, not grudging.

Paul concludes this section of his letter with a number of principles concerning generosity and giving. When dealing with wealth, it is easy to become covetous, and Paul's guidelines serve as reminders of what is really important.

First, he quotes a proverb to teach that the way a person sows is the way he or she reaps (9:6–7). Giving generously is the way to have an abundant return, and the key is an attitude of delight. If people enjoy giving, they do it more frequently and more willingly.

Second, Paul states that when people give generously, God allows them to reap bountifully (9:8–9). When someone shows grace to others by giving, God replenishes the grace so that he or she has more to give.

Paul's third principle is that when people sow generously, they reap more than monetary gain (8:10–14). Cheerful giving transcends financial matters and results in a harvest of righteousness. It is regarded by God as a pleasing spiritual sacrifice. Needy believers may not even know the fellow Christians who give to them, yet they can praise God as the ultimate source.

Finally, Paul suggests that no matter how generous one's giving, it pales when compared with the generosity of God, who gave His only Son (9:15). Even when writing about money, Paul's mind remains on the cross of Christ. The gift of salvation should never cease to produce awe and gratitude, and any degree of generosity believers demonstrate is rooted in the generosity of God.

Take It Home

In this section, Paul has dealt with some difficult matters. He wants believers to do the right thing no matter how hard it might be, whether it involves writing a letter that is certain to create sorrow (7:8–10) or cheerfully giving away one's money (9:6–7). Can you think of something difficult you need to do and have been avoiding. . .perhaps something that can potentially help someone else in the long run, even if it creates hard feelings in the meantime? If so, prayerfully consider if the time is right for you to take action based on Paul's exhortations in this passage.

2 CORINTHIANS 10:1–11:33

MINISTRY: GENUINE AND OTHERWISE

Setting Up the Section

So far in this letter, Paul's writing has been authoritative, but rather gentle. After Titus's report from Corinth, Paul must have discovered that he had a lot of support from the believers there. Still, his critics were outspoken, so here he begins to defend himself more emphatically—letting his readers know he feels no shame or regret for his methods or other aspects of ministry.

Critical Observation

Paul's tone changes dramatically in the last four chapters of the letter, causing some scholars to suggest that this section was not an original part of the letter. They claim that perhaps these chapters were originally the severe and sorrowful letter that Paul wrote to the Corinthians earlier (2:4; 7:8), and that later copyists attached it to the end of 2 Corinthians. While possible, this solution is doubtful. It is more likely that Paul's tone changes here because he now turns from addressing the whole church (which has reconciled with him) to those church members who are still opposing him.

🖹 10:1–18

PAUL'S ASSESSMENT OF HIS MINISTRY

It seems that every church has its critics, and Corinth was certainly no exception. Paul's letter has hinted at his knowledge of these critics, even as he has tried to encourage and enlighten the majority of believers who would be reading his Epistle.

This passage begins with an accusation that has been leveled against him in his absence: Some said he was only bold and authoritative when writing letters, and would be far less impressive in person (10:1, 10). Paul responds to this charge, yet he was not one to speak impulsively. Rather, his appeal is meek. *Meekness* is a term generally used in regard to those in authority. Meekness involves humility, gentleness, and a confidence that God will defend and vindicate the person so that he or she need not become defensive when challenged or criticized. Both Jesus and Moses were known for their meekness, humility, and gentle demeanor.

In contrast, the false apostles in Corinth sounded authoritative and assertive. They modeled themselves after the world's standards (10:2) and seemed to be somewhat successful. Even today, certain believers seem to respect aggressive leaders more than quiet, humble ones. Although Paul was usually meek, he assures the Corinthians he would be just as bold as necessary when in person. If they took care of their problems in the meantime, however, he wouldn't need to be harsh.

Paul goes on to rebut the use of worldly tactics in the church. The secular world relies on certain things for authority: schooling, status, personal connections, oratorical skill, and so forth. The church, however, uses different "weapons" (10:3-6). The only authoritative source of doctrine is the Word of God, so Paul battles against all arguments and pretensions that oppose God's truth.

In addition to his concern about preserving and promoting the truths of scripture as a basis for doctrine, Paul knew scripture was also the basis for Christian living. The final test of any proposed "truth" is whether or not it results in obeying Christ's commands. Any teaching that turns believers from what is clearly and emphatically taught about God in the Bible is a falsehood. If the Corinthian believers learned to be more diligent and completely obedient, then Paul would be better able to confront the acts of disobedience being committed by the false apostles (10:6).

At this point, Paul begins to get a bit more specific about the accusations that his accusers had leveled at him. They said he referred too frequently to his apostolic authority (10:7-8), yet he did so to assure the Corinthians that his authority came from God and not any other source. His critics could not make the same claim. They also said his letters were just a forceful attempt to cover for his lack of personal charisma (10:9-11). But the false apostles were setting their own standards rather than conforming to biblical ones. They sought to elevate themselves by misrepresenting their own accomplishments and minimizing the value of others. While Paul is honest about his ministry, he is never self-promoting. His attention is always given to building up the church—not his own reputation, image, or power (10:12-16). And any boasting is only to give credit to God (10:17-18).

📄 11:1–15

NECESSARY "FOOLISHNESS"

Paul felt it foolish to spend so much time talking about himself, yet it was the right thing to do in order to answer the accusations of his critics. His concern for the believers in Corinth motivated his actions. Anything that prevented them from being further deceived was well worth any potential discomfort he might feel (11:1-3).

Critical Observation

Paul's language throughout this section is direct, sometimes strong, and definitely personal. He borders on sarcasm and hyperbole. His "foolishness" (11:1) is actually a wise course of action. Those he calls "super-apostles" (11:5) were really false apostles. But the Corinthians were clear about his meaning.

Paul poses himself as the father of the bride, so to speak. The Corinthian believers are the bride, and Paul desires to proudly present them to the groom, Jesus Christ (11:2). Yet his concern for them is not merely parental paranoia. They were facing a very real and immediate danger: Spiritual seduction had historically been a trap for God's people, and Paul didn't want history to repeat itself in Corinth.

The Corinthians had been naively tolerant of the false teachings of the self-proclaimed apostles. Since Paul now had their attention, he quickly set himself apart from those he called "super-apostles" (11:5). Was he inferior to the others, as some had charged? Not at all. The difference was a matter of presentation and style. While the false apostles were proud of their speaking ability, Paul didn't purport to be a trained speaker. What set him apart (and above) the others was the content of his message. God had revealed things to Paul that the others knew nothing about (11:5–6). Evidence of this fact is found throughout his letters as he presents and explains the gospel.

The false apostles had no problem finding people to support them financially, while Paul demanded no payment from the Corinthians. So the ironic charge of the false apostles was that Paul's ministry was worthless. Paul again rebuts their ridiculous charges. If what they said was true, then he was robbing the Macedonian churches because they willingly supported him. Paul knew that by continuing to serve without expecting payment he not only verified that the gift of the gospel is free, but also demonstrated that the so-called apostles in Corinth were operating out of greed and self-interest (11:7–12). The self-centered church leaders were trying to position themselves above Paul, when, in reality, they were nowhere near his level of wisdom, integrity, and devotion.

Paul follows with some of his harshest words for the false apostles. Not only were they deceitful, they were servants of Satan who masqueraded as enlightened leaders (11:13–15).

📄 11:16–33

THREE COMPARISONS

Paul continues to compare himself to the false apostles in Corinth using three different standards. The first was the way they treated people under their authority. In this regard, Paul resorts to sarcasm to explain that he isn't strong enough to exploit or take advantage of others the way the leaders in Corinth were doing (11:16–21). Even though the believers there were willing to put up with such domineering tactics, Paul would not resort to that. If they wanted to shame him for such "weakness," so be it.

The second comparison was the Jewish credentials of the leaders. The others were Hebrews, Israelites, and Abraham's descendants (11:21–22). But Paul was also those things, plus more (Philippians 3:4–6).

The third comparison was the crucial difference: the personal price paid to service others (11:23–33). If Paul didn't quite measure up to his critics (by their standards) on the first point, and was an even match on the second, here he far outperformed them.

Paul's lengthy list of sufferings (11:23–33) is his most detailed. Several of the incidents are mentioned in the account of his missionary travels in Acts or in other places, such as his escape from Damascus in a basket, the stoning, and some of the beatings

(Acts 9:23–25; 14:19; 16:22–24). Others we know nothing about. For instance, Acts only tells of one shipwreck of Paul—not three—and it occurred *after* the writing of this letter. So clearly scripture reveals only a small percentage of all Paul experienced at the hands of others.

Demystifying 2 Corinthians

The Mosaic Law prohibited punishment of more than forty lashes (Deuteronomy 25:2–3). It had become Jewish custom to stop at thirty-nine in case of a miscount, so as not to unintentionally break the law (11:24).

As the Corinthian Christians read this list of Paul's sufferings, surely they realized that these were the credentials of a genuine apostle. They were definitely not things the false apostles would have chosen to boast of, even if they had been willing to endure such hardships. Clearly, Paul could have avoided many of these gruesome circumstances if he had backed down when opposed or simply hadn't worked so hard to communicate the gospel to others. Yet he was not only eager to carry the message of Christ's love and forgiveness to as many as possible, he was also willing to suffer along the way.

And still, Paul takes no personal credit. He boasts only in his weakness (11:30), realizing that his ability to endure is through the grace and power of God.

Take It Home

It can be easy to criticize other people before acknowledging the suffering they are going through. Paul's critics in Corinth did so intentionally, but current believers may do so without knowing it. Can you think of some other believer whom others may tend to look down on without giving proper regard to his or her difficult circumstances in life? If so, look for opportunities to prompt the critics to consider the person's situation and respond with more grace and mercy.

2 CORINTHIANS 12:1–13:14

INEXPRESSIBLE GLORY AND UNAVOIDABLE THORNS

Setting Up the Section

Paul has turned up the heat in his defense against the accusations of his critics, coming on stronger as he boasts in what God has done through him. As he closes the letter, he provides some additional proof of the authenticity of his ministry. He also shares a personal problem, but one that further verifies his role as an apostle.

📖 12:1–6

PAUL'S INCREDIBLE VISION

The fact that Paul says he will "go on" to visions and revelations (12:1) suggests that this is yet another aspect of the bragging of the false apostles in Corinth. It was easy enough for them to *say* that their teachings came from God, which would not only greatly reduce questions and resistance from those who heard them, but also make them appear spiritually superior. However, Paul is about to relate an experience that far outweighs any claims made by the religious phonies, yet he couples it with another story that diminishes his personal glory and shows that he was part of a truly spiritual event.

Demystifying 2 Corinthians

Paul had invoked an oath to testify that he was not lying about what he was saying (11:31). The oath would also apply to his statements about his revelation of the third heaven. As incredible as his story sounded, his oath attested that God knew he was telling the truth.

Although Paul begins to write in third person (12:2–3), he soon makes it clear that he is referring to himself (12:7). He couldn't be sure whether he had undergone a bodily experience as well as a spiritual one, yet he was certain of what had taken place.

He was transported to the third heaven, or paradise (12:2, 4). People referred to the earth's atmosphere as the first heaven, and the stars and realms of outer space as the second heaven. Beyond that was the third heaven, where one would find the presence of God. (Jesus passed through the heavens when returning to God at His ascension [Hebrews 4:14].) Paradise was the place where believers were united with God between death and resurrection (Luke 23:43). While there, Paul heard things that he wasn't even allowed to describe. The experience was surely an encouragement to Paul and a confirmation of his relationship with God.

The false apostles would surely have capitalized on such an experience—both financially and in terms of spiritual status. Yet while Paul relates the event as indisputable evidence that he was a called apostle, he understates it as much as possible. By using third person he doesn't say *I* saw and *I* heard great things. He summarizes all that happened to him in only a few sentences. He remains vague and refuses to provide details that would have drawn people to him as storyteller rather than to the significance of the event itself. He allows fourteen years to pass before he tells anyone what had happened. And when he finally does, he doesn't emphasize the vision, but his own weakness (12:5).

📖 12:7–10

PAUL'S THORN IN THE FLESH

Paul's weakness is evident in what he refers to as a thorn in his flesh (12:7). It was probably some sort of Satan-inspired, God-allowed physical malady. After being privileged to witness heavenly events, even Paul would be tempted to become arrogant, and this impediment was a continual reminder that it was God's grace that kept Paul active—not Paul's own strength or wisdom.

Paul never reveals exactly the problem that he was forced to deal with. It seems likely that it was more than a mere irritation, but rather a nagging, persistent, painful problem that could never quite be put out of mind. It may have been something that affected his appearance, perhaps causing embarrassment. It's also likely that it affected his spirit, attitude, and outlook.

Although Paul willingly endured much suffering, he was no masochist. Just as Jesus had prayed to somehow avoid His agonizing death on the cross (Matthew 26:39), Paul prayed that God would remove his thorn. Three times he pleaded, but was told that Jesus' power was made perfect in his weakness (12:9).

Critical Observation

Some people believe that suffering is a result of God's displeasure toward a person, and that faith is all that is needed to heal one's physical problems. Yet Paul's thorn was not the result of sin in his life or a lack of faith. In his case, Paul suffered from a physically painful ailment of some kind because God had a higher purpose for him.

Rather than removing Paul's thorn, God gave Paul sufficient grace to sustain him throughout his lifelong affliction. Paul's thorn in the flesh was actually an ongoing method by which God's power would be demonstrated. So Paul stopped petitioning God to remove the problem and began to praise God for giving it to him. It was in his human weakness that he learned to find God's strength (12:10).

PAUL'S CLOSING ARGUMENT

Like an attorney about to see the jury leave to deliberate, Paul provides his readers a closing argument before ending his letter. He shouldn't have had to defend himself so thoroughly, and he felt foolish for doing so. But his action was necessary because the Corinthians hadn't come to his defense as soon as the "super-apostles" began to criticize him (12:11–13).

Paul reminds the Corinthians yet again that he intends to visit them soon, and assures them that he is not coming with an expectation of personal gain. In fact, he would go out of his way to ensure that neither he nor his associates placed any financial demands on the believers in Corinth (12:14–18).

Paul hopes that his third visit will not create a difficult situation for the Corinthians (12:14). As their spiritual father, he plans to provide for them rather than vice versa. Yet he also suspects he might find a number of problems when he arrives (12:20–21). At this point, Paul reverses his approach to accountability. He had been conscientiously defending his actions to the Corinthians, but now he explains that they would be accountable for *their* actions. Paul had verified that he was indeed an apostle of Jesus Christ, and as such, he sets down truths the Corinthians should accept and live by.

According to the Mosaic Law, any legal accusation had to have more than one witness (Deuteronomy 19:15). Paul was accusing the Corinthians of improper behavior, so it was significant that this would be his third visit, each time with an accompanying witness to what they were doing. He was prepared, if necessary, to be a strict disciplinarian when he arrived (13:1–4).

And although Paul tells the Corinthians to examine themselves in regard to their faith, he doesn't provide a checklist of any kind for them to consider (13:6–9). They were to confirm their relationship with Jesus (13:5) and their commitment to God's truth (13:8). Paul never suggests anything is necessary for one's salvation other than Christ.

Paul's frankness with the Corinthians has a specific purpose: He wants to give them the opportunity to repent and straighten out their spiritual lives before his arrival. If they do, he will have no reason to be harsh with them. If they don't, he will use his God-given authority to discipline them (13:10).

Yet he ends this deeply personal letter with a positive appeal and a reminder of God's grace, love, and fellowship (13:11–14). His final benediction is an assurance of the work of God the Father, God the Son, and God the Holy Spirit.

Take It Home

Do you have any kind of physical problem that might be somewhat comparable to Paul's thorn in the flesh? If so, do you tend to feel a bit resentful because of it, or do you usually tolerate it reasonably well? Can you think of ways to learn to see your human weaknesses as a catalyst for God's grace and strength in your life?

CONTRIBUTING EDITORS:

Dr. Peter Barnes is the pastor of Westlake Hills Presbyterian Church in Austin, Texas. He has a Master of Divinity degree from Gordon-Conwell Theological Seminary, and a Doctor of Ministry from Fuller Theological Seminary. He is author of *The Missional Church: Restoring a Vision for the Mission of God through the Local Church in the 21st Century*. Peter and his wife, Lorie, have three adult sons.

Robert Deffinbaugh, Th.M. graduated from Dallas Theological Seminary with his Th.M. in 1971. Bob is a teacher and elder at Community Bible Chapel in Richardson, Texas, and a regular contributor to the online studies found at Bible.org.

CONSULTING EDITOR:

Dr. Mark Strauss is a professor at Bethel Seminary's San Diego Campus. He is the author of *Distorting Scripture? The Challenge of Bible Translation and Gender Accuracy; The Essential Bible Companion;* and *Four Portraits, One Jesus: An Introduction to Jesus and the Gospels*. He is presently revising the commentary on Mark's Gospel for Expositor's Bible Commentary.